Program Arcade Games

WITH PYTHON AND PYGAME

Paul Vincent Craven

©2013 Paul Vincent Craven

Paul Vincent Craven, Ph.D.
Carver Science Building
Simpson College
Indianola, IA 50125

Thanks to Becky Beaman for all of the editing work. Thanks to Simpson College for being the excellent college that it is.

First Edition: April 2013

To order this product, use ISBN: 978-1484052259

Dedicated to everyone who loves to learn.

Contents

Before getting started...

If you already know *why* you want to learn to program games and just want to learn *how* to get started, then you can skip over this section down to the next section on how to install the software you need.

As you start to learn to program, you might soon find that it looks like *work*. We all know we'd rather skip work and go farming for gold in World of Warcraft or Eve Online or some other game, right? So why learn to program? What does a person get out of it?

1. Learn to Make Games and Get Paid

Learn how to make games and get paid? Ok, *I* won't pay you, but if you learn to program, there are plenty of people that *will* pay you. Here's how to profit:

Figure 1.: Bags of money

1. Learn to program games.

2. Have fun making your own games.

3. Select favorite job offer.

4. Profit.

Look, no ??? in this plan!

Think about it. You can *play* games, but anyone can do that. Being great at a video game really isn't much of an accomplishment in life if you think about it. Or you can learn to *create* games. People care about that.

While you may be studing how to program games, tell your parents and co-workers you are studying *computer science*. It sounds better.

1.1. Why Study Computer Science?

Back to money. According to the National Association of Colleges and Employers (NACE), Computer Engineering is the best-paid degree, Computer Science is third best paying degree, and Information Science is the 10th. Most of the other degrees are also in technology-related and involve software:

Top-Paid Bachelor's Degrees	
Major	Average Salary Offer
Computer Engineering	$70,400
Chemical Engineering	$66,400
Computer Science	$64,400
Aerospace Engineering	$64,000
Mechanical Engineering	$62,900
Electrical/Electronics & Communications Engineering	$62,300
Civil Engineering	$57,600
Finance	$57,300
Construction Science	$56,600
Information Sciences & Systems	$56,100

(Data is from the NACE January 2013 Salary Survey.)

Computer engineers work at integrating computer programs with hardware. In today's engineering market, most of those engineering jobs will need to know some computer programming.

What is Information Science? This is a degree for people who like computers and technology but never really liked programming. This book aims to make sure that isn't you. Programming is fun, and who wants to settle for only 10th in the list of best-paying degrees?

While learning to program games, you can be studying towards one of the best paying four-year degrees you can get. And let's be honest, those engineering degrees usually take five years. Computer science is a great bet for a career.

Not only are computer science graduates getting high-paying offers, they are the most likely to get an offer when applying. According to NACE more than 56 percent of majors get an offer when applying. This is because there are few students going into a field that is in high-demand. To get an idea how Science Technology Engineering and Math (STEM) jobs compare to the students, see Figure 2 and Figure 3.

What about a two-year school to learn programming? After all, two year schools offer a cheaper alternative to four year colleges. Way cheaper. But I'll offer the following data as a caution about choosing a two year school:

Average salary by education level	
Vocational/Tech School	$59,729
Some College	$72,197
College Graduate (4-Year)	$81,539
Master's Degree	$98,911
Doctoral Degree	$112,772

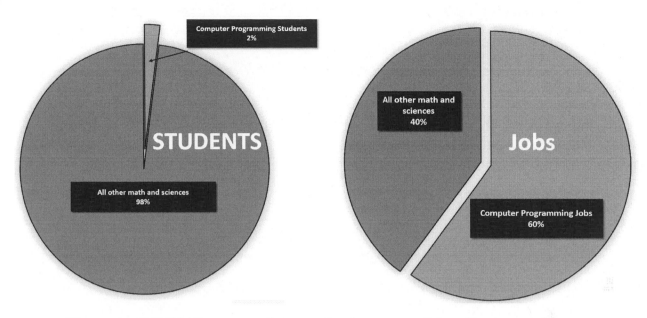

Figure 2.: STEM/Computer Science Graduates vs. Jobs. Source: code.org

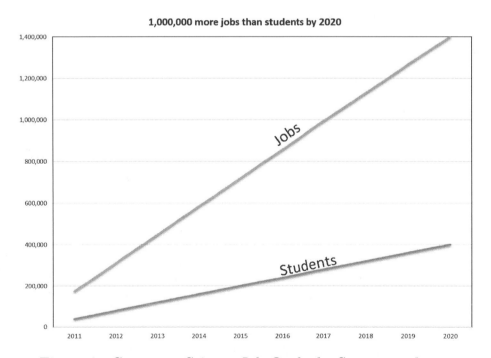

Figure 3.: Computer Science Job Outlook. Source: code.org

According to Dice.com's survey data, people in a technology career who graduate from a two-year school averaged $21,000 less than people who went to a four-year school. In fact, they did worse than dropouts from four-year colleges! So go to a four-year school and skip the two-year school entirely. (Data is according to the 2011-2012 Dice Technical Salary Survey. Note that the salary listed is not the average *starting* salary. The numbers represent the average salary of all workers, no matter how experienced.) Of course, I think Simpson College has the best Computer Science department in the midwest:
`http://simpson.edu/computer-science`

1.2. Get The Most From This Class

> You can't be a great basketball player without practice.

Looking to make your time here worthwhile? Answer the chapter questions! Don't skip them. They are necessary to understand the material.

Do the labs! This is even more important. Learning by only reading the material is about as useful as trying to become an expert basketball player only by reading a book.

Practice! You might see other people that don't have to practice. It isn't fair. Or, you might be smarter than other people, and they start doing better than you because they work at it and you don't. That's not fair either. That's life. Get used to it. Practice.

Are you taking this as a class? Great! Did you know you can save time and *copy* the answers and labs from the Internet? You can also buy yourself a gym membership and send someone else to work out for you. It makes about as much sense.

Seriously, what on earth are you thinking copying from someone else? If you aren't going to do the work drop out now and start filling out McDonald's applications.

If reading isn't your learning style, most of the information is available through videos. You can skip the text entirely and just watch the videos by checking out the YouTube playlist:
`http://www.youtube.com/playlist?list=PL1D91F4E6E79E73E1`
You *can't* learn without doing the work though. Do the reading. Ask questions. Do the labs. Ask questions. Do the worksheets. Ask questions. Listen to the videos. And ask your teacher questions.

1.3. Send Feedback

This is the text I use with the Simpson College class:
`Computer Science 150 Fundamentals of Computing I`
There is a print version and an on-line version. The on-line version is at:
`http://ProgramArcadeGames.com`

The goal of the text, website, worksheets, labs, and videos is to teach basic computer science concepts and get students programming their own games as soon as possible.

> ✎ **Want to keep this resource free?**
> **Drop me a note!**

If you are using it for self-study or for another class, please drop me a note. The more people that use this resource, the more effort I'll put into improving it.

I've heard from a few high schools that use this material. If you are a student at one of these high schools, and liked this material, consider checking out **Simpson College**. We'd love the chance to be able to work with you. Contact myself or **admissions**for more information.

If you notice any errors or omissions in the book, please send me an e-mail. I'd like this to be the best resource possible.

Dr. Paul Vincent Craven
Department Head, Computer Science Department
Simpson College, Indianola, Iowa, USA
`paul.craven@simpson.edu`

2. Installing and Starting Python

To get started, two programs need to be installed, Python and Pygame. Python is the computer language we will program in, and Pygame is a library of commands that will help make writing games easier.

2.1. Windows Installation

If you are working with a computer that already has Python and Pygame set up on it, you can skip this step. But if you want to set up Python and Pygame on your own Windows computer, don't worry. It is very easy.

1. Run the Python installer downloaded from:
   `http://ProgramArcadeGames.com/python-3.3.1.msi`

2. Run the Pygame installer downloaded from:
   `http://ProgramArcadeGames.com/pygame-1.9.2a0.win32-py3.3.msi`

Once everything has been installed, start Python up by selecting the Integrated Development Environment (IDLE) as shown in Figure 4

The original files provided here come from the Python download page at:
`http://www.python.org/download/`

Figure 4.: Starting Python

...and the Pygame file originally comes from:
https://bitbucket.org/pygame/pygame/downloads

2.2. Mac Installation

Python and Pygame run on the Mac. I've never created a tutorial on it. Given the headaches that former students have gone through to get Pygame to work on the Mac, I recommend running Python/Pygame under Windows emulation instead.

2.3. Unix Installation

Unix distributions may come with a Pygame package, or the ability to easily get one. If you want to compile from source, this is what I've used on Linux Mint:

```
# Load required packages
sudo apt-get install mercurial libsdl1.2-dev libsmpeg-dev
sudo apt-get install libasound2-doc libglib2.0-doc python-dev
sudo apt-get install libsdl-ttf2.0-dev  libsdl-image1.2-dev
sudo apt-get install libsdl-mixer1.2-dev libportmidi-dev
sudo apt-get install libavformat-dev libswscale-dev

# Use mercurial to clone current code
hg clone https://bitbucket.org/pygame/pygame

# Build and install
cd pygame
sudo python setup.py
```

2.4. Optional Wing IDE

The biggest risk on UNIX platforms is that your default Python version might be in the 2.x series, and that code won't work with the code examples here in the book. Make sure you have and are using Python 3.3.x.

While not necessary, I also highly recommend installing and using "Wing IDE 101" at: http://wingware.com/downloads/wingide-101/

The Wing IDE is a free version of a commercial development environment for Python. For this class, there is no need for all the bells-and-whistles the commercial version comes with, but they are nice. You will see that I often used this editor while recording the videos.

3. Viewing File Extensions

It is a great idea to change your windows configuration to show file extensions. A file usually has the a name like `Book report.docx` where the `.docx` tells the computer it is a Microsoft Word compatible document. By default Windows hides the `.docx` extension if there is a program installed to handle it. If you are programming, this hiding part of the file name can be annoying.

For Windows 7, to show file extensions, open up your computer's control panel. Find the selection for "Folder Options." Click the "View" tab, and then unselect the option for "Hide extensions for known file types."

For Windows 8, bring up a file explorer by hitting the Winodws-E key. Then click the "view" tab and make sure "File name extensions" has been checked.

1. Create a Custom Calculator

(Hi! If you don't already have a machine with Python and Pygame installed, then `hop back` to the "forward" section to download and install them so you can get started.)

1.1. Introduction

One of the simplest things that can be done with Python is to use it as a fancy calculator. Wait, a calculator isn't a game. Why are we talking about calculators? Boring....

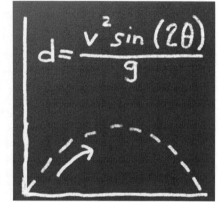

Hey, to calculate objects dropping, bullets flying, and high scores, we need calculations. Plus, any true geek will consider a calculator as a toy rather than a torture device! Let's start our game education with calculators. Don't worry, we'll start graphics by Chapter 5.

A simple calculator program can be used to ask the user for information and then calculate boring things like mortgage payments, or more exciting things like the trajectory of mud balls as they are flung through the air.

As our first example we will calculate kinetic energy, something we might need to do as part of a game physics engine.

The best thing about doing this as a program is the ability to hide the complexities of an equation. All the user needs to do is supply the information and he or she can get the result in an easy-to-understand format. Any similar custom calculator could run on a smart phone, allowing a person to easily perform the calculation on the go.

1.2. Printing

1.2.1. Printing Text

How does a program print something to the screen?

```
print("Hello World.")
```

```
7% Python Shell                                                    ▭ ▢ ✕
File  Edit  Shell  Debug  Options  Windows  Help
Python 3.1.2 (r312:79149, Mar 21 2010, 00:41:52) [MSC v.1500 32 bit (Intel)] on
win32
Type "copyright", "credits" or "license()" for more information.
>>> ============================= RESTART =================================
>>>
This program calculates the kinetic energy of a moving object.
Enter the object's mass in kilograms: 5
Enter the object's speed in meters per second: 10
The object has 250.0 joules of energy.
>>> |
                                                                  Ln: 9 Col: 4
```

Figure 1.1.: Using Python to calculate kinetic energy

This program prints out "Hello World" to the screen. Go ahead and enter it into IDLE prompt and see how it works. Try printing other words and phrases as well. The computer will happily print out just about anything you like, true or not.

What does the "Hello World" program look like in other computer programming languages? Check out Wikipedia. They keep a nice set of "Hello World" programs written in many different computer programming languages:

http://en.wikipedia.org/wiki/Hello_world_program_examples

It is interesting to see how many different computer languages there are. You can get an idea how complex a language is by how easy the "Hello World" program is.

Remember, the command for printing in Python is easy. Just use `print`. After the `print` command are a set of parentheses ( ). Inside these parentheses is what should be printed to the screen. Using parentheses to pass information to a function is standard practice in math, and computer languages.

Math students learn to use parentheses evaluating expressions like $sin(\theta) = cos(\frac{\pi}{2} - \theta)$. sin and cos are functions. Data passed to these functions is inside the parenthesis. What is different in our case is that the information being passed is text.

Notice that there are *double quotes* around the text to be printed. If a print statement has quotes around text, the computer will print it out just as it is written. For example, this program will print 2+3:

```
print("2+3")
```

1.2.2. Printing Results of Expressions

This next program does not have quotes around $2 + 3$, and the computer will evaluate it as a *mathematical expression*. It will print 5 rather than 2+3.

```
print(2+3)
```

The code below will generate an error because the computer will try to evaluate "Hello World" as a mathematical expression, and that doesn't work at all:

```
print(Hello World)
```

The code above will print out an error `SyntaxError:  invalid syntax` which is computer-speak for not knowing what "Hello" and "World" mean.

Also, please keep in mind that this is a single-quote: ' and this is a double-quote: " If I ask for a double-quote, it is a common mistake to write "" which is really a double double-quote.

1.2.3. Printing Multiple Items

A print statement can output multiple things at once, each item separated by a comma. For example this code will print out `Your new score is 1040`

```
print("Your new score is", 1030+10)
```

The next line of code will print out `Your new score is 1030+10`. The numbers are not added together because they are inside the quotes. Anything inside quotes, the computer treats as text. Anything outside the computer thinks is a mathematical statement or computer code.

```
print("Your new score is", "1030+10")
```

✎Does a comma go inside or outside the quotes?

This next code example doesn't work at all. This is because there is no comma separating the text between the quotes, and the 1030+10. At first, it may appear that there is a comma, but the comma is *inside* the quotes. The comma that separates the terms to be printed must be *outside* the quotes. If the programmer wants a comma to be printed, then it must be inside the quotes:

```
print("Your new score is," 1030+10)
```

This next example does work, because there is a comma separating the terms. It prints:
`Your new score is, 1040`
Note that only one comma prints out. Commas outside the quotes separate terms, commas inside the quotes are printed. The first comma is printed, the second is used to separate terms.

```
print("Your new score is,", 1030+10)
```

1.3. Escape Codes

If quotes are used to tell the computer the start and end of the string of text you wish to print, how does a program print out a set of double quotes? For example:

```
print("I want to print a double quote " for some reason.")
```

This code doesn't work. The computer looks at the quote in the middle of the string and thinks that is the end of the text. Then it has no idea what to do with the commands `for some reason` and the quote and the end of the string confuses the computer even further.

It is necessary to tell the computer that we want to treat that middle double quote as text, not as a quote ending the string. This is easy, just prepend a baskslash in front of quotes to tell the computer it is part of a string, not a character that terminates a string. For example:

```
print("I want to print a double quote \" for some reason.")
```

This combination of the two characters \" is called an *escape code*. Almost every language has them. Because the backslash is used as part of an escape code, the backslash itself must be escapted. For example, this code does not work correctly:

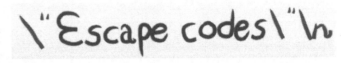

```
print("The file is stored in C:\new folder")
```

Why? Because \n is an escape code. To print the backslash it is necessary to escape it like so:

```
print("The file is stored in C:\\new folder")
```

There are a few other important escape codes to know. Here is a table of the important escape codes:

Escape code	Description
\'	Single Quote
\"	Double Quote
\t	Tab
\r	CR: Carriage Return (move to the left)
\n	LF: Linefeed (move down)

What is a "Carriage Return" and a "Linefeed"? Try this example:

```
print("This\nis\nmy\nsample.")
```

The output from this command is:

```
This
is
my
sample.
```

The \n is a linefeed. It moves "cursor" where the computer will print text down one line. The computer stores all text in one big long line. It knows to display the text on different lines because of the placement of \n characters.

To make matters more complex, different operating systems have different standards on what makes a line ending.

Escape codes	Description
\r\n	CR+LF: Microsoft Windows
\n	LF: UNIX based systems, and newer Macs.
\r	CR: Older Mac based systems

Usually your text editor will take care of this for you. Microsoft Notepad doesn't though, and UNIX files opened in notepad look terrible because the line endings don't show up at all, or show up as black boxes.

1.4. Comments

✏ Comments are important (even if the computer ignores them)

Sometimes code needs some extra explanation to the person reading it. To do this, we add "comments" to the code. The comments are meant for the human reading the code, and not for the computer.

There are two ways to create a comment. The first is to use the # symbol. The computer will ignore any text in a Python program that occurs after the #. For example:

```
# This is a comment, it begins with a # sign
# and the computer will ignore it.

print("This is not a comment, the computer will")
print("run this and print it out.")
```

The # sign between quotes is not treated as a comment. A programmer can disable a line of code by putting a # sign in front of it. It is also possible to put a comment in at the end of a line.

```
print("A # sign between quotes is not a comment.")

# print("This is a comment, even if it is computer code.")

print("Hi") # This is an end-of-line comment
```

It is possible to comment out multiple lines of code using three single quotes in a row to delimit the comments.

```
print("Hi")
'''
This is
a
multi
line
comment. Nothing
Will run in between these quotes.
print("There")
'''
print("Done")
```

Most professional Python programmers will only use this type of multi-line comment for something called *docstrings*. Docstrings allow documentation to be written along side the code and later be automatically pulled out into printed documentation, websites, and Integrated Development Environments (IDEs). For general comments, the # tag works best.

Even if you are going to be the only one reading the code that you write, comments can help save time. Adding a comment that says "Handle alien bombs" will allow you to quickly remember what that section of code does without having to read and decipher it.

1.5. Assignment Operators

How do we store the score in our game? Or keep track of the health of the enemy? What we need to do this is the *assignment operator*. (An *operator* is a symbol like + or −.) This stores a value into a *variable* to be used later on. The code below will assign 10 to the variable x, and then print the value stored in x.

Look at the example below.

Listing 1.1: Assigning and using variables

```
1 # Create a variable x
2 # Store the value 10 into it.
3 x = 10
4
5 # This prints the value stored in x.
6 print(x)
7
8 # This prints the letter x, but not the value in x
9 print("x")
10
11 # This prints "x= 10"
12 print("x=",x)
```

┌───┐
│ ✍ **Variables go outside the quotes.**   │
│   │
└───┘

Note: The listing above also demonstrates the difference between printing an **x** *inside* quotes and an **x** *outside* quotes. If an **x** is inside quotation marks, then the computer prints **x**. If an **x** is outside the quotation marks then the computer will print the value of **x**. Getting confused on the "inside or outside of quotes" question is very common for those learning to program.

An assignment statement (a line of code using the = opera-tor) is different than the algebraic equality your learned about in math. Do not think of them as the same. On the left side of an assignment operator must be exactly one variable. Nothing else may be there.

$pi = 3.14159$

On the right of the equals sign/assignment operator is an *expression*. An expression is anything that evaluates to a value. Examine the code below.

```
x = x + 1
```

The code above obviously can't be an algebraic equality. But it is valid to the computer because it is an assignment statement. Mathematical equations are different than assignment statements even if they have variables, numbers, and an equals sign.

The code above statement takes the current value of x, adds one to it, and stores the result back into x.

Expanding our example, the statement below will print the number 6.

```
x = 5
x = x + 1
print(x)
```

Statements are run sequentially. The computer does not "look ahead." In the code below, the computer will print out 5 on line 2, and then line 4 will print out a 6. This is because on line 2, the code to add one to x has not been run yet.

```
1 x = 5
2 print(x) # Prints 5
3 x = x + 1
4 print(x) # Prints 6
```

The next statement is valid and will run, but it is pointless. The computer will add one to x, but the result is never stored or printed.

```
x + 1
```

The code below will print 5 rather than 6 because the programmer forgot to store the result of x + 1 back into the variable x.

```
x = 5
x + 1
print(x)
```

The statement below is not valid because on the left of the equals sign is more than just a variable:

```
x + 1 = x
```

Python has other types of assignment operators. They allows a programmer to modify a variable easily. For example:

```
x += 1
```

The above statement is equivalent to writing the code below:

```
x = x + 1
```

There are also assignment operators for addition, subtraction, multiplication and division.

1.6. Variables

Variables start with a lower case letter.

Variables *should* start with a lower case letter. Variables *can* start with an upper case letter or an underscore, but those are special cases and should not be done on a normal basis. After the first lower case letter, the variable may include uppercase and lowercase letters, along with numbers and underscores. Variables may not include spaces.

Variables are case sensitive. This can be confusing if a programmer is not expecting it. In the code below, the output will be 6 rather than 5 because there are two different variables, x and X.

```
x = 6
X = 5
print(x)
```

The official style guide for Python (yes, programmers really wrote a book on style) says that multi-word variable names in Python should be separated by underscores. For example, use `hair_style` and not `hairStyle`. Personally, if you are one of my students, I don't care about this rule too much because the next language we introduce, Java, has the exact opposite style rule. I used to try teaching Java style rules while in this class, but then I started getting hate-mail from Python lovers. These people came by my website and were shocked, *shocked* I tell you, about my poor style.

Joan Rivers has nothing on these people, so I gave up and try to use proper style guides now.

Here are some example variable names that are ok, and not ok to use:

Legal variable names	Illegal variable names	Legal, but not proper
first_name	first name	FirstName
distance	9ds	firstName
ds9	%correct	X

All upper-case variable names like MAX_SPEED are allowed only in circumstances where the variable's value should *never* change. A variable that isn't variable is called a *constant*.

1.7. Operators

For more complex mathematical operations, common mathematical operators are available. Along with some not-so-common ones:

operator	operation	example equation	example code
+	addition	$3 + 2$	a = 3 + 2
-	subtraction	$3 - 2$	a = 3 - 2
*	multiplication	$3 \cdot 2$	a = 3 * 2
/	division	$\frac{10}{2}$	a = 10 / 2
//	floor division	N/A	a = 10 // 3
**	power	2^3	a = 2 ** 3
%	modulus	N/A	a = 8 % 3

"Floor division" will always round the answer down to the nearest integer. For example, 11//2 will be 5, not 5.5, and 99//100 will equal 0.

Multiplication by juxtaposition does not work in Python. The following two lines of code will not work:

```
# This does not work
x = 5y
x = 5(3/2)
```

It is necessary to use the multiplication operator to get these lines of code to work:

```
# This does work
x = 5 * y
x = 5 * (3 / 2)
```

1.7.1. Operator Spacing

There can be any number of spaces before and after an operator, and the computer will understand it just fine. For example each of these three lines are equivilant:

```
1 x=5*(3/2)
2 x = 5 * ( 3 / 2 )
3 x        =5        5*(     3/    2)
```

The official style guide for Python says that there should be a space before and after each operator. (You've been dying to know, right? Ok, the official style guide for python code is here: PEP-8.) Of the three lines of code above, the most "stylish" one would be line 2.

1.8. Order of Operations

Python will evaluate expressions using the same order of operations that are expected in standard mathematical expressions. For example this equation does not correctly calculate the average:

```
average=90+86+71+100+98/5
```

The first operation done is 98/5. The computer calculates:

$90 + 86 + 71 + 100 + \frac{98}{5}$
rather than the desired:

$$\frac{90 + 86 + 71 + 100 + 98}{5}$$

By using parentheses this problem can be fixed:

```
average=(90+86+71+100+98)/5
```

1.9. Trig Functions

Trigonometric functions are used to calculate sine and cosine in equations. By default, Python does not know how to calculate sine and cosine, but it can once the proper library has been imported. Units are in radians.

```
# Import the math library
# This line is done only once, and at the very top
# of the program.
from math import *

# Calculate x using sine and cosine
x = sin(0) + cos(0)
```

1.10. Custom Equation Calculators

A program can use Python to calculate the mileage of a car that drove 294 miles on 10.5 gallons of gas.

```
m = 294 / 10.5
print(m)
```

This program can be improved by using variables. This allows the values to easily be changed in the code without modifying the equation.

```
m = 294
g = 10.5
m2 = m / g # This uses variables instead
print(m2)
```

> ✎ **Good variable names are important**

By itself, this program is actually difficult to understand. The variables **m** and **g** don't mean a lot without some context. The program can be made easier to understand by using appropriately named variables:

```
milesDriven = 294
gallonsUsed = 10.5
mpg = milesDriven / gallonsUsed
print(mpg)
```

Now, even a non-programmer can probably look at the program and have a good idea of what it does. Another example of good versus bad variable naming:

```
# Hard to understand
ir = 0.12
b = 12123.34
i = ir * b

# Easy to understand
interestRate = 0.12
accountBalance = 12123.34
interestAmount = interestRate * accountBalance
```

In the IDLE editor it is possible to edit a prior line without retyping it. Do this by moving the cursor to that line and hitting the "enter" key. It will be copied to the current line.

Entering Python code at the >>> prompt is slow and can only be done one line at a time. It is also not possible to save the code so that another person can run it. Thankfully, there is an even better way to enter Python code.

Python code can be entered using a script. A script is a series of lines of Python code that will be executed all at once. To create a script, open up a new window as shown in Figure 1.2.

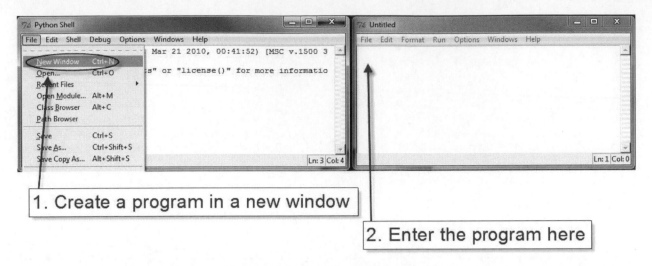

Figure 1.2.: Entering a script

Enter the Python program for calculating gas mileage, and then save the file. Save the file to a flash drive, network drive, or some other location of your choice. Python programs should always end with .py. See Figure 1.3.

Run the program typed in by clicking on the "Run" menu and selecting "Run Module". Try updating the program to different values for miles driven and gallons used.

> ✍ **Caution, common mistake!**

From this point forward, almost all code entered should be in a script/module. Do *not* type your program out on the IDLE >>> prompt. Code typed here is not saved. If this happens, it will be necessary to start over. This is a very common mistake for new programmers.

This program would be even more useful if it would interact with the user and ask the user for the miles driven and gallons used. This can be done with the **input** statement. See the code below:

```
# This code almost works
milesDriven = input("Enter miles driven:")
gallonsUsed = input("Enter gallons used:")
mpg = milesDriven / gallonsUsed
print("Miles per gallon:", mpg)
```

Running this program will ask the user for miles and gallons, but it generates a strange error as shown in Figure 1.4.

The reason for this error can be demonstrated by changing the program a bit:

```
milesDriven = input("Enter miles driven:")
gallonsUsed = input("Enter gallons used:")
```

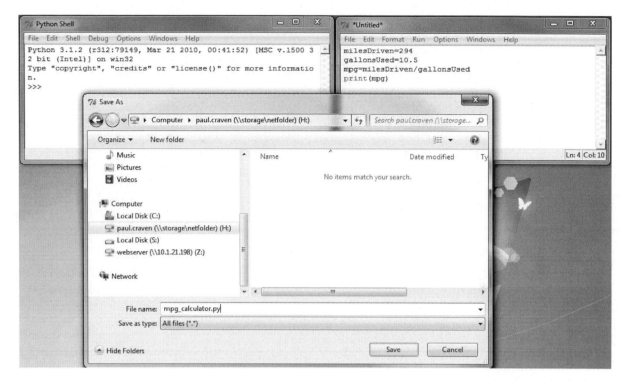

Figure 1.3.: Saving a script

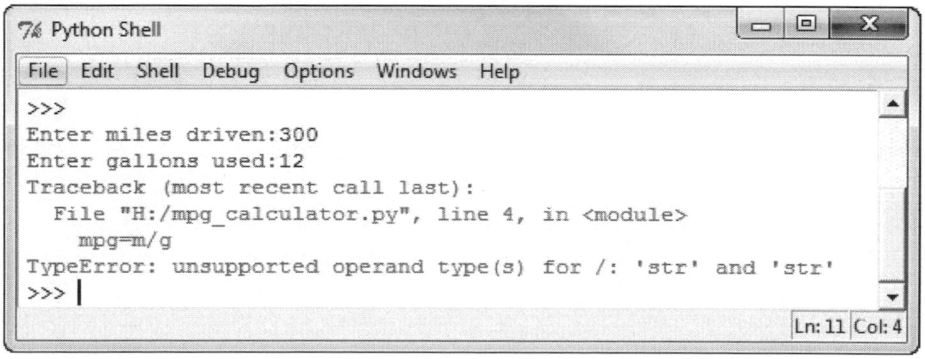

Figure 1.4.: Error running MPG program

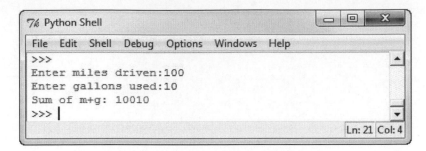

Figure 1.5.: Incorrect Addition

```
x = milesDriven + gallonsUsed
print("Sum of m+g:",x)
```

Running the program above results in the output shown in Figure 1.5.

The program doesn't add the two numbers together, it just puts one right after the other. This is because the program does not know the user will be entering numbers. The user might enter "Bob" and "Mary", and adding those two variables together would be "BobMary"; which would make more sense.

✎Input must be converted to numbers

To tell the computer these are numbers, it is necessary to surround the **input** function with an **int( )** or a **float( )**. Use the former for integers, and the latter for floating point numbers.

The final working program:

Listing 1.2: calculate_miles_per_gallon.py

```
1  # Sample Python/Pygame Programs
2  # Simpson College Computer Science
3  # http://programarcadegames.com/
4  # http://simpson.edu/computer-science/
5
6  # Explanation video: http://youtu.be/JK5ht5_m6Mk
7
8  # Calculate Miles Per Gallon
9  print("This program calculates mpg.")
10
11 # Get miles driven from the user
12 milesDriven=input("Enter miles driven:")
13 # Convert text entered to a
14 # floating point number
15 milesDriven=float(milesDriven)
16
17 #Get gallons used from the user
```

14

```
18 gallonsUsed=input("Enter gallons used:")
19 # Convert text entered to a
20 # floating point number
21 gallonsUsed=float(gallonsUsed)
22
23 # Calculate and print the answer
24 mpg=milesDriven/gallonsUsed
25 print ("Miles per gallon:",mpg)
```

And another example, calculating the kinetic energy of an object:

Listing 1.3: calculate_kinetic_energy.py

```
1 # Sample Python/Pygame Programs
2 # Simpson College Computer Science
3 # http://programarcadegames.com/
4 # http://simpson.edu/computer-science/
5
6 # Calculate Kinetic Energy
7
8 print("This program calculates the kinetic energy of a moving object.")
9 m_string=input("Enter the object's mass in kilograms: ")
10 m=float(m_string)
11 v_string=input("Enter the object's speed in meters per second: ")
12 v=float(v_string)
13
14 e=0.5*m*v*v
15 print("The object has "+str(e)+" joules of energy.")
```

To shorten a program, it is possible to nest the **input** statement into the **float** statement. For example these lines of code:

```
milesDriven=input("Enter miles driven:")
milesDriven=float(milesDriven)
```

Perform the same as this line:

```
milesDriven=float(input("Enter miles driven:"))
```

In this case, the output of the **input** function is directly fed into the **float** function. Either one works, and it is a matter of programmer's preference which to choose. It is important, however, to be able to understand both forms.

1.11. Review Questions

1. Write a line of code that will print your name.

2. How do you enter a comment in a program?

3. What do the following lines of code output?

```
print(2 / 3)
print(2 // 3)
```

4. Write a line of code that creates a variable called **pi** and sets it to an appropriate value.

5. Why does this code not work?

```
A = 22
print(a)
```

6. All of the variable names below can be used. But which of these is the *better* variable name to use?

```
a
A
Area
AREA
area
areaOfRectangle
AreaOfRectangle
```

7. Which of these variables names are not allowed in Python? (More than one might be wrong.)

```
apple
Apple
APPLE
Apple2
1Apple
account number
account_number
account.number
accountNumber
account#
```

8. Why does this code not work?

```
print(a)
a=45
```

9. Explain the mistake in this code:

```
pi = float(3.14)
```

10. Explain the mistake in the following code:

```
radius = input("Radius:")
x = 3.14
pi = x
area = pi  * radius ** 2
```

11. Explain the mistake in the following code:

    ```
    a = ((x)*(y))
    ```

12. Explain the mistake in the following code:

    ```
    radius = input(float("Enter the radius:"))
    ```

13. Explain the mistake in the following code:
    `area = `π`*radius**2`

14. Write a line of code that will ask the user for the length of a square's side and store the result in a variable. Make sure to convert the value to an integer.

15. Write a line of code that prints the area of the square, using the number the user typed in that you stored in question 9.

16. Do the same as in questions 14 and 15, but with the formula for the area of an ellipse.
    $s = \pi ab$
    where a and b are the lengths of the major radii.

17. Do the same as in questions 14 and 15, but with a formula to find the pressure of a gas.
    $$P = \frac{nRT}{V}$$
    where n is the number of moles, T is the absolute temperature, V is the volume, and R is the gas constant 8.3144.

    See `http://en.wikipedia.org/wiki/Gas_constant` for more information on the gas constant.

1.12. Lab

Complete **Lab 1** before continuing. This lab covers the material in this chapter and has you apply what you've learned.

2. What is a Computer Language?

What makes a computer language? Why do computers have them? Why are there so many different computer languages?

Like understanding how an engine works isn't necessary to drive a car, it isn't necessary to understand the answer to these questions to do basic programming. However to progress to an advanced level, it is necessary to understand how a computer works. This provides a brief explanation to get started with.

2.1. Short History of Programming

Computers are electronic, and they are digital. To a computer everything is in terms of no voltage potiential along a wire, or some voltage available. No voltage means a zero to the computer, and some voltage means a one. Computers can't actually count higher than that without combining multiple ones and zeros.

In the early days, switches were used to load ones or zeros into computer memory. Figure 2.1, `courtesy of Wikimedia Commons`, shows an Altair 8800. The front panel switches were used to load in the program. The lights showed the output. There was no monitor.

Each set of on/off switches represented a number. Each number would represent data or an instruction for the computer to perform. This system of only using ones and zeros to represent numbers is called the binary number system. This type of computer language is called a 1GL, or first generation programming language.

Binary numbers are usually represented in groups of four. For example:

```
1010 0010 0011
```

An improvement over entering programs via switches was the use of hexidecimal codes. The decimal numbers used by most people use the digits 0-9. Hexidecimal uses the numbers 0-9 and A-F to represent a set of four switches, or the numbers 0-15.

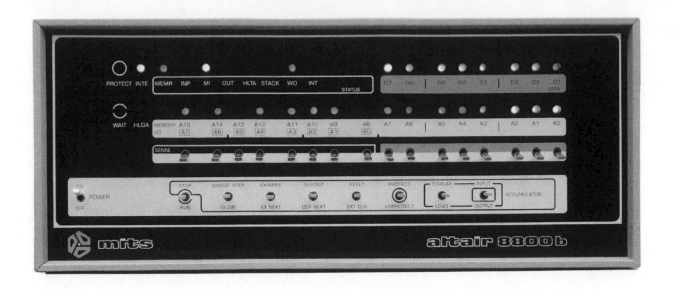

Figure 2.1.: Altair 8800

Binary	Decimal	Hexidecimal
0	0	0
1	1	1
10	2	2
11	3	3
100	4	4
101	5	5
110	6	6
111	7	7
1000	8	8
1001	9	9
1010	10	A
1011	11	B
1100	12	C
1101	13	D
1110	14	E
1111	15	F
1 0000	16	10
1 0001	17	11

In order to make entering programs easier, later computers allowed users to enter programs using assembly language. Each command used a mnemonic, and a program called a compiler would change the mnemonics into the numbers that represented the commands. This type of language is called a 2GL language, or second generation language.

Figure 2.2 shows part of an example assembly language program, also courtesy of the Wikimedia Commons.

While this was an improvement, it still wasn't very easy to program. The next generation of languages allowed for higher-level abstractions. The first of the third generation languages (COBOL, FORTRAN and LISP) were a lot easier to understand and program.

The second and third generation languages used a program called a *compiler*. A compiler takes the program typed in by the user (called *source code*) and turns it into machine code. The programmer then runs the machine code. The original source code is not run.

If there are several pieces of source code in a program, they can be linked together into one program with the use of a program called a *linker*. The linker is run on the machine code generated by the compiler to generate a final program. This final program is what the user runs, and the original source code is not needed.

A disadvantage of compiling to machine language is that the program only works for that particular type of machine. Programs compiled for Windows computers do not work on Apple Macintosh computers, or Linux computers.

Because the whole compile and link steps could be complex for new programmers, some languages instead ran using *interpreters*. These programs look at the source code and interpret it to machine language instructions on the fly. It also allows the same programs to run on Windows, Mac, and Unix computers, provided there is an interpreter available for each platform.

The drawback of using interpreters is that it is slower to operate through an interpreter than in the machine's native language.

Python is an example of an interpreted language. It is easier to develop in Python than C, but Python runs slower and must have a Python interpreter to work.

Languages such as Java use a system where programs are compiled to machine code that runs on a Java Virtual Machine (JVM), rather than the actual machine. Another popular language that does this is C#, a Common Language Infrastructure (CLI) language that runs on the Virtual Execution System (VES) virtual machine. A full discussion of these is beyond the scope of this book, but feel free to read up on them.

There are many different computer languages today. Because computers perform so many different types of tasks, different languages have been developed that specialize in different tasks. Languages such as C are good for operating systems and small embedded computers. Other languages like PHP specialize in creating web pages. Python is a general purpose language that specializes in being easy-to-use.

The company Tiobe keeps track of the popularity of various programming language in their index that is updated each month. It is a good idea to look here, and at job placement boards like DICE to keep up to date with what languages employers are looking for.

Thankfully almost all languages share the same common elements, and once one language has

```
MONITOR FOR 6802 1.4            9-14-80  TSC ASSEMBLER  PAGE   2


C000                     ORG     ROM+$0000 BEGIN MONITOR
C000 8E 00 70  START     LDS     #STACK

               *****************************************
               * FUNCTION: INITA - Initialize ACIA
               * INPUT: none
               * OUTPUT: none
               * CALLS: none
               * DESTROYS: acc A

0013           RESETA    EQU     %00010011
0011           CTLREG    EQU     %00010001

C003 86 13     INITA     LDA A   #RESETA    RESET ACIA
C005 B7 80 04            STA A   ACIA
C008 86 11               LDA A   #CTLREG    SET 8 BITS AND 2 STOP
C00A B7 80 04            STA A   ACIA

C00D 7E C0 F1            JMP     SIGNON     GO TO START OF MONITOR

               *****************************************
               * FUNCTION: INCH - Input character
               * INPUT: none
               * OUTPUT: char in acc A
               * DESTROYS: acc A
               * CALLS: none
               * DESCRIPTION: Gets 1 character from terminal

C010 B6 80 04  INCH      LDA A   ACIA       GET STATUS
C013 47                  ASR A              SHIFT RDRF FLAG INTO CARRY
C014 24 FA               BCC     INCH       RECIEVE NOT READY
C016 B6 80 05            LDA A   ACIA+1     GET CHAR
C019 84 7F               AND A   #$7F       MASK PARITY
C01B 7E C0 79            JMP     OUTCH      ECHO & RTS

               *****************************************
               * FUNCTION: INHEX - INPUT HEX DIGIT
               * INPUT: none
               * OUTPUT: Digit in acc A
               * CALLS: INCH
               * DESTROYS: acc A
               * Returns to monitor if not HEX input

C01E 8D F0     INHEX     BSR     INCH       GET A CHAR
C020 81 30               CMP A   #'0        ZERO
C022 2B 11               BMI     HEXERR     NOT HEX
C024 81 39               CMP A   #'9        NINE
C026 2F 0A               BLE     HEXRTS     GOOD HEX
C028 81 41               CMP A   #'A
C02A 2B 09               BMI     HEXERR     NOT HEX
C02C 81 46               CMP A   #'F
C02E 2E 05               BGT     HEXERR
C030 80 07               SUB A   #7         FIX A-F
C032 84 0F     HEXRTS    AND A   #$0F       CONVERT ASCII TO DIGIT
C034 39                  RTS

C035 7E C0 AF  HEXERR    JMP     CTRL       RETURN TO CONTROL LOOP
```

Figure 2.2.: Example assembly language

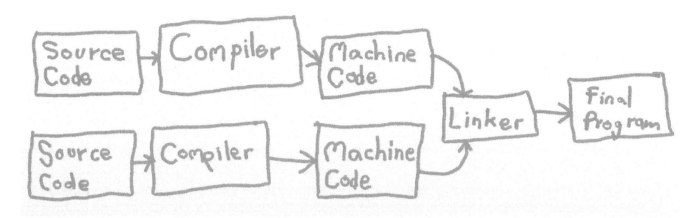

Figure 2.3.: Compilers and linkers

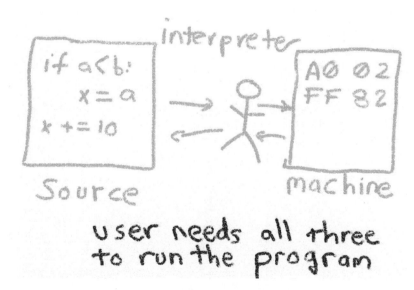

Figure 2.4.: Interpreter

been learned, the same theories will apply to the other languages.

For an entertaining history of computing, I recommend watching: `Triumph of the Nerds` by Robert X Cringley, a three part series on the orgins of computing. The movies are entertaining enough that your entire family might enjoy them. I also recommend the book `Accidental Empires` if you are more into reading than video.

What happens after those videos? They don't even cover the birth of the Internet! Then check out the video series `Nerds 2.0.1` also by Robert X Cringely.

2.2. Review Questions

1. Give an example of a binary number. (While a number such as "1" can be a binary, decimal, and hexidecimal number, try coming up with an example that better illustrates the differences between the different bases of numbers.)

2. Give an example of a decimal number.

3. Give an example of a hexidecimal number.

4. Convert the numbers 1, 10, 100, 1000, and 10000 from binary to decimal.

5. What is a compiler?

6. What is source code?

7. What is machine language?

8. What is a first generation language?

9. What is a second generation language?

10. What is a third generation language?

11. What is an interpreter?

3. Quiz Games and If Statements

How do we tell if a player has beat the high score? How can we tell if he has run out of lives? How can we tell if she has the key required to open the locked door?

What we need is the `if` statement. The `if` statement is also known as a *conditional statement*. (You can use the term "conditional statement" when you want to impress everyone how smart you are.) The `if` statement allows a computer to make a decision. Is it hot outside? Has the spaceship reached the edge of the screen? Has too much money been withdrawn from the account? A program can test for these conditions with the `if` statement.

3.1. Basic Comparisons

Here are a few examples of `if` statements. The first section sets up two variables (a and b) for use in the `if` statements. Then two `if` statements show how to compare the variables to see if one is greater than the other.

Listing 3.1: Example if statements: less than, greater than

```
1  # Variables used in the example if statements
2  a = 4
3  b = 5
4
5  # Basic comparisons
6  if a < b:
7      print ("a is less than b")
8
9  if a > b:
10     print ("a is greater than b")
11
12 print("Done")
```

Since a is less than b, the first statement will print out if this code is run. If the variables a and b were both equal to 4, then neither of the two `if` statements above would print anything out. The number 4 is not greater than 4, so the `if` statement would fail.

To show the flow of a program a *flowchart* may be used. Most people can follow a flowchart even without an introduction to programming. See how well you can understand Figure 3.1.

This book skips an in-depth look at flowcharting because it is boring. But if you want to be a superstar programmer, please read more about it at:

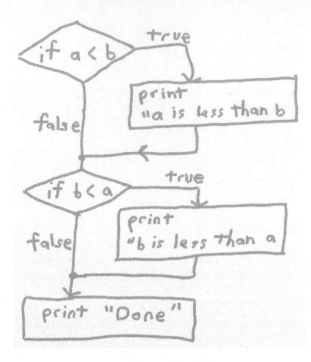

Figure 3.1.: Flowchart

http://en.wikipedia.org/wiki/Flowchart

The prior example checked for greater than or less than. Numbers that were equal would not pass the test. To check for a values greater than *or equal*, the following examples show how to do this:

Listing 3.2: Example if statements: less than or equal, greater than or equal

```
1 if a <= b:
2     print ("a is less than or equal to b")
3
4 if a >= b:
5     print ("a is greater than or equal to b")
```

The <= and >= symbols must used in order, and there may not be a space between them. For example, =< will not work, nor will <=.

When writing these statements out on a test, some students like to use the ≤ symbol. For example:

if a ≤ b:

This ≤ symbol doesn't actually work in a program. Plus most people don't know how to easily type it on the keyboard. (Just in case you are curious, to type it hold down the 'alt' key while typing 243 on the number pad.) So when writing out code, remember that it is <= and not ≤. Many people lose points on tests for this reason; don't be that person.

The next set of code checks to see if two items are equal or not. The operator for equal is ==
and the operator for not equal is !=. Here they are in action.

```
1 # Equal
2 if a == b:
3     print ("a is equal to b")
4
5 # Not equal
6 if a != b:
7     print ("a and b are not equal")
```

Caution! Common mistake.

NOTE: It is very easy to mix up when to use == and =. Use == if you are asking if they are
equal, use = if you are assigning a value.

The two most common mistakes in mixing the = and ==operators are demonstrated below:

```
1 # This is wrong
2 a == 1
3
4 # This is also wrong
5 if a = 1:
6     print ("A is one")
```

Stop! Please take a moment to go back and carefully study the last two code examples. Save
time later by making sure you understand when to use = and ==. Don't guess.

3.2. Indentation

Indentation matters. Each line under the if statement that is indented will only be executed if
the statement is true:

```
1 if a == 1:
2     print("If a is one, this will print.")
3     print("So will this.")
4     print("And this.")
5
6 print("This will always print because it is not indented.")
```

Indentation must be the same. This code doesn't work.

```
1 if a == 1:
2   print("Indented two spaces.")
3     print("Indented four. This will generate an error.")
4     print("The computer will want you to make up your mind.")
```

Once an if statement has been finished, it is not possible to re-indent to go back to it. The test has to be performed again.

```
1 if a == 1:
2     print("If a is one, this will print.")
3     print("So will this.")
4
5 print("This will always print because it is not indented.")
6     print("This will generate an error. Why it is indented?")
```

3.3. Using And/Or

An if statement can check multiple conditions by chaining together comparisons with **and** and **or**. These are also considered to be *operators* just like + or - are.

Listing 3.4: Example if statements, using "and" and "or"

```
1 # And
2 if a < b and a < c:
3     print ("a is less than b and c")
4
5 # Non-exclusive or
6 if a < b or a < c:
7     print ("a is less than either a or b (or both)")
```

Repeat yourself please.

A common mistake is to omit a variable when checking it against multiple conditions. The code below does not work because the computer does not know what to check against the variable c. It will not assume to check it against a.

```
1 # This is not correct
2 if a < b or < c:
3     print ("a is less than b and c")
```

3.4. Boolean Variables

Python supports Boolean variables. What are Boolean variables? Boolean variables can store either a **True** or a value of **False**. **Boolean algebra**was developed by **George Boole**in back in 1854. If only he knew how important his work would become as the basis for modern computer logic!

An `if` statement needs an expression to evaluate to **True** or **False**. What may seem odd is that it does not actually need to do any comparisons if a variable already evaluates to **True** or **False**.

Listing 3.5: If statements and Boolean data types

```
1 # Boolean data type. This is legal!
2 a = True
3 if a:
4     print ("a is true")
```

Back when I was in school it was popular to say some false statement. Wait three seconds, then shout "NOT!" Well, even your computer thinks that is lame. If you are going to do that, you have to start with the **not** operator. The following code uses the **not** to flip the value of **a** between true and false.

Listing 3.6: The not operator example 1

```
1 # How to use the not function
2 if not(a):
3     print ("a is false")
```

Because **not** is an operator and not a function, the parentheses aren't necessary. This is also legal:

Listing 3.7: The not operator example 2

```
1 # How to use the not function
2 if not a:
3     print ("a is false")
```

It is also possible to use Boolean variables with **and** and **or** operators.

Listing 3.8: Using "and" with Boolean variables

```
1 a = True
2 b = False
3
4 if a and b:
5     print ("a and b are both true")
```

> ✎ **Who knew True/False could be hard?**

It is also possible to assign a variable to the result of a comparison. In the code below, the variables **a** and **b** are compared. If they are equal, **c** will be **True**, otherwise **c** will be **False**.

Listing 3.9: Assigning values to Boolean data types

```
1 a = 3
2 b = 3
3 # This next line is strange-looking, but legal.
4 # c will be true or false, depending if
5 # a and b are equal.
6 c = a == b
7 # Prints value of c, in this case True
8 print(c)
```

> ✏️ Zero means False. Everything else is True.

It is possible to create an `if` statement with a condition that does not evaluate to true or false. This is not usually desired, but it is important to understand how the computer handles these values when searching for problems.

The statement below is legal and will cause the text to be printed out because the values in the `if` statement are non-zero:

```
1 if 1:
2     print ("1")
3 if "A":
4     print ("A")
```

The code below will not print out anything because the value in the if statement is zero which is treated as False. Any value other than zero is considered true.

```
1 if 0:
2     print ("Zero")
```

In the code below, the first `if` statement appears to work. The problem is that it will always trigger as true even if the variable `a` is not equal to `b`. This is because `b` by itself is considered true.

```
1 a = "c"
2 if a == "B" or "b":
3     print ("a is equal to b. Maybe.")
4
5 # This is a better way to do the if statement.
6 if a == "B" or a == "b":
7     print ("a is equal to b.")
```

3.5. Else and Else If

Below is code that will get the temperature from the user and print if it is hot.

```
1 temperature = int(input("What is the temperature in Fahrenheit? "))
2 if temperature > 90:
```

```
3     print("It is hot outside")
4 print ("Done")
```

If the programmer wants code to be executed if it is not hot, she can use the **else** statement. Notice how the **else** is lined up with the **i** in the **if** statement, and how it is followed by a colon just like the **if** statement.

In the case of an **if...else** statement, one block of code will always be executed. The first block will be executed if the statement evaluates to **True**, the second block if it evaluates to **False**.

Listing 3.10: Example if/else statement

```
1 temperature = int(input("What is the temperature in Fahrenheit? "))
2 if temperature > 90:
3     print("It is hot outside")
4 else:
5     print("It is not hot outside")
6 print ("Done")
```

It is possible to chain several **if** statements together using the **else...if** statement. Python abbreviates this as **elif**.

Listing 3.11: Example if/elif/else statement

```
1 temperature = int(input("What is the temperature in Fahrenheit? "))
2 if temperature > 90:
3     print("It is hot outside")
4 elif temperature < 30:
5     print("It is cold outside")
6 else:
7     print("It is not hot outside")
8 print ("Done")
```

In the code below, the program will output "It is hot outside" even if the user types in 120 degrees. Why? How can the code be fixed?

If you can't figure it out, see the video.

Listing 3.12: Example of improper ordering if/elif/else

```
1 temperature = int(input("What is the temperature in Fahrenheit? "))
2 if temperature > 90:
3     print("It is hot outside")
4 elif temperature > 110:
5     print("Oh man, you could fry eggs on the pavement!")
6 elif temperature < 30:
7     print("It is cold outside")
8 else:
9     print("It is ok outside")
10 print ("Done")
```

3.6. Text Comparisons

It is possible to use an `if` statement to check text. (Note, if Eclipse is used rather than the recommended IDLE program, the example does not work because the input will contain an extra carriage return at the end.)

Listing 3.13: Case sensitive text comparison

```
1 userName = input("What is your name? ")
2 if userName == "Paul":
3     print("You have a nice name.")
4 else:
5     print("Your name is ok.")
```

The prior example will only match if the user enters "Paul". It will not work if the user enters "paul" or "PAUL".

A common mistake is to forget the quotes around the string being compared. In the example below, the computer will think that `Paul` is a variable that stores a value. It will flag an error because it has no idea what is stored in the variable `Paul`.

Listing 3.14: Incorrect comparison

```
1 userName = input("What is your name? ")
2 if userName == Paul: # This does not work because quotes are missing
3     print("You have a nice name.")
4 else:
5     print("Your name is ok.")
```

3.6.1. Multiple Text Possibilities

When comparing a variable to multiple possible strings of text, it is important to remember that the comparison must include the variable. For example:

```
# This does not work! It will always be true
if userName == "Paul" or "Mary":
```

Instead, the code should read:

```
# This does work
if userName == "Paul" or userName == "Mary":
```

This is because any value other than zero, the computer assumes to mean `True`. So to the computer `"Mary"` is the same thing as `True` and so it will run the code in the `if` statement.

3.6.2. Case Insensitive Comparisons

If the program needs to match regardless as to the case of the text entered, the easiest way to do that is to convert everything to lower case. This can be done with the `lower`command.

The example below will take whatever the user enters, convert it to lower case, and then do the comparison. Important: Don't compare it against a string that has uppercase. If the user input is converted to lowercase, then compared against uppercase letters, there is no way a match can occur.

Listing 3.15: Case-insensitive text comparison

```
1 userName = input("What is your name? ")
2 if userName.lower() == "paul":
3     print("You have a nice name.")
4 else:
5     print("Your name is ok.")
```

3.7. Example `if` Statements

The next set of example code below runs through all the concepts talked about earlier. The video traces through each line of code and explains how it works.

The video uses an integrated editor called Eclipse. The default version of Eclipse doesn't work with Python, but the PyDev version does. The PyDev editor is available for free from: http://pydev.org/

The editor is complex, but it has many options and can be a powerful environment to work in. Some programmers like using environments such as PyDev that can have so many plug-ins that will do everything but bring you coffee. Some developers prefer a minimilistic environment that doesn't "get in the way."

Listing 3.16: if_statement_examples.py

```
1 # Sample Python/Pygame Programs
2 # Simpson College Computer Science
3 # http://programarcadegames.com/
4 # http://simpson.edu/computer-science/
5
6 # Explanation video: http://youtu.be/pDpNSck2aXQ
7
8 # Variables used in the example if statements
9 a = 4
10 b = 5
11 c = 6
12
13 # Basic comparisons
14 if a < b:
15     print("a is less than b")
16
17 if a > b:
```

```
18     print("a is greater than than b")
19
20 if a <= b:
21     print("a is less than or equal to b")
22
23 if a >= b:
24     print("a is greater than or equal to b")
25
26 # NOTE: It is very easy to mix when to use == and =.
27 # Use == if you are asking if they are equal, use =
28 # if you are assigning a value.
29 if a == b:
30     print("a is equal to b")
31
32 # Not equal
33 if a != b:
34   printt ("a and b are not equal")
35
36 # And
37 if a < b and a < c:
38     print("a is less than b and c")
39
40 # Non-exclusive or
41 if a < b or a < c:
42     print("a is less than either a or b (or both)")
43
44
45 # Boolean data type. This is legal!
46 a = True
47 if a:
48     print("a is true")
49
50 if not a:
51     print("a is false")
52
53 a = True
54 b = False
55
56 if a and b:
57     print("a and b are both true")
58
59 a = 3
60 b = 3
61 c = a == b
62 print(c)
63
64 # These are also legal and will trigger as being true because
65 # the values are not zero:
```

```
66 if 1:
67     print("1")
68 if "A":
69     print("A")
70
71 # This will not trigger as true because it is zero.
72 if 0:
73     print("Zero")
74
75 # Comparing variables to multiple values.
76 # The first if statement appears to work, but it will always
77 # trigger as true even if the variable a is not equal to b.
78 # This is because "b" by itself is considered true.
79 a = "c"
80 if a == "B" or "b":
81     print("a is equal to b. Maybe.")
82
83 # This is the proper way to do the if statement.
84 if a == "B" or a == "b":
85     print("a is equal to b.")
86
87 # Example 1: If statement
88 temperature = int(input("What is the temperature in Fahrenheit? "))
89 if temperature > 90:
90     print("It is hot outside")
91 print("Done")
92
93 # Example 2: Else statement
94 temperature = int(input("What is the temperature in Fahrenheit? "))
95 if temperature > 90:
96     print("It is hot outside")
97 else:
98     print("It is not hot outside")
99 print("Done")
100
101 #Example 3: Else if statement
102 temperature = int(input("What is the temperature in Fahrenheit? "))
103 if temperature > 90:
104     print("It is hot outside")
105 elif temperature < 30:
106     print("It is cold outside")
107 else:
108     print("It is not hot outside")
109 print("Done")
110
111 # Example 4: Ordering of statements
112 # Something with this is wrong. What?
113 temperature = int(input("What is the temperature in Fahrenheit? "))
```

```
114 if temperature > 90:
115     print("It is hot outside")
116 elif temperature > 110:
117     print("Oh man, you could fry eggs on the pavement!")
118 elif temperature < 30:
119     print("It is cold outside")
120 else:
121     print("It is ok outside")
122 print("Done")
123
124 # Comparisons using string/text
125 # Note, this example does not work when running under Eclipse
126 # because the input will contain an extra carriage return at the
127 # end. It works fine under IDLE.
128 userName = input("What is your name? ")
129 if userName == "Paul":
130     print("You have a nice name.")
131 else:
132     print("Your name is ok.")
```

3.8. Review Questions

1. Correct the following code:

    ```
    1 temperature = float (input("Temperature")
    2 if temperature > 90:
    3     print("It is hot outside.")
    ```

2. There are two things wrong with this code. One prevents it from running, and the other is subtle.

    ```
    1 x == 4
    2 if x >= 0:
    3     print("x is positive.")
    4 else:
    5     print("x is not positive.")
    ```

3. There are four things wrong with this code. Copy it into a script in IDLE and find the errors.

    ```
    1 answer = input("What is the name of Dr. Bunsen Honeydew's assistant?")
    2 if a = "Beaker":
    3     print("Correct!")
    4     else
    5     print("Incorrect! It is Beaker.")
    ```

4. Correct the following code:

```
1 userInput = input("A cherry is a:")
2 print("A. Dessert topping")
3 print("B. Desert topping")
4 if userInput=="A":
5     print("Correct!")
```

5. What three things are wrong with the following code?

```
1 x = input("Enter a number:")
2 if x = 3
3     print ("You entered 3")
```

6. This program doesn't work correctly. What is wrong?

```
1 x = input("How are you today?")
2 if x == "Happy" or "Glad":
3     print ("That is good to hear!")
```

7. Look at the code below. Write you best guess on what it will print. Next, run the code and see if you are correct:

```
1 x = 5
2 y = x == 6
3 z = x == 5
4 print("x=",x)
5 print("y=",y)
6 print("z=",z)
7 if y:
8     print ("Fizz")
9 if z:
10     print ("Buzz")
```

8. Correct the following code:

```
1 answer = input("True or False, is 3+4 equal to 7?")
2 a = True
3 b = False
4 if a:
5     print("Correct")
6 else:
7     print("Incorrect")
```

9. Write a Python program that will take in a number from the user and print if it is positive, negative, or zero.

10. Write a Python program that will take in a number from a user and print out "Success" if it is greater than -10 and less than 10, inclusive.

3.9. Lab

Complete Lab 2 "Create-a-Quiz" to create your own quiz program and make sure that you've learned how to properly use the `if` statement.

4. Guessing Games with Random Numbers and Loops

The last step before we start with graphics is learning how to loop a section of code. Most games "loop." They repeat the same code over and over. For example the number guessing game below loops for each guess that the user makes:

```
Hi! I'm thinking of a random number between 1 and 100.
--- Attempt 1
Guess what number I am thinking of: 50
Too high.
--- Attempt 2
Guess what number I am thinking of: 25
Too high.
--- Attempt 3
Guess what number I am thinking of: 17
Too high.
--- Attempt 4
Guess what number I am thinking of: 9
Too low.
--- Attempt 5
Guess what number I am thinking of: 14
Too high.
--- Attempt 6
Guess what number I am thinking of: 12
Too high.
--- Attempt 7
Guess what number I am thinking of: 10
Too low.
Aw, you ran out of tries. The number was 11.
```

Wait, what does this have to do with graphics and video games? A lot. Each *frame* the game displays is one time through a loop. You may be familiar with the frames-per-second (FPS) statistic that games show. The FPS represents the number of times the computer updates the screen each second. The higher the rate, the smoother the game. (Although an FPS rate past 60 is faster than most screens can update, so there isn't much point to push it past that.) Figure 4.1 shows the game Eve Online and a graph showing how many frames per second the computer is able to display.

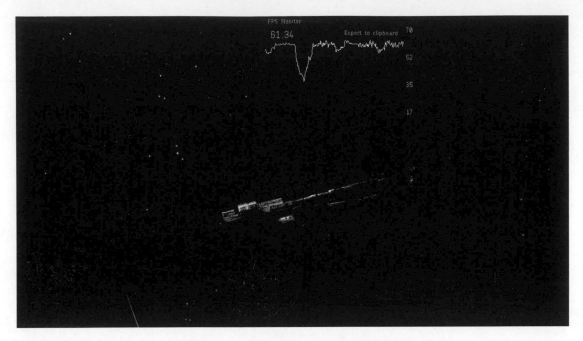

Figure 4.1.: FPS in video games

The loop in these games works like the flowchart in Figure 4.2. Despite the complexities of modern games, the inside of this loop is similar to the calculator program we did in Chapter 1. Get user input. Perform calculations. Output the result. In a video game, we try to repeat this up to 60 times per second.

There can even be loops inside of other loops. A real "loop the loop." Take a look at the "Draw Everything" box in Figure 4.2. This set of code loops through and draws each object in the game. That loop is inside of the larger loop that draws each frame of the game, which looks like Figure 4.3.

There are two major types of loops in Python, `for` loops and `while` loops. If you want to repeat a certain number of times, use a `for` loop. If you want to repeat until something happens (like the user hits the quit button) then use a `while` loop.

For example, a `for` loop can be used to print all student records since the computer knows how many students there are. A `while` loop would need to be used to check for when a user hits the mouse button since the computer has no idea how long it will have to wait.

4.1. For Loops

The `for` loop example below runs the `print` statement five times. It could just as easily run 100 or 1,000,000 times just by changing the 5 to the desired number of times to loop. Note the similarities of how the `for` loop is written to the `if` statement. Both end in a colon, and both

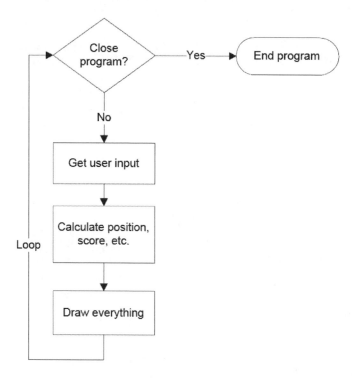

Figure 4.2.: Game loop

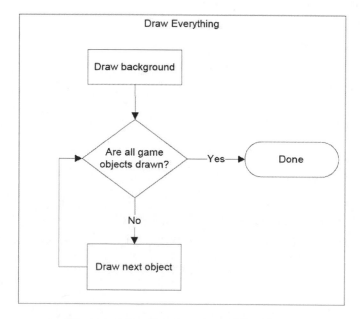

Figure 4.3.: Draw everything loop

use indentation to specify which lines are affected by the statement.

Listing 4.1: Loop to print five times

```
1 for i in range(5):
2     print ("I will not chew gum in class.")
```

Output:

```
I will not chew gum in class.
I will not chew gum in class.
I will not chew gum in class.
I will not chew gum in class.
I will not chew gum in class.
```

The i on line 1 is a variable that keeps track of how many times the program has looped. It is a new variable and can be named any legal variable name. Programmers often use i as for the variable name, because the i is short for *increment*. This variable helps track when the loop should end.

The **range** function controls how many times the code in the loop is run. In this case, five times.

The next example code will print "Please," five times and "Can I go to the mall?" only once. "Can I go to the mall?" is not indented so it is not part of the **for** loop and will not print until the **for** loop completes.

```
1 for i in range(5):
2     print ("Please,")
3 print ("Can I go to the mall?")
```

Output:

```
Please,
Please,
Please,
Please,
Please,
Can I go to the mall?
```

This next code example takes the prior example and indents line 3. This change will cause the program to print "Please," and "Can I go to the mall?" five times. Since the statement has been indented "Can I go to the mall?" is now part of the **for** loop and will repeat five times just line the word "Please,".

```
1 for i in range(5):
2     print ("Please,")
3     print ("Can I go to the mall?")
```

Output:

```
Please,
Can I go to the mall?
Please,
Can I go to the mall?
Please,
Can I go to the mall?
Please,
Can I go to the mall?
Please,
Can I go to the mall?
```

The code below will print the numbers 0 to 9. Notice that the loop starts at 0 and does not include the number 10. It is natural to assume that `range(10)` would include 10, but it stops just short of it.

Listing 4.2: Print the numbers 0 to 9

```
1 for i in range(10):
2     print(i)
```

Output:

```
0
1
2
3
4
5
6
7
8
9
```

A program does not need to name the variable `i`, it could be named something else. For example a programmer might use `lineNumber` if she was processing a text file.

If a programmer wants to go from 1 to 10 instead of 0 to 9, there are a couple ways to do it. The first way is to send the `range` function two numbers instead of one. The first number is the starting value, the second is just beyond the ending value.

It does take some practice to get used to the idea that the `for` loop will include the first number, but not the second number listed. The example below specifies a range of `(1,11)`, and the numbers 1 to 10 are printed. The starting number 1 is included, but not the ending number of 11.

Listing 4.3: Print the numbers 1 to 10, version 1

```
1 for i in range(1,11):
2     print(i)
```

Output:

```
1
2
3
4
5
6
7
8
9
10
```

Another way to print the numbers 1 to 10 is to still use `range(10)` and have the variable i go from 0 to 9. But just before printing out the variable the programmer adds one to it. This also works to print the numbers 1 to 10. Either method works just fine.

Listing 4.4: Print the numbers 1 to 10, version 2

```
1 # Print the numbers 1 to 10.
2 for i in range(10):
3     print(i + 1)
```

4.1.1. Counting By Numbers Other Than One

If the program needs to count by 2's or use some other increment, that is easy. Just like before there are two ways to do it. The easiest is to supply a third number to the range function that tells it to count by 2's. The second way to do it is to go ahead and count by 1's, but multiply the variable by 2. The code example below shows both methods.

Listing 4.5: Two ways to print the even numbers 2 to 10

```
1 # Two ways to print the even numbers 2 to 10
2 for i in range(2,12,2):
3     print(i)
4
5 for i in range(5):
6     print ((i + 1) * 2)
```

Output:

```
2
4
6
8
10
2
4
6
```

```
8
10
```

It is also possible to count backwards down towards zero by giving the range function a negative step. In the example below, start at 10, go down to but not including 0, and do it by -1 increments. The hardest part of creating these loops is to accidentally switch the start and end numbers. The program starts at the larger value, so it goes first. Normal `for` loops that count up start with the smallest value listed first in the `range` function.

Listing 4.6: Count down from 10 to 1

```
1 for i in range(10,0,-1):
2     print(i)
```

Output:

```
10
9
8
7
6
5
4
3
2
1
```

If the numbers that a program needs to iterate through don't form an easy pattern, it is possible to pull numbers out of a list:

Listing 4.7: Print numbers out of a list

```
1 for i in [2,6,4,2,4,6,7,4]:
2     print(i)
```

This prints:

```
2
6
4
2
4
6
7
4
```

4.1.2. Nesting Loops

Try to predict what the code below will print. Then enter the code and see if you are correct.

```
# What does this print? Why?
for i in range(3):
    print ("a")
for j in range(3):
  print ("b")
```

This next block of code is almost identical to the one above. The second `for` loop has been indented one tab stop so that it is now *nested* inside of the first for loop. This changes how the code runs significantly. Try it and see.

```
1 # What does this print? Why?
2 for i in range(3):
3     print("a")
4     for j in range(3):
5         print("b")
6
7 print("Done")
```

I'm not going to tell you what the code does, go to a computer and see.

4.1.3. Keeping a Running Total

A common operation in working with loops is to keep a running total. This "running total" code pattern is used a lot in this book. Keep a running total of a score, total a person's account transactions, use a total to find an average, etc. You might want to bookmark this code listing because we'll refer back to it several times. In the code below, the user enters five numbers and the code totals up their values.

Listing 4.8: Keep a Running Total
```
1 total = 0
2 for i in range(5):
3     newNumber = int(input("Enter a number: " ))
4     total += newNumber
5 print("The total is: ",total)
```

Note that line 1 creates the variable `total`, and sets it to an initial amount of zero. It is easy to forget the need to create and initialize the variable to zero. Without it the computer will complain when it hits line 4. It doesn't know how to add `newNumber` to `total` because `total` hasn't been given a value yet.

A common mistake is to use `i` to `total` instead of `newNumber`. Remember, we are keeping a running total of the values entered by the user, not a running total of the current loop count.

Speaking of the current loop count, we can use the loop count value to solve some mathematical operations. For example:

$$s = \sum_{n=1}^{100} n$$

If you aren't familiar with this type of formula, it is just a fancy way of stating:

$s = 1 + 2 + 3 + 4 + 5 \ldots 98 + 99 + 100$

The code below adds all the numbers from 1 to 100. It demonstrates a common pattern where a running total is kept inside of a loop. This also uses a separate variable `sum` to track the running total.

Listing 4.9: Sum all numbers 1 to 100

```
1 # What is the value of sum?
2 sum = 0
3 for i in range(1,101):
4     sum = sum + i
5 print(sum)
```

Here's a different variation. This takes five numbers from the user and counts the number of times the user enters a zero:

```
1 total = 0
2 for i in range(5):
3     newNumber = int(input( "Enter a number: "))
4     if newNumber == 0:
5         total += 1
6 print("You entered a total of",total,"zeros")
```

A programmer that understands the nested `for` loops and running totals should be able to predict the output of the code below.

```
1 # What is the value of a?
2 a = 0
3 for i in range(10):
4     a=a+1
5 print(a)
6
7 # What is the value of a?
8 a = 0
9 for i in range(10):
10     a = a + 1
11 for j in range(10):
12     a = a + 1
13 print(a)
14
15 # What is the value of a?
16 a = 0
17 for i in range(10):
18     a = a + 1
19     for j in range(10):
20         a = a + 1
21 print(a)
```

Don't go over this section too fast. Give it a try and predict the output of the code above. Then copy it into a Python program and run it to see if you are right. If you aren't, figure out why.

4.2. Example for Loops

This example code covers common for loops and shows how they work.

Listing 4.10: for_loop_examples.py

```python
# Sample Python/Pygame Programs
# Simpson College Computer Science
# http://programarcadegames.com/
# http://simpson.edu/computer-science/

# Print 'Hi' 10 times
for i in range(10):
    print ("Hi")

# Print 'Hello' 5 times and 'There' once
for i in range(5):
    print ("Hello")
print ("There")

# Print 'Hello' 'There' 5 times
for i in range(5):
    print ("Hello")
    print ("There")

# Print the numbers 0 to 9
for i in range(10):
    print (i)

# Two ways to print the numbers 1 to 10
for i in range(1,11):
    print (i)

for i in range(10):
    print (i+1)

# Two ways to print the even numbers 2 to 10
for i in range(2,12,2):
    print (i)

for i in range(5):
    print ((i+1)*2)
```

```
37
38 # Count down from 10 down to 1 (not zero)
39 for i in range(10,0,-1):
40     print(i)
41
42 # Print numbers out of a list
43 for i in [2,6,4,2,4,6,7,4]:
44     print(i)
45
46 # What does this print? Why?
47 for i in range(3):
48     print ("a")
49     for j in range(3):
50         print ("b")
51
52 # What is the value of a?
53 a=0
54 for i in range(10):
55     a=a+1
56 print(a)
57
58 # What is the value of a?
59 a=0
60 for i in range(10):
61     a=a+1
62 for j in range(10):
63     a=a+1
64 print(a)
65
66 # What is the value of a?
67 a=0
68 for i in range(10):
69     a=a+1
70     for j in range(10):
71         a=a+1
72 print(a)
73
74 # What is the value of sum?
75 sum=0
76 for i in range(1,101):
77     sum = sum + i
```

4.3. While Loops

A `for` loop is used when a program knows it needs to repeat a block of code for a certain number of times. A `while` loop is used when a program needs to loop until a particular condition occurs.

Oddly enough, a `while` loop can be used anywhere a `for` loop is used. It can be used to loop until an increment variable reaches a certain value. Why have a `for` loop if a `while` loop can do everything? The `for` loop is simpler to use and code. A `for` loop that looks like this:

Listing 4.11: Using a for loop to print the numbers 0 to 9

```
1 for i in range(10):
2     print(i)
```

...can be done with a `while` loop that looks like this:

Listing 4.12: Using a while loop to print the numbers 0 to 9

```
1 i = 0
2 while i < 10:
3     print(i)
4     i = i + 1
```

Line 1 of the `while` loop sets up a "sentinel" variable that will be used to count the number of times the loop has been executed. This happens automatically in a `for` loop eliminating one line of code. Line 2 contains the actual `while` loop. The format of the `while` loop is very similar to the `if` statement. If the condition holds, the code in the loop will repeat. Line 4 adds to the increment value. In a `for` loop this happens automatically, eliminating another line of code. As one can see from the code, the `for` loop is more compact than a `while` loop and is easier to read. Otherwise programs would do everything with a `while` loop.

A common mistake is to confuse the `for` loop and the `while` loop. The code below shows a programmer that can't quite make up his/her mind between a `for` loop or a `while` loop.

Listing 4.13: Example of a confused loop

```
1 while range(10):
2     print(i)
```

> **Don't use range with a while loop!**

The `range` function only works with the `for` loop. Do not use it with the `while` loop!

4.3.1. Using Increment Operators

Increment operators are often used with while loops. It is possible to short-hand the code:

```
i = i + 1
```

With the following:

```
i += 1
```

In the **while** loop it would look like:

```
1 i = 0
2 while i < 10:
3     print(i)
4     i += 1
```

This can be done with subtraction and multiplication as well. For example:

```
  i *= 2
```

Is the same as:

```
  i = i * 2
```

See if you can figure out what would this print:

```
1 i = 1
2 while i <= 2 ** 32:
3     print(i)
4     i *= 2
```

4.3.2. Looping Until User Wants To Quit

A very common operation is to loop until the user performs a request to quit:

Listing 4.14: Looping until the user wants to quit

```
1 quit = "n"
2 while quit == "n":
3     quit = input ("Do you want to quit? ")
```

There may be several ways for a loop to quit. Using a Boolean variable to trigger the event is a way of handling that. Here's an example:

Listing 4.15: Looping until the game is over or the user wants to quit

```
1 done = False
2 while not done:
3     quit = input ("Do you want to quit? ")
4     if quit == "y" :
5         done = True;
6
7     attack = input ("Does your elf attack the dragon? ")
8     if attack == "y":
9         print ("Bad choice, you died.")
10         done = True;
```

This isn't perfect though, because if the user says she wants to quit, the code will still ask if she wants to attack the dragon. How could you fix this?

Here is an example of using a **while** loop where the code repeats until the value gets close enough to zero:

```
1 value = 0
2 increment = 0.5
3 while value < 0.999:
4     value += increment
5     increment *= 0.5
6     print(value)
```

4.3.3. Common Problems With while Loops

The programmer wants to count down from 10. What is wrong and how can it be fixed?

```
1 i = 10
2 while i == 0:
3     print(i)
4     i -= 1
```

What is wrong with this loop that tries to count to 10? What will happen when it is run? How should it be fixed?

```
1 i = 1
2 while i < 10:
3     print(i)
```

4.4. Example while Loops

Here's a program that covers the different uses of the **while** loop that we just talked about.

Listing 4.16: while_loop_examples.py

```
1 # Sample Python/Pygame Programs
2 # Simpson College Computer Science
3 # http://programarcadegames.com/
4 # http://simpson.edu/computer-science/
5
6 # A while loop can be used anywhere a for loop is used:
7 i = 0
8 while i < 10:
9     print(i)
10     i = i + 1
11
12 # This is the same as:
13 for i in range(10):
14     print(i)
```

```python
15
16 # It is possible to short hand the code:
17 # i=i+1
18 # With the following:
19 # i += 1
20 # This can be done with subtraction, and multiplication as well.
21 i = 0
22 while i < 10:
23     print(i)
24     i += 1
25
26 # What would this print?
27 i = 1
28 while i <= 2**32:
29     print(i)
30     i *= 2
31
32
33
34 # A very common operation is to loop until the user performs
35 # a request to quit
36 quit = "n"
37 while quit == "n":
38     quit = input ("Do you want to quit? ")
39
40
41 # There may be several ways for a loop to quit. Using a boolean
42 # to trigger the event is a way of handling that.
43 done = False
44 while not done:
45     quit = input ("Do you want to quit? ")
46     if quit == "y":
47         done = True;
48
49     attack = input ("Does your elf attach the dragon? ")
50     if attack == "y":
51         print("Bad choice, you died.")
52         done = True;
53
54 value = 0
55 increment = 0.5
56 while value < 0.999:
57     value += increment
58     increment *= 0.5
59     print(value)
60
61
62 # -- Common problems with while loops --
```

```
63
64 # The programmer wants to count down from 10
65 # What is wrong and how to fix it?
66 i = 10
67 while i == 0:
68     print (i)
69     i -= 1
70
71 # What is wrong with this loop that tries
72 # to count to 10? What will happen when it is run?
73 i = 1
74 while i < 10:
75     print (i)
```

4.5. Random Numbers

Random numbers are heavily used in computer science for programs that involve games or simulations.

4.5.1. The `randrange` Function

By default, Python does not know how to make random numbers. It is necessary to have Python import a code library that can create random numbers. So to use random numbers, the first thing that should appear at the top of the program is an **import** statement:

```
import random
```

Just like with pygame, it is important not to create a file with the same name as what is being imported. Creating a file called **random.py** will cause Python to start importing that file instead of the system library that creates random numbers.

After this, random numbers can be created with the **randrange** function. For example, this code creates random numbers from 0 to 49. By default the lower bound is 0.

Listing 4.17: Random number from 0 to 49

```
my_number = random.randrange(50)
```

The next code example generates random numbers from 100 to 200. Just line the **range** funciton The second parameter specifies an upper-bound that is not inclusive. Therefore if you want random numbers up to and including 200, specify 201.

Listing 4.18: Random number from 100 to 200

```
my_number = random.randrange(100,201)
```

If a program needs to select a random item from a list, that is easy:

Listing 4.19: Picking a random item out of a list

```
my_list = ["rock","paper","scissors"]
random_index = random.randrange(3)
print(my_list[random_index])
```

4.5.2. The `random` Function

All of the prior code generates integer numbers. If a floating point number is desired, a programmer may use the **random** function.

The code below generates a random number from 0 to 1 such as 0.4355991106620656.

Listing 4.20: Random floating point number from 0 to 1

```
my_number=random.random()
```

With some simple math, this number can be adjusted. For example, the code below generates a random floating point number between 10 and 15:

Listing 4.21: Random floating point number between 10 and 15

```
my_number=random.random()*5+10
```

4.6. Non-Looping Review Questions

1. Cross out the variable names that are not legal in Python.

   ```
   pi
   PI
   fred
   Fred
   GreatBigVariable
   greatBigVariable
   great_big_variable
   great.big.variable
   2x
   x2x
   total%
   #left
   ```

2. Circle variable names that might be legal, but would not be proper.

   ```
   pi
   PI
   fred
   Fred
   ```

```
GreatBigVariable
greatBigVariable
great_big_variable
great.big.variable
2x
x2x
total%
#left
```

3. Give an example of a Python expression:

4. What is an "operator" in Python?

5. What does the following program print out?

```
x = 3
x + 1
print(x)
```

6. Correct the following code:

```
user_name = input("Enter your name: )"
```

7. Correct the following code:

```
value = int(input(print("Enter your age")))
```

8. Correct the following code:

```
temperature = float (input("Temperature"))
if temperature > = 90
    print("It is hot outside.")
```

9. Correct the following code:

```
1 print("Welcome to Oregon Trail!")
2 userInput = input("What is your occupation?")
3
4 print("A. Banker")
5 print("B. Carpenter")
6 print("C. Farmer")
7
8 if userInput = A:
9     money = 100
10 else if userInput = B:
11     money = 70
12 else if userInput = C:
13     money = 50
```

10. What is wrong with this code?

```
1 x = input ("Enter a number:")
2 if x > 100
3     print ("You entered a large number.")
4 else
5   print ("You didn't enter a large number.")
```

11. Write a program that asks the user how many quarters and nickels they have, then prints the total amount of money those coins are worth.

4.7. Looping Review Questions

1. Write a Python program that will use a `for` loop to print your name 10 times, and then the word "Done" at the end.

2. Write a Python program that will use a `for` loop to print "Red" and then "Gold" 20 times.

3. Write a Python program that will use a `for` loop to print the even numbers from 2 to 100, inclusive.

4. Write a Python program that will use a `while` loop to count from 10 down to, and including, 0. Then print the words "Blast off!"

5. There are four things wrong with this program. Find and correct them.

```
1 print("This program takes three numbers and returns the sum.")
2 total = 0
3
4 for i in range(3):
5     x = input("Enter a number: ")
6     total = total + i
7     print("The total is:",x)
```

6. Write a Python program that:

   - asks the user for seven numbers
   - prints the total sum of the numbers
   - prints the count of the positive entries, the number entries equal to zero, and the number of negative entries.

4.8. Random Numbers Review Questions

1. Write a program that prints a random integer from 1 to 10 (inclusive).

2. Write a program that prints a random floating point number somewhere between 1 and 10 (inclusive).

3. Coin flip tosser

   - Create a program that will print a random 0 or 1.
   - Instead of 0 or 1, print heads or tails.
   - Add a loop so that the program does this 50 times.
   - Create a running total for the number of heads flipped, and the number of tails.

4. Write a program that plays rock, paper, scissors

   - Create a program that randomly prints 0, 1, or 2.
   - Expand the program so it randomly prints rock, paper, or scissors using if statements. Don't select from a list, as shown in the chapter.
   - Add to the program so it first asks the user their choice.
     - It will be easier if you have them enter 1, 2, or 3.
   - Add conditional statement to figure out who wins.

5. Introduction to Graphics

Now that you can create loops, it is time to move on to learning how to create graphics. This chapter covers:

- How the computer handles x, y coordinates. It isn't like the coordinate system you learned in math class.
- How to specify colors. With millions of colors to choose from, telling the computer what color to use isn't as easy as just saying "red."
- How to open a blank window for drawing. Every artist needs a canvas.
- How to draw lines, rectangles, ellipses, and arcs.

5.1. Computer Coordinate Systems

The Cartesian coordinate system, shown in Figure 5.1 (`Wikimedia Commons`), is the system most people are used to when plotting graphics. This is the system taught in school. The computer uses a similar, but somewhat different, coordinate system. Understanding why it is different requires a quick bit of computer history.

During the early '80s, most computer systems were text-based and did not support graphics. Figure 5.2 (`Wikimedia Commons`) shows an early spreadsheet program run on an Apple][computer that was popular in the '80s. When positioning text on the screen, programmers started at the top calling it line 1. The screen continued down for 24 lines and across for 40 characters.

Even with plain text, it was possible to make rudimentary graphics by just using characters on the keyboard. See this kitten shown in Figure 5.3 and look carefully at how it is drawn. When making this art, characters were still positioned starting with line 1 at the top.

Later the character set was expanded to include boxes and other primitive drawing shapes. Characters could be drawn in different colors. As shown in Figure 5.4 the graphics got more advanced. Search the web for "ASCII art" and many more examples can be found.

Once computers moved to being able to control individual pixels for graphics, the text-based coordinate system stuck.

The x coordinates work the same as the Cartesian coordinates system. But the y coordinates are reversed. Rather than the zero y coordinate at the bottom of the graph like in Cartesian graphics, the zero y coordinate is at the top of the screen with the computer. As the y values go up, the computer coordinate position moved down the screen, just like lines of text rather

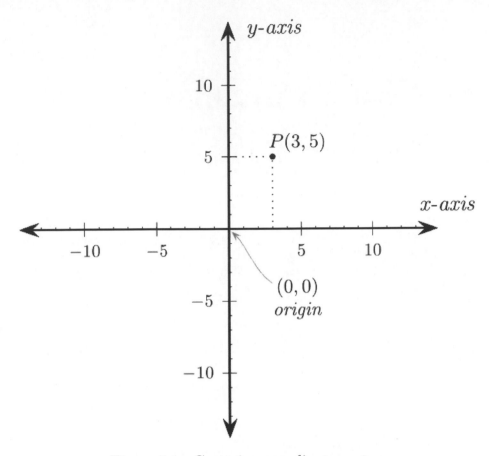

Figure 5.1.: Cartesian coordinate system

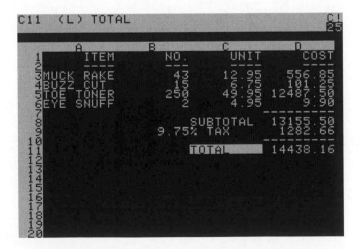

Figure 5.2.: Early Apple text screen

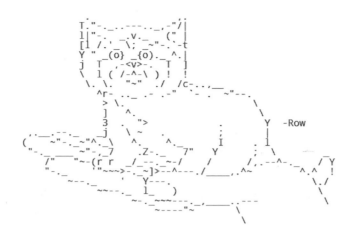

Figure 5.3.: Text screen

Figure 5.4.: Spaceware text screen

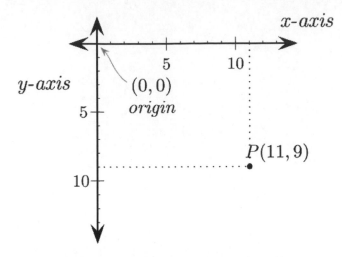

Figure 5.5.: Computer coordinate system

than standard Cartesian graphics. See Figure 5.5.

Also, note the screen covers the lower right quadrant, where the Cartesian coordinate system usually focuses on the upper right quadrant. It is possible to draw items at negative coordinates, but they will be drawn off-screen. This can be useful when part of a shape is off screen. The computer figures out what is off-screen and the programmer does not need to worry too much about it.

5.2. Pygame Library

To make graphics easier to work with, we'll use the Pygame. Pygame is a library of code other people have written, and makes it simple to:

- Draw graphic shapes
- Display bitmapped images
- Animate
- Interact with keyboard, mouse, and gamepad
- Play sound
- Detect when objects collide

The first code a Pygame program needs to do is load and initialize the Pygame library. Every program that uses Pygame should start with these lines:

Listing 5.1: Importing and initializing Pygame

```
# Import a library of functions called 'pygame'
import pygame
# Initialize the game engine
```

```
pygame.init()
```

If you haven't installed Pygame yet, directions for installing Pygame are available in the **before you begin** section. If Pygame is not installed on your computer, you will get an error when trying to run `import pygame`.

> ✎ **Don't name any file "pygame.py"**

Important: The `import pygame` looks for a library file named `pygame`. If a programmer creates a new program named `pygame.py`, the computer will import that file instead! This will prevent any pygame programs from working until that `pygame.py` file is deleted.

5.3. Colors

Next, we need to add variables that define our program's colors. Colors are defined in a list of three colors: red, green, and blue. Have you ever heard of an RGB monitor? This is where the term comes. Red-Green-Blue. With older monitors, you could sit really close to the monitor and make out the individual RGB colors. At least before your mom told you not to sit so close to the TV. This is hard to do with today's high resolution monitors.

Each element of the RGB triad is a number ranging from 0 to 255. Zero means there is none of the color, and 255 tells the monitor to display as much of the color as possible. The colors combine in an additive way, so if all three colors are specified, the color on the monitor appears white. (This is different than how ink and paint work.)

Lists in Python are surrounded by either square brackets or parentheses. (Chapter 7 covers lists in detail and the difference between the two types.) Individual numbers in the list are separated by commas. Below is an example that creates variables and sets them equal to lists of three numbers. These lists will be used later to specify colors.

Listing 5.2: Defining colors

```
# Define some colors
black   = (   0,   0,   0)
white   = ( 255, 255, 255)
green   = (   0, 255,   0)
red     = ( 255,   0,   0)
```

Using the interactive shell in IDLE, try defining these variables and printing them out. If the five colors above aren't the colors you are looking for, you can define your own. To pick a color, find an on-line "color picker" like the one shown in Figure 5.6. One such color picker is at: `http://www.colorpicker.com/`

Extra: Some color pickers specify colors in hexadecimal. You can enter hexadecimal numbers if you start them with 0x. For example:

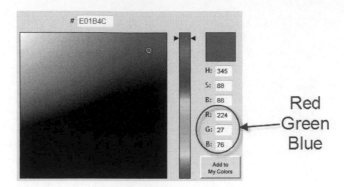

Figure 5.6.: Color picker

```
white = (0xFF, 0xFF, 0xFF)
```

Eventually the program will need to use the value of π when drawing arcs, so this is a good time in our program to define a variable that contains the value of π. (It is also possible to import this from the math library as `math.pi`.)

```
pi = 3.141592653
```

5.4. Open a Window

So far, the programs we have created only printed text out to the screen. Those programs did not open any windows like most modern programs do. The code to open a window is not complex. Below is the required code, which creates a window sized to a width of 700 pixels, and a height of 500:

Listing 5.3: Opening and setting the window size

```
# Set the width and height of the screen
size = (700,500)
screen = pygame.display.set_mode(size)
```

Why `set_mode`? Why not `open_window`? The reason is that this command can actually do a lot more than open a window. It can also create games that run in a full-screen mode. This removes the start menu, title bars, and gives the game control of everything on the screen. Because this mode is slightly more complex to use, and most people prefer windowed games anyway, we'll skip a detailed discussion on full-screen games. But if you want to find out more about full-screen games, check out the documentation on pygame's `display` command.

Also, why `size=(700,500)` and not `size=700,500`? The same reason why we put parentheses around the color definitions. Python can't normally store two numbers (a height and width) into one variable. The only way it can is if the numbers are stored as a list. Lists need either parentheses or square brackets. (Technically, parenthesis surrounding a set of numbers is more accurately called a *tuple* or an *immutable list*. Lists surrounded by square brackets are just called lists. An experienced Python developer would cringe at calling a list of numbers surrounded by parentheses a list rather than a tuple.) Lists are covered in detail in Chapter 7.

To set the title of the window (which shown in the title bar) use the following line of code:

Listing 5.4: Setting the window title

```
pygame.display.set_caption("Professor Craven's Cool Game")
```

5.5. Interacting With the User

With just the code written so far, the program would create a window and immediately hang. The user can't interact with the window, even to close it. All of this needs to be programmed. Code needs to be added so that the program waits in a loop until the user clicks "exit."

This is the most complex part of the program, and a complete understanding of it isn't needed yet. But it is necessary to have an *idea* of what it does, so spend some time studying it and asking questions.

Listing 5.5: Setting up the main program loop

```
1  #Loop until the user clicks the close button.
2  done = False
3
4  # Used to manage how fast the screen updates
5  clock = pygame.time.Clock()
6
7  # -------- Main Program Loop -----------
8  while done == False:
9      # ALL EVENT PROCESSING SHOULD GO BELOW THIS COMMENT
10     for event in pygame.event.get(): # User did something
11         if event.type == pygame.QUIT: # If user clicked close
12             done = True # Flag that we are done so we exit this loop
13     # ALL EVENT PROCESSING SHOULD GO ABOVE THIS COMMENT
14
15
16     # ALL GAME LOGIC SHOULD GO BELOW THIS COMMENT
17
18     # ALL GAME LOGIC SHOULD GO ABOVE THIS COMMENT
19
20
21     # ALL CODE TO DRAW SHOULD GO BELOW THIS COMMENT
22
23     # ALL CODE TO DRAW SHOULD GO ABOVE THIS COMMENT
24
```

```
25      # Limit to 20 frames per second
26      clock.tick(20)
```

Eventually we will add code to handle the keyboard and mouse clicks. That code will go between the comments for event processing. Code for determining when bullets are fired and how objects move will go between the comments for game logic. We'll talk about that in later chapters. Code to draw will go in between the appropriate draw-code comments.

5.5.1. The Event Processing Loop

Pay Attention!

Alert! One of the most frustrating problems programmers have is to mess up the event processing loop. This "event processing" code handles all the keystrokes, mouse button clicks, and several other types of events. For example your loop might look like:

Listing 5.6: Sample event loop - Good

```
1      for event in pygame.event.get():
2          if event.type == pygame.QUIT:
3              print("User asked to quit.")
4          if event.type == pygame.KEYDOWN:
5              print("User pressed a key.")
6          if event.type == pygame.KEYUP:
7              print("User let go of a key.")
8          if event.type == pygame.MOUSEBUTTONDOWN:
9              print("User pressed a mouse button")
```

The events (like pressing keys) all go together in a list. The program uses a `for` loop to loop through each event. Using a chain of `if` statements the code figures out what type of event occured, and the code to handle that event goes in the `if` statement.

All the `if` statements should go together, in one `for` loop. A common mistake when doing copy and pasting of code is to not merge loops from two programs, but to have two event loops.

Listing 5.7: BAD event loop example

```
1      # Here is one event loop
2      for event in pygame.event.get():
3          if event.type == pygame.QUIT:
4              print("User asked to quit.")
5          if event.type == pygame.KEYDOWN:
6              print("User pressed a key.")
7          if event.type == pygame.KEYUP:
8              print("User let go of a key.")
9
```

```
10      # Here the programmer has copied another event loop
11      # into the program. This is BAD. The events were already
12      # processed.
13      for event in pygame.event.get():
14          if event.type == pygame.QUIT:
15              print("User asked to quit.")
16          if event.type == pygame.MOUSEBUTTONDOWN:
17              print("User pressed a mouse button")
```

The `for` loop on line 2 grabbed all of the user events. The `for` loop on line 13 won't grab any events because they were already processed in the prior loop.

Another typical problem is to start drawing, and then try to finish the event loop:

Listing 5.8: BAD Sample event loop

```
1       for event in pygame.event.get():
2           if event.type == pygame.QUIT:
3               print("User asked to quit.")
4           if event.type == pygame.KEYDOWN:
5               print("User pressed a key.")
6
7
8       pygame.rect.draw(screen,green,[50,50,100,100])
9
10      # This is code that processes events. But it is not in the
11      # 'for' loop that processes events. It will not act reliably.
12      if event.type == pygame.KEYUP:
13          print("User let go of a key.")
14      if event.type == pygame.MOUSEBUTTONDOWN:
15          print("User pressed a mouse button")
```

This will cause the program to ignore some keyboard and mouse commands. Why? The `for` loop processes all the events in a list. So if there are two keys that are hit, the `for` loop will process both. In the example above, the `if` statements are not in the `for` loop. If there are multiple events, the `if` statements will only run for the last event, rather than all events.

5.5.2. Processing Each Frame

The basic logic and order for each frame of the game:
- While not done:
  - For each event (keypress, mouse click, etc.):
    * Use a chain of `if` statements to run code to handle each event.
  - Run calculations to determine where objects move, what happens when objects collide, etc.
  - Clear the screen
  - Draw everything

It makes the program easier to read and understand if these steps aren't mixed togther. Don't do some calculations, some drawing, some more calculations, some more drawing. Also, see how this is similar to the calculator done in chapter one. Get user input, run calculations, and output the answer. That same pattern applies here.

The code for drawing the image to the screen happens inside the while loop. With the clock tick set at 10, the contents of the window will be drawn 10 times per second. If it happens too fast the computer is sluggish because all of its time is spent updating the screen. If it isn't in the loop at all, the screen won't redraw properly. If the drawing is outside the loop, the screen may initially show the graphics, but the graphics won't reappear if the window is minimized, or if another window is placed in front.

5.6. Ending the Program

Right now, clicking the "close" button of a window while running this Pygame program in IDLE will still cause the program to crash. This is a hassle because it requires a lot of clicking to close a crashed program.

The problem is, even though the loop has exited, the program hasn't told the computer to close the window. By calling the command below, the program will close any open windows and exit as desired.

Listing 5.9: Proper shutdown of a Pygame program

```
pygame.quit()
```

5.7. Clearing the Screen

The following code clears whatever might be in the window with a white background. Remember that the variable white was defined earlier as a list of 3 RGB values.

Listing 5.10: Clear the Screen

```
# Clear the screen and set the screen background
screen.fill(white)
```

This should be done before any drawing command is issued. Clearing the screen *after* the program draws graphics results in the user only seeing a blank screen.

When a window is first created it has a black background. It is still important to clear the screen because there are several things that could occur to keep this window from starting out cleared. A program should not assume it has a blank canvas to draw on.

5.8. Flipping the Screen

Very important! You must flip the display after you draw. The computer will not display the graphics as you draw them because it would cause the screen to flicker. This waits to display the screen until the program has finished drawing. The command below "flips" the graphics to the screen.

Failure to include this command will mean the program just shows a blank screen. Any drawing code after this flip will not display.

Listing 5.11: Flipping the Pygame display

```
# Go ahead and update the screen with what we've drawn.
pygame.display.flip()
```

5.9. Open a Blank Window

Let's bring everything we've talked about into one full program. This code can be used as a base template for a Pygame program. It opens up a blank window and waits for the user to press the close button.

Listing 5.12: pygame_base_template.py

```
1  # Sample Python/Pygame Programs
2  # Simpson College Computer Science
3  # http://programarcadegames.com/
4  # http://simpson.edu/computer-science/
5
6  # Explanation video: http://youtu.be/vRB_983kUMc
7
8  import pygame
9
10 # Define some colors
11 black    = (   0,   0,   0)
12 white    = ( 255, 255, 255)
13 green    = (   0, 255,   0)
14 red      = ( 255,   0,   0)
15
16 pygame.init()
17
18 # Set the width and height of the screen [width,height]
19 size = [700,500]
20 screen = pygame.display.set_mode(size)
21
22 pygame.display.set_caption("My Game")
23
```

```
24 #Loop until the user clicks the close button.
25 done = False
26
27 # Used to manage how fast the screen updates
28 clock = pygame.time.Clock()
29
30 # -------- Main Program Loop -----------
31 while done == False:
32     # ALL EVENT PROCESSING SHOULD GO BELOW THIS COMMENT
33     for event in pygame.event.get(): # User did something
34         if event.type == pygame.QUIT: # If user clicked close
35             done = True # Flag that we are done so we exit this loop
36     # ALL EVENT PROCESSING SHOULD GO ABOVE THIS COMMENT
37
38
39     # ALL GAME LOGIC SHOULD GO BELOW THIS COMMENT
40
41     # ALL GAME LOGIC SHOULD GO ABOVE THIS COMMENT
42
43
44
45     # ALL CODE TO DRAW SHOULD GO BELOW THIS COMMENT
46
47     # First, clear the screen to white. Don't put other drawing commands
48     # above this, or they will be erased with this command.
49     screen.fill(white)
50
51     # ALL CODE TO DRAW SHOULD GO ABOVE THIS COMMENT
52
53     # Go ahead and update the screen with what we've drawn.
54     pygame.display.flip()
55
56     # Limit to 20 frames per second
57     clock.tick(20)
58
59 # Close the window and quit.
60 # If you forget this line, the program will 'hang'
61 # on exit if running from IDLE.
62 pygame.quit()
```

5.10. Drawing Introduction

Here is a list of things that you can draw:
http://www.pygame.org/docs/ref/draw.html
A program can draw things like rectangles, polygons, circles, ellipses, arcs, and lines. We will

also cover how to display text with graphics. Bitmapped graphics such as images are covered in Chapter 12. If you decide to look at that pygame reference, you might see a function definition like this:

```
pygame.draw.rect(Surface, color, Rect, width=0): return Rect
```

A frequent cause of confusion is the part of the line that says `width=0`. What this means is that if you do not supply a width, it will default to zero. Thus this function call:

```
pygame.draw.rect(screen, red, [55,500,10,5])
```

Is the same as this function call:

```
pygame.draw.rect(screen, red, [55,500,10,5], 0)
```

The : `return Rect` is telling you that the function returns a rectangle, the same one that was passed in. You can just ignore this part.

What will not work, is attempting to copy the line and put `width=0` in the quotes.

```
# This fails and the error the computer gives you is
# really hard to understand.
pygame.draw.rect(screen, red, [55,500,10,5], width=0)
```

5.11. Drawing Lines

The code example below shows how to draw a line on the screen. It will draw on the screen a green line from (0,0) to (100,100) that is 5 pixels wide. Remember that **green** is a variable that was defined earlier as a list of three RGB values.

Listing 5.13: Drawing a single line

```
1 # Draw on the screen a green line from (0,0) to (100,100)
2 # that is 5 pixels wide.
3 pygame.draw.line(screen,green,[0,0],[100,100],5)
```

Use the base template from the prior example and add the code to draw lines. Read the comments to figure out exactly where to put the code. Try drawing lines with different thicknesses, colors, and locations. Draw several lines.

5.12. Drawing Lines With Loops and Offsets

Programs can repeat things over and over. The next code example draws a line over and over using a loop. Programs can use this technique to do multiple lines, and even draw an entire car.

Putting a line drawing command inside a loop will cause multiple lines being drawn to the screen. But here's the catch. If each line has the same starting and ending coordinates, then each line will draw *on top* of the other line. It will look like only one line was drawn.

To get around this, it is necessary to offset the coordinates each time through the loop. So the first time through the loop the variable `y_offset` is zero. The line in the code below is drawn from (0,10) to (100,110). The next time through the loop `y_offset` increased by 10. This causes the next line to be drawn to have new coordinates of (0,20) and (100,120). This continues each time through the loop shifting the coordinates of each line down by 10 pixels.

Listing 5.14: Drawing a series of lines

```
1 # Draw on the screen several green lines from (0,10) to (100,110)
2 # 5 pixels wide using a while loop
3 y_offset = 0
4 while y_offset < 100:
5     pygame.draw.line(screen,red,[0,10+y_offset],[100,110+y_offset],5)
6     y_offset = y_offset+10
```

This same code could be done even more easily with a **for** loop:

Listing 5.15: Drawing a series of lines

```
1 # Draw on the screen several green lines from (0,10) to (100,110)
2 # 5 pixels wide using a for loop
3 for y_offset in range(0,100,10):
4     pygame.draw.line(screen,red,[0,10+y_offset],[100,110+y_offset],5)
```

Run this code and try using different changes to the offset. Try creating an offset with different values. Experiment with different values until exactly how this works is obvious.

For example, here is a loop that uses sine and cosine to create a more complex set of offsets and produces the image shown in Figure 5.7.

Listing 5.16: Complex offsets

```
1 for i in range(200):
2
3     radians_x = i/20
4     radians_y = i/6
5
6     x=int( 75 * math.sin(radians_x)) + 200
7     y=int( 75 * math.cos(radians_y)) + 200
8
9     pygame.draw.line(screen,black,[x,y],[x+5,y], 5)
```

Multiple elements can be drawn in one **for** loop, such as this code which draws the multiple X's shown in Figure 5.8.

Listing 5.17: Complex offsets

```
1     for x_offset in range(30,300,30):
2         pygame.draw.line(screen,black,[x_offset,100],[x_offset-10,90], 2 )
3         pygame.draw.line(screen,black,[x_offset,90],[x_offset-10,100], 2 )
```

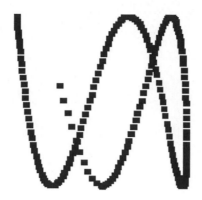

Figure 5.7.: Complex Offsets

Figure 5.8.: Multiple X's

5.13. Drawing a Rectangle

When drawing a rectangle, the computer needs coordinates for the upper left rectangle corner (the origin), and a height and width.

Figure 5.9 shows a rectangle (and an ellipse, which will be explained later) with the origin at (20,20), a width of 250 and a height of 100. When specifying a rectangle the computer needs a list of these four numbers in the order of (x, y, width, height).

The next code example draws this rectangle. The first two numbers in the list define the upper left corner at (20,20). The next two numbers specify first the width of 250 pixels, and then the height of 100 pixels.

The 2 at the end specifies a line width of 2 pixels. The larger the number, the thicker the line around the rectangle. If this number is 0, then there will not be a boarder around the rectangle. Instead it will be filled in with the color specified.

Listing 5.18: Drawing a rectangle

```
1 # Draw a rectangle
2 pygame.draw.rect(screen,black,[20,20,250,100],2)
```

5.14. Drawing an ellipse

An ellipse is drawn just like a rectangle. The boundaries of a rectangle are specified, and the computer draws an ellipses inside those boundaries.

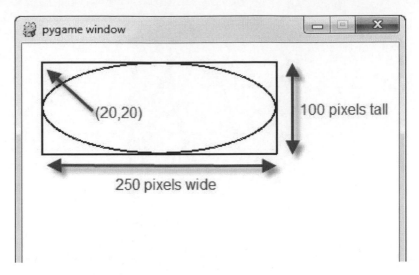

Figure 5.9.: Drawing an ellipse

The most common mistake in working with an ellipse is to think that the starting point specifies the center of the ellipse. In reality, nothing is drawn at the starting point. It is the upper left of a rectangle that contains the ellipse.

Looking back at Figure 5.9 one can see an ellipse 250 pixels wide and 100 pixels tall. The upper left corner of the 250x100 rectangle that contains it is at (20,20). Note that nothing is actually drawn at (20,20). With both drawn on top of each other it is easier to see how the ellipse is specified.

Listing 5.19: Drawing an ellipse

```
1 # Draw an ellipse, using a rectangle as the outside boundaries
2 pygame.draw.ellipse(screen,black,[20,20,250,100],2)
```

5.15. Drawing an Arc

What if a program only needs to draw part of an ellipse? That can be done with the `arc` command. This command is similar to the `ellipse` command, but it includes start and end angles for the arc to be drawn. The angles are in radians.

The code example below draws four arcs showing four difference quadrants of the circle. Each quadrant is drawn in a different color to make the arcs sections easier to see. The result of this code is shown in Figure 5.10.

Listing 5.20: Drawing arcs

```
1 # Draw an arc as part of an ellipse. Use radians to determine what
```

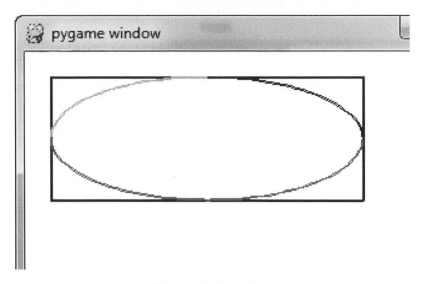

Figure 5.10.: Arcs

```
2 # angle to draw.
3 pygame.draw.arc(screen,green,[100,100,250,200],  pi/2,      pi,  2)
4 pygame.draw.arc(screen,black,[100,100,250,200],     0,   pi/2,  2)
5 pygame.draw.arc(screen,red,  [100,100,250,200],3*pi/2,   2*pi,  2)
6 pygame.draw.arc(screen,blue, [100,100,250,200],    pi, 3*pi/2,  2)
```

5.16. Drawing a Polygon

The next line of code draws a polygon. The triangle shape is defined with three points at (100,100) (0,200) and (200,200). It is possible to list as many points as desired. Note how the points are listed. Each point is a list of two numbers, and the points themselves are nested in another list that holds all the points. This code draws what can be seen in Figure 5.11.

Listing 5.21: Drawing a polygon

```
1 # This draws a triangle using the polygon command
2 pygame.draw.polygon(screen,black,[[100,100],[0,200],[200,200]],5)
```

5.17. Drawing Text

Text is slightly more complex. There are three things that need to be done. First, the program creates a variable that holds information about the font to be used, such as what typeface and how big.

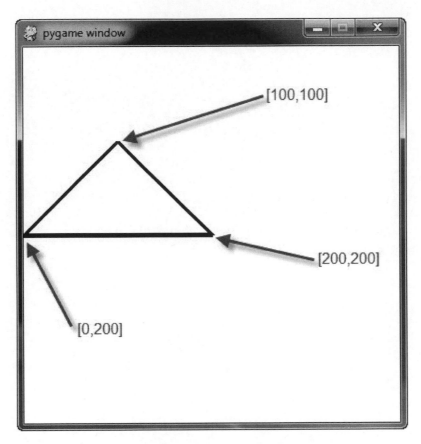

Figure 5.11.: Polygon

Second, the program creates an image of the text. One way to think of it is that the program carves out a "stamp" with the required letters that is ready to be dipped in ink and stamped on the paper.

The third thing that is done is the program tells where this image of the text should be stamped (or "blit'ed") to the screen.

Here's an example:

Listing 5.22: Drawing text on the screen

```
1 # Select the font to use. Default font, 25 pt size.
2 font = pygame.font.Font(None, 25)
3
4 # Render the text. "True" means anti-aliased text.
5 # Black is the color. The variable black was defined
6 # above as a list of [0,0,0]
7 # Note: This line creates an image of the letters,
8 # but does not put it on the screen yet.
9 text = font.render("My text",True,black)
10
11 # Put the image of the text on the screen at 250x250
12 screen.blit(text, [250,250])
```

Want to print the score to the screen? That is a bit more complex. This does not work:

```
text = font.render("Score: ",score,True,black)
```

Why? A program can't just add extra items to `font.render` like the `print` statement. Only one string can be sent to the command, therefore the actual value of score needs to be appended to the "Score: " string. But this doesn't work either:

```
text = font.render("Score: "+score,True,black)
```

If score is an integer variable, the computer doesn't know how to add it to a string. You, the programmer, must convert the score to a string. Then add the strings together like this:

```
text = font.render("Score: "+str(score),True,black)
```

Now you know how to print the score. If you want to print a timer, that requires print formatting, discussed in a chapter later on. Check in the **example code** for section on-line for the `timer.py` example:

ProgramArcadeGames.com/python_examples/f.php?file=timer.py

5.18. Full Program Listing

This is a full listing of the program discussed in this chapter. This program, along with other programs, may be downloaded from:

http://ProgramArcadeGames.com/index.php?chapter=example_code

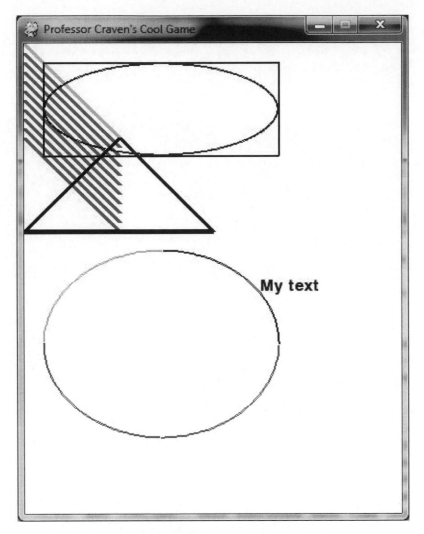

Figure 5.12.: Result of example program

Listing 5.23: simple_graphics_demo.py

```python
1   # Sample Python/Pygame Programs
2   # Simpson College Computer Science
3   # http://programarcadegames.com/
4   # http://simpson.edu/computer-science/
5
6   # Import a library of functions called 'pygame'
7   import pygame
8
9   # Initialize the game engine
10  pygame.init()
11
12  # Define the colors we will use in RGB format
13  black = [  0,  0,  0]
14  white = [255,255,255]
15  blue =  [  0,  0,255]
16  green = [  0,255,  0]
17  red =   [255,  0,  0]
18
19  pi = 3.141592653
20
21  # Set the height and width of the screen
22  size = [400,500]
23  screen = pygame.display.set_mode(size)
24
25  pygame.display.set_caption("Professor Craven's Cool Game")
26
27  #Loop until the user clicks the close button.
28  done = False
29  clock = pygame.time.Clock()
30
31  while done == False:
32
33      # This limits the while loop to a max of 10 times per second.
34      # Leave this out and we will use all CPU we can.
35      clock.tick(10)
36
37      for event in pygame.event.get(): # User did something
38          if event.type == pygame.QUIT: # If user clicked close
39              done=True # Flag that we are done so we exit this loop
40
41      # All drawing code happens after the for loop and but
42      # inside the main while done==False loop.
43
44      # Clear the screen and set the screen background
45      screen.fill(white)
46
```

```
47      # Draw on the screen a green line from (0,0) to (100,100)
48      # 5 pixels wide.
49      pygame.draw.line(screen,green,[0,0],[100,100],5)
50
51      # Draw on the screen several green lines from (0,10) to (100,110)
52      # 5 pixels wide using a loop
53      for y_offset in range(0,100,10):
54          pygame.draw.line(screen,red,[0,10+y_offset],[100,110+y_offset],5)
55
56
57      # Draw a rectangle
58      pygame.draw.rect(screen,black,[20,20,250,100],2)
59
60      # Draw an ellipse, using a rectangle as the outside boundaries
61      pygame.draw.ellipse(screen,black,[20,20,250,100],2)
62
63      # Draw an arc as part of an ellipse.
64      # Use radians to determine what angle to draw.
65      pygame.draw.arc(screen,black,[20,220,250,200], 0, pi/2, 2)
66      pygame.draw.arc(screen,green,[20,220,250,200], pi/2, pi, 2)
67      pygame.draw.arc(screen,blue, [20,220,250,200], pi,3*pi/2, 2)
68      pygame.draw.arc(screen,red, [20,220,250,200],3*pi/2, 2*pi, 2)
69
70      # This draws a triangle using the polygon command
71      pygame.draw.polygon(screen,black,[[100,100],[0,200],[200,200]],5)
72
73      # Select the font to use. Default font, 25 pt size.
74      font = pygame.font.Font(None, 25)
75
76      # Render the text. "True" means anti-aliased text.
77      # Black is the color. This creates an image of the
78      # letters, but does not put it on the screen
79      text = font.render("My text",True,black)
80
81      # Put the image of the text on the screen at 250x250
82      screen.blit(text, [250,250])
83
84      # Go ahead and update the screen with what we've drawn.
85      # This MUST happen after all the other drawing commands.
86      pygame.display.flip()
87
88  # Be IDLE friendly
89  pygame.quit()
```

5.19. Review Questions

After answering the review questions below, try writing a computer program that creates an image of your own design. For details, see the `Create-a-Picture` lab.

1. Before a program can use any functions like `pygame.display.set_mode()`, what two things must happen?

2. What does the `pygame.display.set_mode()` function do?

3. What is `pygame.time.Clock` used for?

4. What does this `for event in pygame.event.get()` loop do?

5. For this line of code:

   ```
   pygame.draw.line(screen,green,[0,0],[100,100],5)
   ```

   - What does `screen` do?
   - What does `[0,0]` do? What does `[100,100]` do?
   - What does 5 do?

6. Explain how the computer coordinate system differs from the standard Cartesian coordinate system.

7. Explain how `white = ( 255, 255, 255)` represents a color.

8. When drawing a rectangle, what happens if the specified line width is zero?

9. Sketch the ellipse drawn in the code below, and label the origin coordinate, the length, and the width:

   ```
   pygame.draw.ellipse(screen,black,[20,20,250,100],2)
   ```

10. Describe, in general, what are the three steps needed when printing text to the screen using graphics?

11. What are the coordinates of the polygon that the code below draws?

    ```
    pygame.draw.polygon(screen,black
        ,[[50,100],[0,200],[200,200],[100,50]],5)
    ```

12. What does `pygame.display.flip()` do?

13. What does `pygame.quit()` do?

5.20. Lab

Complete `Lab 3` "Create-a-Picture" to create your own picture, and show you understand how to use loops and graphics.

6. Back to Looping

Games involve a lot of complex loops. This is a "challenge chapter" to learn how to be an expert with loops. If you can understand the problems in this chapter by the end of it, you can certify yourself as a loop expert.

If becoming a loop expert isn't your goal, at least make sure you can write out the answers for the first eight problems. That will give you enough knowledge to continue this book. (Besides, being a loop expert never got anyone a date. Except for that guy in the Groundhog Day movie.)

There are video explanations for the answers on-line, and the answer code "animates." Just hit the "step" button to see how the code operates.

6.1. Print Statement End Characters

By default, the **print** statement puts a *carriage return* at the end of what is printed out. As we explained back in the first chapter, the carriage return is a character that moves the next line of output to be printed to the next line. Most of the time this is what we want. Sometimes it isn't. If we want to continue printing on the same line, we can change the default character printed at the end. This is an example before we change the ending character:

```
print("Pink")
print("Octopus")
```

...which will print out:

```
Pink
Octopus
```

But if we wanted the code output to print on the same line, it can be done by using a new option to set the **end** character. For example:

```
print("Pink", end="")
print("Octopus")
```

This will print:

```
PinkOctopus
```

We can also use a space instead of setting it to an empty string:

```
print("Pink", end=" ")
print("Octopus")
```

This will print:

```
Pink Octopus
```

Here's another example, using a variable:

```
i = 0
print(i, end=" ")
i = 1
print(i, end=" ")
```

This will print:

```
0 1
```

6.2. Advanced Looping Problems

1. Write code that will print ten asterisks (*) like the following:

   ```
   * * * * * * * * * *
   ```

   Have this code print using a **for** loop, and print each asterisk individually, rather than just printing ten asterisks with one **print** statement. This can be done in two lines of code, a **for** loop and a **print** statement.

   When you have figured it out, or given up, here is the answer:
   `ProgramArcadeGames.com/chapters/06_back_to_looping/problem_1.php`

2. Write code that will print the following:

   ```
   * * * * * * * * * *
   * * * * *
   * * * * * * * * * * * * * * * * * * * *
   ```

   This is just like the prior problem, but also printing five and twenty stars. Copy and paste from the prior problem, adjusting the **for** loop as needed.

   When you have figured it out, or given up, here is the answer:
   `ProgramArcadeGames.com/chapters/06_back_to_looping/problem_2.php`

3. Use two **for** loops, one of them nested inside the other, to print the following 10x10 rectangle:

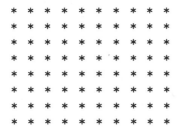

```
* * * * * * * * * *
* * * * * * * * * *
* * * * * * * * * *
* * * * * * * * * *
* * * * * * * * * *
* * * * * * * * * *
* * * * * * * * * *
* * * * * * * * * *
```

To start, take a look at Problem 1. The code in Problem 1 generates one line of asterisks. It needs to be repeated ten times. Work on this problem for at least ten minutes before looking at the answer.

When you have figured it out, or given up, here it is:
ProgramArcadeGames.com/chapters/06_back_to_looping/10x10box.php

4. Use two **for** loops, one of them nested, to print the following 5x10 rectangle:

```
* * * * *
* * * * *
* * * * *
* * * * *
* * * * *
* * * * *
* * * * *
* * * * *
* * * * *
* * * * *
```

This is a lot like the prior problem. Experiment with the ranges on the loops to find exactly what the numbers passed to the **range** function control.

When you have figured it out, or given up, here is the answer:
ProgramArcadeGames.com/chapters/06_back_to_looping/problem_4.php

5. Use two **for** loops, one of them nested, to print the following 20x5 rectangle:

```
* * * * * * * * * * * * * * * * * * * *
* * * * * * * * * * * * * * * * * * * *
* * * * * * * * * * * * * * * * * * * *
* * * * * * * * * * * * * * * * * * * *
* * * * * * * * * * * * * * * * * * * *
```

Again, like Problem 3 and Problem 4, but with different range values.

When you have figured it out, or given up, here is the answer:
ProgramArcadeGames.com/chapters/06_back_to_looping/problem_5.php

6. Write code that will print the following:

```
0 1 2 3 4 5 6 7 8 9
0 1 2 3 4 5 6 7 8 9
0 1 2 3 4 5 6 7 8 9
0 1 2 3 4 5 6 7 8 9
0 1 2 3 4 5 6 7 8 9
0 1 2 3 4 5 6 7 8 9
0 1 2 3 4 5 6 7 8 9
0 1 2 3 4 5 6 7 8 9
0 1 2 3 4 5 6 7 8 9
0 1 2 3 4 5 6 7 8 9
```

Use two nested loops. Print the first line with a loop, and not with:

```
print("0 1 2 3 4 5 6 7 8 9")
```

Tip: First, create a loop that prints the first line. Then enclose it in another loop that repeats the line 10 times. Use either i or j variables for what the program prints. This example and the next one helps reinforce what those index variables are doing.

Work on this problem for at least ten minutes before looking at the answer. The process of spending ten minutes working on the answer is far more important than the answer itself.

ProgramArcadeGames.com/chapters/06_back_to_looping/number_square_answer.php

7. Adjust the prior program to print:

```
0 0 0 0 0 0 0 0 0 0
1 1 1 1 1 1 1 1 1 1
2 2 2 2 2 2 2 2 2 2
3 3 3 3 3 3 3 3 3 3
4 4 4 4 4 4 4 4 4 4
5 5 5 5 5 5 5 5 5 5
6 6 6 6 6 6 6 6 6 6
7 7 7 7 7 7 7 7 7 7
8 8 8 8 8 8 8 8 8 8
9 9 9 9 9 9 9 9 9 9
```

Answer:
ProgramArcadeGames.com/chapters/06_back_to_looping/problem_7.php

8. Write code that will print the following:

```
0
0 1
0 1 2
0 1 2 3
0 1 2 3 4
0 1 2 3 4 5
```

```
0 1 2 3 4 5 6
0 1 2 3 4 5 6 7
0 1 2 3 4 5 6 7 8
0 1 2 3 4 5 6 7 8 9
```

Tip: This is just problem 6, but the inside loop no longer loops a fixed number of times. Don't use `range(10)`, but adjust that range amount.

After working at least ten minutes on the problem, here is the answer:
ProgramArcadeGames.com/chapters/06_back_to_looping/top_right_triangle.php

Make sure you can write out the code for this and the prior problems. Yes, this practice is work, but it will pay off later and you'll save time in the long run.

9. Write code that will print the following:

```
0 1 2 3 4 5 6 7 8 9
  0 1 2 3 4 5 6 7 8
    0 1 2 3 4 5 6 7
      0 1 2 3 4 5 6
        0 1 2 3 4 5
          0 1 2 3 4
            0 1 2 3
              0 1 2
                0 1
                  0
```

This one is difficult. Tip: Two loops are needed inside the outer loop that controls each row. First, a loop prints spaces, then a loop prints the numbers. Loop both these for each row. To start with, try writing just one inside loop that prints:

```
0 1 2 3 4 5 6 7 8 9
0 1 2 3 4 5 6 7 8
0 1 2 3 4 5 6 7
0 1 2 3 4 5 6
0 1 2 3 4 5
0 1 2 3 4
0 1 2 3
0 1 2
0 1
0
```

Then once that is working, add a loop after the outside loop starts and before the already existing inside loop. Use this new loop to print enough spaces to right justify the other loops.

After working at least ten minutes on the problem, here is the answer:
ProgramArcadeGames.com/chapters/06_back_to_looping/bottom_left_triangle.php

10. Write code that will print the following (Getting the alignment is hard, at least get the numbers):

```
1    2    3    4    5    6    7    8    9
2    4    6    8   10   12   14   16   18
3    6    9   12   15   18   21   24   27
4    8   12   16   20   24   28   32   36
5   10   15   20   25   30   35   40   45
6   12   18   24   30   36   42   48   54
7   14   21   28   35   42   49   56   63
8   16   24   32   40   48   56   64   72
9   18   27   36   45   54   63   72   81
```

Tip: Start by adjusting the code in problem 1 to print:

```
0  0  0  0  0  0  0  0  0  0
0  1  2  3  4  5  6  7  8  9
0  2  4  6  8  10  12  14  16  18
0  3  6  9  12  15  18  21  24  27
0  4  8  12  16  20  24  28  32  36
0  5  10  15  20  25  30  35  40  45
0  6  12  18  24  30  36  42  48  54
0  7  14  21  28  35  42  49  56  63
0  8  16  24  32  40  48  56  64  72
0  9  18  27  36  45  54  63  72  81
```

Then adjust the code to print:

```
1  2  3  4  5  6  7  8  9
2  4  6  8  10  12  14  16  18
3  6  9  12  15  18  21  24  27
4  8  12  16  20  24  28  32  36
5  10  15  20  25  30  35  40  45
6  12  18  24  30  36  42  48  54
7  14  21  28  35  42  49  56  63
8  16  24  32  40  48  56  64  72
9  18  27  36  45  54  63  72  81
```

Finally, use an `if` to print spaces if the number being printed is less than 10.

After working at least ten minutes on the problem, here is the answer:
`ProgramArcadeGames.com/chapters/06_back_to_looping/multiplication_table.php`

11. Write code that will print the following:

```
        1
      1 2 1
    1 2 3 2 1
  1 2 3 4 3 2 1
1 2 3 4 5 4 3 2 1
```

```
        1 2 3 4 5 6 5 4 3 2 1
      1 2 3 4 5 6 7 6 5 4 3 2 1
    1 2 3 4 5 6 7 8 7 6 5 4 3 2 1
  1 2 3 4 5 6 7 8 9 8 7 6 5 4 3 2 1
```

Tip: first write code to print:

```
1
1 2
1 2 3
1 2 3 4
1 2 3 4 5
1 2 3 4 5 6
1 2 3 4 5 6 7
1 2 3 4 5 6 7 8
1 2 3 4 5 6 7 8 9
```

Then write code to print:

```
1
1 2 1
1 2 3 2 1
1 2 3 4 3 2 1
1 2 3 4 5 4 3 2 1
1 2 3 4 5 6 5 4 3 2 1
1 2 3 4 5 6 7 6 5 4 3 2 1
1 2 3 4 5 6 7 8 7 6 5 4 3 2 1
1 2 3 4 5 6 7 8 9 8 7 6 5 4 3 2 1
```

Then finish by adding spaces to print the final answer.

After working at least ten minutes on the problem, here is the answer:
ProgramArcadeGames.com/chapters/06_back_to_looping/top_triangle.php

12. Write code that will print the following:

```
                1
              1 2 1
            1 2 3 2 1
          1 2 3 4 3 2 1
        1 2 3 4 5 4 3 2 1
      1 2 3 4 5 6 5 4 3 2 1
    1 2 3 4 5 6 7 6 5 4 3 2 1
  1 2 3 4 5 6 7 8 7 6 5 4 3 2 1
1 2 3 4 5 6 7 8 9 8 7 6 5 4 3 2 1
  1 2 3 4 5 6 7 8
    1 2 3 4 5 6 7
      1 2 3 4 5 6
        1 2 3 4 5
```

```
1 2 3 4
  1 2 3
    1 2
      1
```

This can be done by combining problems 11 and 9.

After working at least ten minutes on the problem, here is the answer:
ProgramArcadeGames.com/chapters/06_back_to_looping/three_quarters.php

13. Write code that will print the following:

```
                1
              1 2 1
            1 2 3 2 1
          1 2 3 4 3 2 1
        1 2 3 4 5 4 3 2 1
      1 2 3 4 5 6 5 4 3 2 1
    1 2 3 4 5 6 7 6 5 4 3 2 1
  1 2 3 4 5 6 7 8 7 6 5 4 3 2 1
1 2 3 4 5 6 7 8 9 8 7 6 5 4 3 2 1
  1 2 3 4 5 6 7 8 7 6 5 4 3 2 1
    1 2 3 4 5 6 7 6 5 4 3 2 1
      1 2 3 4 5 6 5 4 3 2 1
        1 2 3 4 5 4 3 2 1
          1 2 3 4 3 2 1
            1 2 3 2 1
              1 2 1
                1
```

After working at least ten minutes on the problem, here is the answer:
ProgramArcadeGames.com/chapters/06_back_to_looping/full_diamond.php

6.3. Basic Review

1. What does this program print out?

```
x = 0
while x < 10:
    print(x)
    x = x + 2
```

2. What does this program print out?

```
x = 1
while x < 64:
    print(x)
    x = x * 2
```

3. What does this program print out?

```
x = 5
while x >= 0:
    print(x)
    if x == "1":
        print ("Blast off!")
    x = x - 1
```

4. Fix the following code:

```
x = input("Enter a number greater than zero: ")

while x <= 0:
    print("Too small. Enter a number greater than zero: ")
```

5. Fix the following code:

```
x = 10

while x < 0:
    print(x)
    x - 1

print ("Blast-off")
```

6. What does this program print out?

```
print(3 == 1 + 2)
x = 5
print(x == 5)
print(3 < 4)
print(4 < 4)
print("Hi" == "Hi")
print("hi" == "Hi")
print("a" < "b")
t = 5 == 5
print(t)
done = False
if done:
    print("I am done.")
else:
    print("I am not done.")
```

6.4. Lab

Complete Lab 4 "Loopy Lab" to make practice writing advanced looping code.

7. Introduction to Lists

7.1. Data Types

So far this book has shown four types of data:
- String (a string is short for "string of characters," which normal people think of as text.)
- Integer
- Floating point
- Boolean

Python can display what type of data a value is with the **type** function. Admittedly, this function isn't terribly useful for the any other programming we will do in this book, but it is good to use the function just this once to demonstrate the types of data introduced so far. Type the following into the interactive IDLE shell. (Don't create a new window and type this in as a program; it won't work.)

```
type(3)
type(3.145)
type("Hi there")
type(True)
```

Output:

```
>>> type(3)
<class 'int'>

>>> type(3.145)
<class 'float'>

>>> type("Hi there")
<class 'str'>

>>> type(True)
<class 'bool'>
```

It is also possible to use the **type** function on a variable to see what kind of data is in it.

```
x = 3
type(x)
```

The two new types of data introduced in this chapter are *Lists* and *Tuples*. Try running the following commands in the interactive Python shell and see what is displayed:

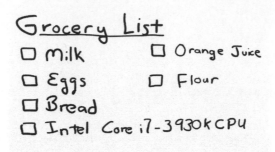

Figure 7.1.: Even computers use lists

```
type(  (2,3,4,5) )
type(  [2,3,4,5] )
```

7.2. Working With Lists

You've created grocery lists, to-do lists, bucket lists, but how do you create a list on the computer?

Try these examples using IDLE's command line. To create a list and print it out, try the following:

```
>>> x = [1,2]
>>> print(x)
[1, 2]
```

To print an individual element in an array:

```
>>> print(x[0])
1
```

This number with the item's location is called the *index*. Note that list locations start at zero. So a list with 10 elements does not have an element in spot [10]. Just spots [0] through [9]. It can be very confusing to create an array of 10 items and then not have an item 10, but most computer languages start counting at 0 rather than 1.

Think of a list as an ice cube tray that holds numbers, as shown in Figure 7.2. The values are stored inside each tray spot, and written on the side of the tray are numbers starting at zero that identify the location of each spot.

Remember, there are two sets of numbers to consider when working with a list of numbers: the position and the value. The position, also known as index, refers to *where* a value is. The value is the actual number stored at that location. When working with an array, make sure to think if you need the *location* or the *value*.

It is easy to get the value given the location, but it is harder to get the location given the value. Chapter 16 is dedicated to answering how to find the location of a particular value.

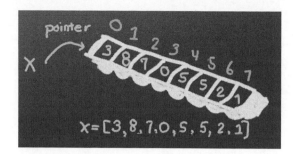

Figure 7.2.: Lists are like ice cube trays

A program can assign new values to an individual element in a list. In the case below, the first spot at location zero (not one) is assigned the number 22.

```
>>> x[0] = 22
>>> print(x)
[22, 2]
```

Also, a program can create a "tuple." This data type works just like a list, but with two differences. First, it is created with parentheses rather than square brackets. Second, it is not possible to change the tuple once created. See below:

```
>>> x = (1,2)
>>> print(x)
(1, 2)
>>> print(x[0])
1
>>> x[0] = 22
Traceback (most recent call last):
  File "<pyshell#18>", line 1, in <module>
    x[0] = 22
TypeError: 'tuple' object does not support item assignment
>>>
```

As can be seen from the output of the code above, we can't assign an item in the tuple a new value. Why would we want this limitation? First, the computer can run faster if it knows the value won't change. Second, some lists we don't want to change, such as a list of RGB colors for red. The color red doesn't change, therefore an immutable tuple is a better choice.

An *array* is a list of objects. It a type of data structure that is very important in computer science. The "list" data type in Python is very similar to an array data structure.

7.3. Iterating Through a List

If a program needs to iterate through each item in a list, such as to print it out, there are two types of **for** loops that can do this.

The first method to iterate through each item in a loop is by using a "for-each" loop. This type of loop takes a collection of items, and loops the code once per item. It will take a *copy* of the item and store it in a variable for processing.

The format of the command:

`for` *item_variable* `in` *list_name* `:`

Here are some examples:

```
my_list = [101,20,10,50,60]
for item in my_list:
    print( item )
```

Output:

```
101
20
10
50
60
```

Programs can store strings in lists too:

```
my_list = ["Spoon", "Fork", "Knife"]
for item in my_list:
    print(item)
```

Output:

```
Spoon
Knife
Fork
```

Lists can even contain other lists. This iterates through each item in the main list, but not in sublists.

```
my_list = [ [2,3], [4,3], [6,7] ]
for item in my_list:
    print(item)
```

Output:

```
[2,3]
[4,3]
[6,7]
```

The other way to iterate through a list is to use an *index variable* and directly access the list rather than through a copy of each item. To use an index variable, the program counts from 0 up to the length of the list. If there are ten elements, the loop must go from 0 to 9 for a total of ten elements.

The length of a list may be found by using the `len` function. Combining that with the `range` function allows the program to loop through the entire list.

```
my_list = [101,20,10,50,60]
for i in range( len(my_list) ):
    print( my_list[i] )
```

Output:

```
101
20
10
50
60
```

This method is more complex, but is also more powerful. Because we are working directly with the list elements, rather than a copy, the list can be modified. The for-each loop does not allow modification of the original list.

7.4. Adding to a List

New items may be added to a list (but not a tuple) by using the **append** command. For example:

```
my_list = [2,4,5,6]
print(my_list)
my_list.append(9)
print(my_list)
```

Output:

```
[2,4,5,6]
[2,4,5,6,9]
```

Side note: If performance while appending is a concern, it is very important to understand how a list is being implemented. For example, if a list is implemented as an *array data type*, then appending an item to the list is a lot like adding a new egg to an full egg carton. A new egg carton must be built with thirteen spots. Then twelve eggs are moved over. Then the thirteenth egg is added. Finally the old egg carton is recycled. Because this can happen behind the scenes in a function, programmers may forget this and let the computer do all the work. It would be more efficient to simply tell the computer to make an egg carton with enough spots to begin with. Thankfully, Python does not implement a list as an array data type. But it is important to pay attention to your next semester data structures class and learn how all of this works.

To create a list from scratch, it is necessary to create a blank list and then use the append function. This example creates a list based upon user input:

Listing 7.1: Creating a list of numbers from user input

```
1 my_list = [] # Empty list
2 for i in range(5):
3     userInput = input( "Enter an integer: ")
```

```
4    userInput = int( userInput )
5    my_list.append(userInput)
6    print(my_list)
```

Output:

```
Enter an integer: 4
[4]
Enter an integer: 5
[4, 5]
Enter an integer: 3
[4, 5, 3]
Enter an integer: 1
[4, 5, 3, 1]
Enter an integer: 8
[4, 5, 3, 1, 8]
```

If a program needs to create an array of a specific length, all with the same value, a simple trick is to use the following code:

Listing 7.2: Create an array with 100 zeros

```
1 # Create an array with 100 zeros.
2 my_list = [0] * 100
```

7.5. Summing or Modifying a List

Creating a running total of an array is a common operation. Here's how it is done:

Listing 7.3: Summing the values in a list v1

```
1  # Copy of the array to sum
2  myArray = [5,76,8,5,3,3,56,5,23]
3
4  # Initial sum should be zero
5  arrayTotal = 0
6
7  # Loop from 0 up to the number of elements
8  # in the array:
9  for i in range( len(myArray) ):
10    # Add element 0, next 1, then 2, etc.
11    arrayTotal += myArray[i]
12
13 # Print the result
14 print( arrayTotal )
```

The same thing can be done by using a `for` loop to iterate the array, rather than count through a range:

Listing 7.4: Summing the values in a list v2

```
1  # Copy of the array to sum
2  myArray = [5,76,8,5,3,3,56,5,23]
3
4  # Initial sum should be zero
5  arrayTotal = 0
6
7  # Loop through array, copying each item in the array into
8  # the variable named item.
9  for item in myArray:
10    # Add each item
11    arrayTotal += item
12
13 # Print the result
14 print( arrayTotal )
```

Numbers in an array can also be changed by using a `for` loop:

Listing 7.5: Doubling all the numbers in a list

```
1  # Copy of the array to modify
2  myArray = [5,76,8,5,3,3,56,5,23]
3
4  # Loop from 0 up to the number of elements
5  # in the array:
6  for i in range( len(myArray) ):
7    # Modify the element by doubling it
8    myArray[i] = myArray[i] * 2
9
10 # Print the result
11 print( myArray )
```

However version 2 *does not work* at doubling the values in an array. Why? Because `item` is a *copy* of an element in the array. The code below doubles the copy, not the original array element.

Listing 7.6: Bad code that doesn't double all the numbers in a list

```
1  # Copy of the array to modify
2  myArray = [5,76,8,5,3,3,56,5,23]
3
4  # Loop through each element in myArray
5  for item in myArray:
6    # This doubles item, but does not change the array
7    # because item is a copy of a single element.
8    item = item * 2
9
10 # Print the result
```

```
11 print( myArray )
```

7.6. Slicing Strings

Strings are actually lists of characters. They can be treated like lists with each letter a separate item. Run the following code with both versions of x:

Listing 7.7: Accessing a string as a list

```
1 x = "This is a sample string"
2 #x = "0123456789"
3
4 print("x=",x)
5
6 # Accessing a single character
7 print("x[0]=",x[0])
8 print("x[1]=",x[1])
9
10 # Accessing from the right side
11 print("x[-1]=",x[-1])
12
13 # Access 0-5
14 print("x[:6]=",x[:6])
15 # Access 6
16 print("x[6:]=",x[6:])
17 # Access 6-8
18 print("x[6:9]=",x[6:9])
```

Strings in Python may be used with some of the mathematical operators. Try the following code and see what Python does:

Listing 7.8: Adding and multiplying strings

```
1 a = "Hi"
2 b = "There"
3 c = "!"
4 print(a + b)
5 print(a + b + c)
6 print(3 * a)
7 print(a * 3)
8 print((a * 2) + (b * 2))
```

It is possible to get a length of a string. It is also possible to do this with any type of array.

Listing 7.9: Getting the length of a string or list

```
1 a = "Hi There"
```

```
2 print(len(a))
3
4 b = [3,4,5,6,76,4,3,3]
5 print(len(b))
```

Since a string is an array, a program can iterate through each character element just like an array:

```
for character in "This is a test.":
    print (character)
```

Exercise: Starting with the following code:

```
months = "JanFebMarAprMayJunJulAugSepOctNovDec"

n = int(input("Enter a month number: "))
```

Print the three month abbreviation for the month number that the user enters. (Calculate the start position in the string, then use the info we just learned to print out the correct substring.)

7.7. Secret Codes

This code prints out every letter of a string individually:

```
plain_text = "This is a test. ABC abc"

for c in plain_text:
    print (c, end=" ")
```

Computers do not actually store letters of a string in memory; computers store a series of numbers. Each number represents a letter. The table that computers use to translate numbers to letters is the American Standard Code for Information Interchange (ASCII). There are many other tables as well, these tables can be used to support cyrillic, kanji, and other international characters. By default, Python uses ASCII.

The ASCII chart covers the numbers 0-255. Each letter is represented by one byte of memory. A partial copy of the ASCII chart is below:

Value	Character	Value	Character	Value	Character	Value	Character
40	(	61	=	82	R	103	g
41	)	62	>	83	S	104	h
42	*	63	?	84	T	105	i
43	+	64	@	85	U	106	j
44	,	65	A	86	V	107	k
45	-	66	B	87	W	108	l
46	.	67	C	88	X	109	m
47	/	68	D	89	Y	110	n
48	0	69	E	90	Z	111	o
49	1	70	F	91	[	112	p
50	2	71	G	92	\	113	q
51	3	72	H	93	]	114	r
52	4	73	I	94	^	115	s
53	5	74	J	95	_	116	t
54	6	75	K	96	`	117	u
55	7	76	L	97	a	118	v
56	8	77	M	98	b	119	w
57	9	78	N	99	c	120	x
58	:	79	O	100	d	121	y
59	;	80	P	101	e	122	z
60	<	81	Q	102	f		

For more information about ASCII see:
http://en.wikipedia.org/wiki/ASCII
This next set of code converts each of the letters in the prior example to its ordinal value using the ASCII chart.

```
plain_text = "This is a test. ABC abc"

for c in plain_text:
    print (ord(c), end=" ")
```

This next program takes each ASCII value and adds one to it. Then it prints the new ASCII value, then converts the value back to a letter.

```
plain_text = "This is a test. ABC abc"

for c in plain_text:
    x = ord(c)
    x = x + 1
    c2 = chr(x)
    print (c2, end="")
```

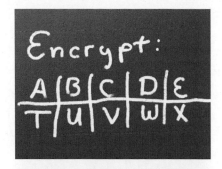

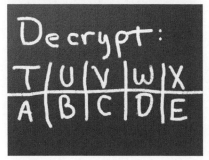

The next code listing takes each ASCII value and adds one to it, then converts the value back to a letter.

Listing 7.10: simple_encryption.py

```
1 # Sample Python/Pygame Programs
2 # Simpson College Computer Science
3 # http://programarcadegames.com/
4 # http://simpson.edu/computer-science/
5
6 # Explanation video: http://youtu.be/sxFIxD8Gd3A
7
8 plain_text="This is a test. ABC abc"
9
10 encrypted_text=""
11 for c in plain_text:
12     x=ord(c)
13     x=x+1
14     c2=chr(x)
15     encrypted_text=encrypted_text+c2
16 print (encrypted_text)
```

Finally, the last code takes each ASCII value and subtracts one from it, then converts the value back to a letter. By feeding this program the output of the previous program, it serves as a decoder for text encoded by the prior example.

Listing 7.11: simple_decryption.py

```
1  # Sample Python/Pygame Programs
2  # Simpson College Computer Science
3  # http://programarcadegames.com/
4  # http://simpson.edu/computer-science/
5
6  # Explanation video: http://youtu.be/sxFIxD8Gd3A
7
8  encrypted_text="Uijt!jt!b!uftu/!BCD!bcd"
9
10 plain_text=""
11 for c in encrypted_text:
12     x=ord(c)
13     x=x-1
14     c2=chr(x)
15     plain_text=plain_text+c2
16 print (plain_text)
```

7.8. Associative Arrays

Python is not limited to using numbers as an array index. It is also possible to use an *associative array*. An associative array works like this:

```
# Create an empty associative array
# (Note the curly braces.)
x = {}

# Add some stuff to it
x["fred"] = 2
x["scooby"] = 8
x["wilma"] = 1

# Fetch and print an item
print(x["fred"])
```

You won't really need associative arrays for this class, but I think it is important to point out that it is possible.

7.9. Review Questions

After answering the questions below, try working on the Loopy Lab. Next, try taking Test 1 from the **sample tests** available on-line.

1. List the four types of data we've covered, and give an example of each:

2. What does this code print out?

```
my_list = [5,2,6,8,101]
print(my_list[1])
print(my_list[4])
print(my_list[5])
```

3. What does this code print out?

```
my_list=[5,2,6,8,101]
for my_item in my_list:
    print (my_item)
```

4. What does this code print out?

```
my_list1 = [5,2,6,8,101]
my_list2 = (5,2,6,8,101)
my_list1[3] = 10
print(my_list1)
my_list2[2] = 10
print(my_list2)
```

5. What does this code print out?

```
word = "Simpson"
for letter in word:
    print (letter)
```

6. What does this code print out?

```
my_text = "The quick brown fox jumped over the lazy dogs."
print("The 3rd spot is: " + my_text[3])
print("The -1 spot is: " + my_text[-1])
```

7. What does the following program print out?

```
s = "0123456789"
print(s[1])
print(s[:3])
print(s[3:])
```

8. Write code that will take a string from the user. Print the length of the string. Print the first letter of the string.

9. Write a loop that will take in a list of five numbers from the user, adding each to an array. Then print the array.

10. Write a program that take an array like the following, and print the average:

```
my_list = [3,12,3,5,3,4,6,8,5,3,5,6,3,2,4]
```

8. Introduction to Animation

8.1. The Bouncing Rectangle

To begin our first animation, let's start with the base pygame program from Chapter 5 that opens up a blank screen. Source for `pygame_base_template.py` can be found here:
`ProgramArcadeGames.com/python_examples/f.php?file=pygame_base_template.py`

We will put together a program to bounce a white rectangle around a screen with a black background. Feel free to pick your own colors, just make sure the background color is different than the rectangle color!

First step, start with the base template and flip the background color from white to black. This code should be around line 46.

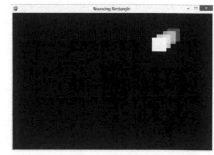

```
screen.fill(black)
```

Next up, draw the rectangle we plan to animate. A simple rectangle will suffice. This code should be placed after clearing the screen, and before flipping it.

```
pygame.draw.rect(screen, white, [50, 50, 50, 50])
```

Each time through the loop the rectangle will be drawn at an (x,y) location of exactly (50,50). This is controlled by the first two 50s in the list. Until those numbers change, the square will not move.

The rectangle will be 50 pixels wide and 50 pixels tall. The dimensions are controlled by the last two numbers in the list. We could also call this rectangle a square, since it has the same width and height. I'll stick with calling it a rectangle because all squares are also rectangles, and depending on the monitor and resolution used, pixels aren't always square. Look up *Pixel Aspect Ratio* if you are really interested in this subject.

How do we keep changing the location rather than have it stuck at (50, 50)? Use a variable, of course! The code below is a first step towards that:

```
rect_x = 50
pygame.draw.rect(screen,white,[rect_x,50,50,50])
```

To move the rectangle to the right, x can be increased by one each frame. This code is close, but it does not quite do it:

```
rect_x = 50
pygame.draw.rect(screen,white,[rect_x,50,50,50])
rect_x += 1
```

The problem with the above code is that rect_x is reset back to 50 each time through the loop. To fix this problem, move the initialization of rect_x up outside of the loop. This next section of code will successfully slide the rectangle to the right.

Listing 8.1: Animating a rectangle sliding to the right

```
# Starting x position of the rectangle
# Note how this is outside the main while loop.
rect_x = 50

# -------- Main Program Loop -----------
while done == False:
  for event in pygame.event.get(): # User did something
    if event.type == pygame.QUIT: # If user clicked close
      done = True # Flag that we are done so we exit this loop

  # Set the screen background
  screen.fill(black)

  pygame.draw.rect(screen, white, [rect_x,50,50,50])
  rect_x += 1
```

To move the box faster, rather than increasing rect_x by 1, increase it by 5:

```
rect_x += 5
```

We can expand this code and increase both x and y, causing the square to move both down and right:

Listing 8.2: Animating a rectangle down and to the right

```
# Starting position of the rectangle
rect_x = 50
rect_y = 50

# -------- Main Program Loop -----------
while done == False:
  for event in pygame.event.get():
    if event.type == pygame.QUIT:
      done = True

  # Set the screen background
  screen.fill(black)

  # Draw the rectangle
```

```
pygame.draw.rect(screen,white,[rect_x,rect_y,50,50])

# Move the rectangle starting point
rect_x += 5
rect_y += 5
```

The direction and speed of the boxes movement can be stored in a vector. This makes it easy for the direction and speed of a moving object to be changed. The next bit of code shows using variables to store the x and y change of (5, 5).

Listing 8.3: Using variables to store object speed

```
# Starting position of the rectangle
rect_x = 50
rect_y = 50

# Speed and direction of rectangle
rect_change_x = 5
rect_change_y = 5

# -------- Main Program Loop -----------
while done == False:
  for event in pygame.event.get(): # User did something
    if event.type == pygame.QUIT: # If user clicked close
      done = True # Flag that we are done so we exit this loop

  # Set the screen background
  screen.fill(black)

  # Draw the rectangle
  pygame.draw.rect(screen,white,[rect_x,rect_y,50,50])

  # Move the rectangle starting point
  rect_x += rect_change_x
  rect_y += rect_change_y
```

Once the box hits the edge of the screen it will keep going. Nothing makes the rectangle bounce off the edge of the screen. To reverse the direction so the rectangle travels towards the right, **rect_change_y** needs to change from 5 to -5 once the rectangle gets to the bottom side of the screen. The rectangle is at the bottom when **rect_y** is greater than the height of the screen. The code below can do the check and reverse the direction:

```
# Bounce the rectangle if needed
if rect_y > 450:
  rect_change_y = rect_change_y * -1
```

Why check **rect_y** against 450? If the screen is 500 pixels high, then checking against 500 would be a logical first guess. But remember the rectangle is drawn starting from the *top left*

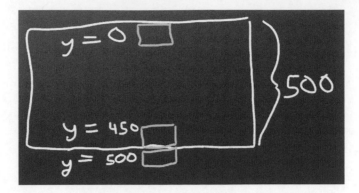

Figure 8.1.: Rectangle location based on y coordinate

corner of the rectangle. If the rectangle was drawn starting at 500, it would draw from 500 to 550, totally off screen before it bounced. See Figure 8.1.

Taking into account that the rectangle is 50 pixels high the correct bounce location is: $500 - 50 = 450$.

The code below will bounce the rectangle off all four sides of a 700x400 window:

Listing 8.4: Bouncing a rectangle

```
# Bounce the rectangle if needed
if rect_y > 450 or rect_y < 0:
  rect_change_y = rect_change_y * -1
if rect_x > 650 or rect_x < 0:
  rect_change_x = rect_change_x * -1
```

Interested in a more complex shape than a rectangle? Several drawing commands can be used based off the **rect_x** and **rect_y**. The code below draws a red rectangle inside the white rectangle. The red rectangle is offset 10 pixels in the x,y directions from the upper left corner of the white rectangle. It also is 20 pixels smaller in both dimensions, resulting in 10 pixels of white surrounding the red rectangle. See Figure 11.1.

```
# Draw a red rectangle inside the white one
pygame.draw.rect(screen, white, [rect_x,rect_y,50,50])
pygame.draw.rect(screen, red, [rect_x+10,rect_y+10,30,30])
```

8.2. Animating Snow

Animating only one item isn't enough? Need to animate more? How about being able to animate hundreds of objects at once? This shows how to use techniques from Section 8.1 to animate many snowflakes falling.

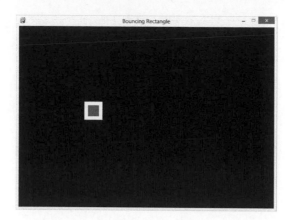

Figure 8.2.: White rectangle with a red square in the middle

8.2.1. Code Explanation

To start this program, begin with the base pygame template that opens up a blank screen. Again, source for `pygame_base_template.py` can be found here:

`ProgramArcadeGames.com/python_examples/show_file.php?file=pygame_base_template.py`

It is possible to create x, y locations for things like stars, snow, or rain by using random numbers. The simplest way to attempt this is using a `for` loop to draw circles in random x, y positions. Try the following code inside of the main `while` loop.

```
for i in range(50):
    x = random.randrange(0, 400)
    y = random.randrange(0, 400)
    pygame.draw.circle(screen, white, [x,y], 2)
```

Try it, this program has an odd problem! Twenty times per second, each time through the loop, it draws the stars in new random locations. Try adjusting the star count and see how it changes the image.

Obviously, we need to randomly position the stars and keep them in the same spot. We don't want to generate new positions twenty times per second. We need to to keep a *list* of where they are. The program can use a python list to do this. This should be done *before* the main loop, otherwise the program will add 50 new stars to the list every 1/20th of a second.

```
for i in range(50):
    x = random.randrange(0,400)
    y = random.randrange(0,400)
    star_list.append([x,y])
```

Once the star locations have been added, they can be accessed like a normal list. The following code would print both the x and y coordinates of the first location, stored in position zero:

```
print(star_list[0])
```

111

What if we wanted just the x or y coordinate? We have lists inside lists. The main list has all the coordinates. Inside of that list, each coordinate is a list of an x (position 0), and a y coordinate (position 1). For example, here are three coordinates:

```
[[34,10],
 [10,50],
 [20,18]]
```

To print the y coordinate at position 0, first select coordinate 0, and then the y value at position 1. The code will look like:

```
print(star_list[0][1])
```

To print the x value of the 21st coordinate (position 20), first select coordinate 20, and then the x value at position 0:

```
print(star_list[20][0])
```

Inside of the main **while** loop, a program may use a **for** loop to draw each of the items in the star list. Remember, **len(star_list)** will return the number of elements in the star list.

```
# Process each star in the list
for i in range(len(star_list)):
    # Draw the star
    pygame.draw.circle(screen, white, star_list[i], 2)
```

Remember, there are two types of **for** loops. The other type of loop can be used, and it would look like:

```
# Process A COPY of each star's location in the list
for xy_coord in star_list:
    # Draw the star
    pygame.draw.circle(screen, white, xy_coord, 2)
```

However, because we plan on modifying the star's location we can't use this type of **for** loop because we'd be modifying the location of a copy of the star's location rather than the actual star's location.

If the program is to have all the objects in the array move down, like snow, then expanding the **for** loop created above will cause the y coordinate to increase:

```
# Process each star in the list
for i in range(len(star_list)):

    # Draw the star
    pygame.draw.circle(screen, white, star_list[i], 2)

    # Move the star down one pixel
    star_list[i][1] += 1
```

This moves the snow downwards, but once off the screen nothing new appears. By adding the code below, the snow will reset to the top of the screen in a random location:

```
      # If the star has moved off the bottom of the screen
      if star_list[i][1] > 400:
        # Reset it just above the top
        y = random.randrange(-50,-10)
        star_list[i][1] = y
        # Give it a new x position
        x = random.randrange(0,400)
        star_list[i][0] = x
```

8.2.2. Full Program Listing

Listing 8.5: animating_snow.py

```
 1  # Sample Python/Pygame Programs
 2  # Simpson College Computer Science
 3  # http://programarcadegames.com/
 4  # http://simpson.edu/computer-science/
 5
 6  # Explanation video: http://youtu.be/Gkhz3FuhGoI
 7
 8  # Import a library of functions called 'pygame'
 9  import pygame
10  import random
11
12  # Initialize the game engine
13  pygame.init()
14
15  black = [ 0, 0, 0]
16  white = [255,255,255]
17
18  # Set the height and width of the screen
19  size = [400,400]
20  screen = pygame.display.set_mode(size)
21  pygame.display.set_caption("Snow Animation")
22
23  # Create an empty array
24  star_list = []
25
26  # Loop 50 times and add a star in a random x,y position
27  for i in range(50):
28      x = random.randrange(0,400)
29      y = random.randrange(0,400)
30      star_list.append([x,y])
31
32  clock = pygame.time.Clock()
33
```

```
34 #Loop until the user clicks the close button.
35 done = False
36 while done == False:
37
38     for event in pygame.event.get(): # User did something
39         if event.type == pygame.QUIT: # If user clicked close
40             done=True # Flag that we are done so we exit this loop
41
42     # Set the screen background
43     screen.fill(black)
44
45     # Process each star in the list
46     for i in range(len(star_list)):
47
48         # Draw the star
49         pygame.draw.circle(screen, white, star_list[i], 2)
50
51         # Move the star down one pixel
52         star_list[i][1] += 1
53
54         # If the star has moved off the bottom of the screen
55         if star_list[i][1] > 400:
56             # Reset it just above the top
57             y=random.randrange(-50, -10)
58             star_list[i][1] = y
59             # Give it a new x position
60             x=random.randrange(0, 400)
61             star_list[i][0] = x
62
63     # Go ahead and update the screen with what we've drawn.
64     pygame.display.flip()
65     clock.tick(20)
66
67 # Be IDLE friendly. If you forget this line, the program will 'hang'
68 # on exit.
69 pygame.quit ()
```

This example shows each snowflake moving the same direction. What if each item needs to be animated separately, with its own direction? If you need this for your game, see Chapter 13 on how to use classes. Lab 8 steps you through how to have hundreds of different items animated, each with their own direction.

8.3. 3D Animation

Extending from a 2D environment into a 3D environment complete with game physics isn't as hard as it would seem. While it is beyond the scope of this class, it is worth while to see how it is done.

Figure 8.3.: Example Blender File

There is a freely available 3D program called *Blender* which has a "game engine" that allows programmers to create 3D games. The 3D objects in the game can have Python code attached to them that controls their actions in the game.

Look at Figure 8.3. This shows a green tray with several objects in it. The blue object is controlled by a Python script that moves it around the tray bumping into the other objects. The script, shown below, has many of the same features that the 2D programs have. There is a main loop, there is a list for x,y locations, and there are variables controlling the vector.

The main program loop is controlled by Blender. The python code shown in the listing is called by Blender for each "frame" the game renders. This is why the Python code does not show a main program loop. It does exist however.

The blue object has a location held in x,y,z format. It can be accessed and changed by using the `blueobject.position` variable. Array position 0 holds x, position 1 holds y, and position 2 holds the z location.

Rather than the `change_x` and `change_y` variables used in the 2D examples in this changer, this Blender example uses the associative array locations:

`blueObject["x_change"]`
`blueObject["y_change"]`

The `if` statements check to see if the blue object has reached the borders of the screen and the direction needs to reverse. Unlike pixels used in the 2D games, locations of objects may be a floating point number type. To position an item between 5 and 6, setting its location to 5.5 is permissable.

Listing 8.6: Example Blender Python program

```
1 # Import Blender Game Engine
2 import bge
```

```
3
4 # Get a reference to the blue object
5 cont = bge.logic.getCurrentController()
6 blueObject = cont.owner
7
8 # Print the x,y coordinates where the blue object is
9 print(blueObject.position[0], blueObject.position[1] )
10
11 # Change x,y coordinates according to x_change and
12 # y_change. x_change and y_change are game properties
13 # associated with the blue object.
14 blueObject.position[0] += blueObject["x_change"]
15 blueObject.position[1] += blueObject["y_change"]
16
17 # Check to see of the object has gone to the edge.
18 # If so reverse direction. Do so with all 4 edges.
19 if blueObject.position[0] > 6 and blueObject["x_change"] > 0:
20     blueObject["x_change"] *= -1
21
22 if blueObject.position[0] < -6 and blueObject["x_change"] < 0:
23     blueObject["x_change"] *= -1
24
25 if blueObject.position[1] > 6 and blueObject["y_change"] > 0:
26     blueObject["y_change"] *= -1
27
28 if blueObject.position[1] < -6 and blueObject["y_change"] < 0:
29     blueObject["y_change"] *= -1
```

Blender may be downloaded from:
http://www.blender.org/

A full blender example file is available at:
ProgramArcadeGames.com/chapters/08_intro_to_animation/simple_block_move.blend.

8.4. Review Questions

8.5. Lab

Complete Lab 5 "Animation" and create your own animation.

9. Functions

9.1. Introduction to Functions

Functions are used for two reasons. First, they make code easier to read and understand. Second, they allow code to be used more than once.

Imagine a set of code that controls a toy car. Suppose the programmer wishes to make the car move forward. To do this, the programmer executes the following commands:

```
turnOnMotor()
pauseOneSecond()
turnOffMotor()
```

By defining a function, the program can improve readability and reuse code multiple times:

```
def moveForward():
    turnOnMotor()
    pauseOneSecond()
    turnOffMotor()
```

By itself, this code will not cause the car to move foward. It does tell the computer *how* to do **moveForward**. You have to *call* the function to actually run the code in the function and get the car to move forward:

```
moveForward()
```

With a whole library of functions defining what the car can do, a final program might look like:

```
moveForward()
turnLeft()
moveForward()
moveForward()
turnRight()
moveForward()
```

Remember that **moveForward** has three lines of code. Each one of these other commands has multiple lines of code. By using functions, we can repeat the commands without repeating all the code contained within, making for a much smaller program.

Function names are very important. If the function names are descriptive, even a non-programmer should be able to read a set of code and get an idea what is happening. Function names follow the same rules as variable names, and should start with a lower case letter.

9.2. Function Parameters

Functions can take *parameters*. These can be used to increase the flexibility of a function by altering what it does based on parameters passed to it. For example, our function called `moveForward()` drives the robot foward for one second. But the function could be changed to take a parameter that specifies how many seconds to move forward. For example `moveForward(3)` would move forward for three seconds and `moveForward(6)` would move for six seconds.

Adjusting the function for the robot might look like:

```
def moveForward(time):
    turnOnMotor()
    for i in range(time):
        pauseOneSecond()
    turnOffMotor()
```

Here is a different function that can be run without a robot car. This function will calculate and print out the volume of a sphere:

Listing 9.1: Function that prints the volume of a sphere

```
1 def volumeSphere(radius):
2     pi = 3.141592653589
3     volume = 4 * pi * radius ** 2
4     print("The volume is", volume)
```

> ✎ **Parameters are assigned values when a function is called, not when it is defined.**

The name of the function is `volumeSphere`. The data going into the functions will be stored in a new variable called `radius`. The resulting volume is printed to the screen. The `radius` variable does not get a value here. Frequently new programmers get confused because parameter variables aren't given a value when the function is defined, so it doesn't look legal. Parameters are given a value when the function is called.

To call this function, use:

```
volumeSphere(22)
```

The `radius` variable in the function is created and initialized with a value of 22. The function's code is run once the execution reaches the call to the function.

What if we need to pass in more than one value? Multiple parameters can be passed to a function, each parameter separated by a comma:

Listing 9.2: Function that prints the volume of a cylinder

```
1 def volumeCylinder(radius, height):
2     pi = 3.141592653589
3     volume = 2 * pi * radius * (radius + height)
4     print("The volume is", volume)
```

That function may be called by:

```
volumeCylinder(12, 3)
```

Parameters are done in order, so `radius` will get the 12, and `height` will get the 3 value.

Unfortunately, these example functions are limited. Why? If a person wanted to use the `volumeCylinder` function to calculate the volume in a six-pack, it wouldn't work. It only prints out the volume of one cylinder. It is not possible to use the function's result for one cylinder's volume in an equation and multiply it by six to get a six-pack volume.

This can be solved by using a `return` statement. For example:

Listing 9.3: Function that returns the volume of a cylinder

```
1 def volumeCylinder(radius, height):
2     pi = 3.141592653589
3     volume = 2 * pi * radius * (radius + height)
4     return volume
```

Return is not a function, and does not use parentheses. Don't do `return(volume)`.

Because of the `return`, this function could be used later on as part of an equation to calculate the volume of a six-pack like this:

```
sixPackVolume = volumeCylinder(2.5, 5) * 6
```

The value returned from `volumeCylinder` goes into the equation and is multiplied by six.

There is a big difference between a function that *prints* a value and a function that *returns* a value. Look at the code below and try it out.

```
# Function that prints the result
def sumPrint(a, b):
    result = a + b
    print(result)

# Function that returns the results
def sumReturn(a, b):
    result = a+b
    return(result)

# This prints the sum of 4+4
sumPrint(4, 4)

# This does not
sumReturn(4, 4)
```

```
# This will not set x1 to the sum
# It actually gets a value of 'None'
x1 = sumPrint(4, 4)

# This will
x2 = sumReturn(4, 4)
```

9.3. Documenting Functions

Functions in Python typically have a comment as the first statement of the function. This comment is delimited using three double quotes, and is called a *docstring*. A function may look like:

Listing 9.4: Documented function that returns the volume of a cylinder

```
1 def volumeCylinder(radius, height):
2     """Returns volume of a cylinder given radius, height."""
3     pi = 3.141592653589
4     volume = 2 * pi * radius * (radius + height)
5     return volume
```

The great thing about using docstrings in functions is that the comment can be pulled out and put into a website documenting your code using a tool like **Sphinx**. Most languages have similar tools that can help make documenting your code a breeze. This can save a lot of time as you start working on larger programs.

9.4. Variable Scope

The use of functions introduces the concept of *scope*. Scope is where in the code a variable is "alive" and can be accessed. For example, look at the code below:

```
# Define a simple function that sets
# x equal to 22
def f():
    x = 22

# Call the function
f()
# This fails, x only exists in f()
print(x)
```

The last line will generate an error because x only exists inside of the f() function. The variable is created when f() is called and the memory it uses is freed as soon as f() finishes.

A more confusing rule is accessing variables created outside of the f() function. In the following code, x is created before the f() function, and thus can be read from inside the f() function.

```
# Create the x variable and set to 44
x = 44

# Define a simple function that prints x
def f():
    print(x)

# Call the function
f()
```

Variables created ahead of a function may be read inside of the function *only if the function does not change the value*. This code, very similar to the code above, will fail. The computer will claim it doesn't know what x is.

```
# Create the x variable and set to 44
x=44

# Define a simple function that prints x
def f():
    x += 1
    print(x)

# Call the function
f()
```

Other languages have more complex rules around the creation of variables and scope than Python does. Because Python is straight-forward it is a good introductory language.

9.5. Pass-by-copy

Functions pass their values by creating a copy of the original. For example:

```
# Define a simple function that prints x
def f(x):
    x += 1
    print(x)

# Set y
y = 10
# Call the function
f(y)
# Print y to see if it changed
print(y)
```

The value of y does not change, even though the f() function increases the value passed to it. Each of the variables listed as a parameter in a function is a brand new variable. The value of that variable is copied from where it is called.

This is reasonably straight forward in the prior example. Where it gets confusing is if both the code that calls the function and the function itself have variables named the same. The code below is identical to the prior listing, but rather than use y it uses x.

```
# Define a simple function that prints x
def f(x):
    x += 1
    print(x)

# Set x
x = 10
# Call the function
f()
# Print x to see if it changed
print(x)
```

The output is the same as the program that uses y. Even though both the function and the surrounding code use x for a variable name, there are actually *two* different variables. There is the variable x that exists inside of the function, and a different variable x that exists outside the function.

9.6. Functions Calling Functions

It is entirely possible for a function to call another function. For example, say the functions like the following were defined:

```
def armOut(whichArm, palmUpOrDown):
  # code would go here

def handGrab(what):
  # code goes here
```

Then another function could be created that calls the other functions:

```
def macarena():
  armOut("right", "down")
  armOut("left", "down")
  armOut("right", "up")
  armOut("left", "up")
  handGrab("right", "left arm")
  handGrab("left", "right arm")
  # etc
```

9.7. Review Questions

9.7.1. Predicting Output

Predict what each block of code will print out:

1. Block 1

```
for i in range(5):
    print(i + 1)
```

2. Block 2

```
for i in range(5):
    print(i)
    i = i + 1
```

3. Block 3

```
x = 0
for i in range(5):
    x += 1
print(x)
```

4. Block 4

```
x = 0
for i in range(5):
    for j in range(5):
        x += 1
print(x)
```

5. Block 5

```
for i in range(5):
    for j in range(5):
        print (i, j)
```

6. Block 6

```
for i in range(5):
    for j in range(5):
        print ("*", end="")
        print ()
```

7. Block 7

```
for i in range(5):
    for j in range(5):
        print ("*", end="")
    print ()
```

8. Block 8

```
for i in range(5):
    for j in range(5):
        print ("*", end="")
print ()
```

9. Block 9

```
# What is the mistake here?
array=[5, 8, 10, 4, 5]
i=0
for i in array:
    i = i + array[i]
print(i)
```

10. Block 10

```
for i in range(5):
    x=0
    for j in range(5):
        x += 1
print (x)
```

11. Block 11

```
import random
play_again = "y"
while play_again == "y":
    for i in range(5):
        print (random.randrange(2), end="")
    print()
    play_again = input("Play again? ")
print ("Bye!")
```

12. Block 12

```
def f1(x):
    print(x)
y = 3
f1(y)
```

13. Block 13

```
def f2(x):
    x = x + 1
    print(x)
y = 3
f2(y)
print(y)
```

14. Block 14

```
def f3(x):
    x = x + 1
    print(x)
x = 3
f3(x)
print(x)
```

15. Block 15

```
def f4(x):
    z = x + 1
    print(z)
x = 3
f4(x)
print(z)
```

16. Block 16

```
def foo(x):
    x = x + 1
    print ("x=", x)

x = 10
print ("x=", x)
foo(x)
print ("x=", x)
```

17. Block 17

```
def f():
    print ("f start")
    g()
    h()
    print ("f end")

def g():
    print ("g start")
    h()
    print ("g end")
```

```
def h():
    print ("h")

f()
```

18. Block 18

```
def foo():
    x = 3
    print ("foo has been called")

x = 10
print ("x=", x)
foo()
print ("x=", x)
```

19. Block 19 (This demonstrates a new concept that won't be fully explained until Chapter 13.)

```
def a(x):
    print ("a", x)
    x = x + 1
    print ("a", x)

x = 1
print("main", x)
a(x)
print("main", x)

def b(y):
    print("b", y[1])
    y[1] = y[1] + 1
    print("b", y[1])

y=[123, 5]
print("main", y[1])
b(y)
print("main",y[1])

def c(y):
    print("c",y[1])
    y = [101,102]
    print("c",y[1])

y = [123,5]
print("main",y[1])
c(y)
```

```
print("main",y[1])
```

If any of the results from these problems are not clear, check out the video on-line that explains it. Each block number is in the comment at the top, so you can skip through the video to the parts you are interested in.

9.7.2. Correcting Code

1. Correct the following code: (Don't let it print out the word "None")

```
def sum(a, b, c):
    print(a + b + c)

print(sum(10, 11, 12))
```

2. Correct the following code: (x should increase by one, but it doesn't.)

```
def increase(x):
    return x + 1

x = 10
print("X is", x, " I will now increase x." )
increase(x)
print("X is now", x)
```

3. Correct the following code:

```
def print_hello:
    print("Hello")

print_hello()
```

4. Correct the following code:

```
def count_to_ten():
    for i in range[10]:
        print(i)

count_to_ten()
```

5. Correct the following code:

```
def sum_list(list):
    for i in list:
        sum = i
        return sum
```

```
list = [45, 2, 10, -5, 100]
print(sum_list(list))
```

6. Correct the following code: (This almost reverses the string. What is wrong?)

```
def reverse(text):
    result = ""
    text_length = len(text)
    for i in range(text_length):
        result = result + text[i * -1]
    return result

text = "Programming is the coolest thing ever."
print(reverse(text))
```

7. Correct the following code:

```
def get_user_choice():
    while True:
        command = input("Command: ")
        if command = f or command = m or command = s or command = d or
            command = q:
            return command

        print("Hey, that's not a command. Here are your options:" )
        print("f - Full speed ahead")
        print("m - Moderate speed")
        print("s - Status")
        print("d - Drink")
        print("q - Quit")

user_command = get_user_choice()
print("You entered:", user_command)
```

For explanations on how to correct the code, see the video on-line. Don't watch the video until spending time trying to figure out how to correct the code, or else it will all be pointless.

9.8. Lab

Complete Lab 6 "Functions" and practice creating your own functions.

10. Wait, What Else Can We Do?

What else can we do with programming skills? Once you finish this course and look around, you might find yourself doing something other than programming video games. Your programming probably won't be in Python. In fact, you might not realize you've got an opportunity to do programming at all.

In this chapter we'll look at different examples of what you can do with your programming skills. Even if you don't become a full-time programmer, you can save yourself a lot of time and effort by creating some small programs on the side that keep you from doing repetitive tasks.

10.1. Arduino Demonstration

It used to be that combining programming skills with electronics to control robotics was difficult. Creating *embedded systems* that combine a small cheap computer that can manage servos, valves, motors, and lights required a very different type of programming. Embedded systems often don't even have an operating system like Microsoft Windows. They might not even have a disk drive!

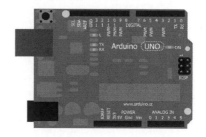

In the last few years programming embedded systems has become so easy that even some grade school kids are doing it. One of the products helping this new movement of do-it-yourselfers is the Arduino. The specifications for the Arduino are free and open, allowing anyone to create their own embedded solutions for very little money.

There are many other companies that sell Arduino kits. If you have a good Radio Shack in your neighborhood, it may have a selection of Arduino computers. Adafruit (one of my favorite companies) sells an excellent starter pack with an Arduino computer, some lights, a motor, a servo, and a few other odds and ends can be purchased for various companies for less than $100. http://adafruit.com/products/170

This experimenter's package can be used to build the following Arduino example that controls nine LED lights, one multi-color LED light, and uses a force sensor to control a servo arm.

Figure 10.1 shows how to hook up one LED light to the Arduino. The LED hooks up to pin 13 on the Arduino. A "resistor" is also placed in-line to keep the electricity from flowing too fast and burning out the LED. Resistors have different values, and the color codes on the resistor

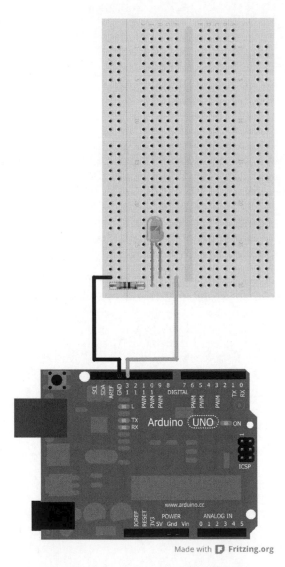

Figure 10.1.: Adruino Example: Hooking up an LED

allow a person to select the correct resistor.

This setup for pin 13 is repeated for pins 13 down to 4, so that a total of 9 LEDs can be hooked up to the Arduino.

If you don't want to be stuck with only one color of LED, you can use a multi-color LED. Multi-color LEDs have three LEDs built into them. One for red, one blue, and one green. Sound familiar? Colors are specified for the LED by controlling how bright red, green, and blue are. This is just like programming our game!

Hooking up the multi-colored LED is shown in Figure 10.2.

Figure 10.3 shows how to hook up a force sensor to control how far a servo arm moves. The force sensor is very sensitive, and based on how gently it is squeezed, the robotic servo arm can do your work. A little more work and you can create your own exoskeleton!

Take a look at the code below. The code is in the computer language "C." You'll find the C language has many things that are similar to what we've learned in Python:

- Instead of using **import** to bring in a library, C uses **#include**.
- C uses curly braces rather than indentation to determine what goes in a loop, function, or conditional statement.
- In the example **setup** is a function definition, just as Python has function definitions.
- Rather than what type of data you want in a variable, C requires you to explicitly state that you are creating a new variable, and what data it will store. For example, **int r** creates a new variable **r** that holds an integer number.
- The Arduino has a **setup** function that has code similar to what we'd put before the main program loop in our Python games.
- The Arduino has a **loop** function that is called over and over. The code in here is the type of code that would go in our main program loop for Python.
- As you can see, there are also **random** number functions in C.
- The **for** loop in C looks different than Python, but the concept is the same.
- C also has **if** statements and uses == to test for equality.

Listing 10.1: Arduino program

```
1  // Import servo library
2  #include <Servo.h>
3
4  // Global Variables
5  long currentPin=4;
6  Servo myservo;
7
8  // Setup function
9  void setup() {
10     // Attach the servo object to pin 3
11     myservo.attach(3);
12     // Set pins 1 to 13 for output.
13     for( int i=1; i <= 13; i++ )
```

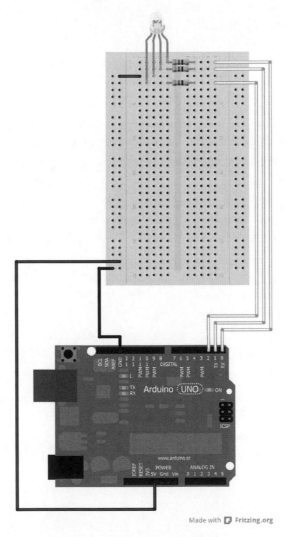

Made with **□** Fritzing.org

Figure 10.2.: Adruino Example: Hooking up an RGB LED

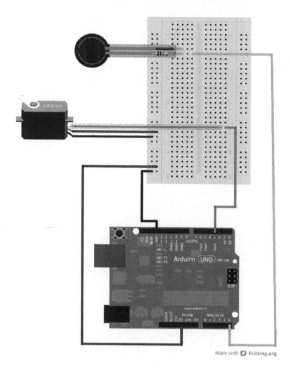

Figure 10.3.: Adruino Example: Force sensor controlling a servo

```
14          pinMode(i, OUTPUT);
15 }
16
17 // Main program loop
18 void loop()
19 {
20     // Loop from pins 4 to 13
21     for( int i=4; i <= 13; i++ ) {
22         // Figure out if the LED should be lit
23         if( currentPin == i ) {
24             digitalWrite(i, HIGH); // On
25         } else {
26             digitalWrite(i, LOW);  // Off
27         }
28     }
29     // Set the next LED to light up next time
30     currentPin += 1;
31     // Reset back to the beginning
32     if( currentPin > 13 ) {
33         currentPin = 4;
34     }
35
36     // Get random color values
```

```
37    int r=random(0,256);
38    int g=random(0,256);
39    int b=random(0,256);
40
41    // Set red, green, and blue parts of LED
42    analogWrite(0, r);
43    analogWrite(1, g);
44    analogWrite(2, b);
45
46    // Read force sensor on pin A5 (possible range 0-1023)
47    int sensorValue = analogRead(A5);
48    // Write out servo position (possible range 0-255)
49    myservo.write(sensorValue / 4);
50
51    // Delay 150ms before we do this again
52    delay(150);
53 }
```

10.2. Excel Macro Demonstration

10.2.1. Introduction

Imagine you graduate from college and start work in the business world. A nightmare! You weren't hired as a VP! You are a lowly peon in the business world set to do menial tasks for someone else. This isn't at all like what the college brochure promised you.

You have to create the same charts, over and over for some financial analyst. He makes too much money to be stuck creating charts, so you have your first job creating these charts for him in Excel.

Wait, boring, repetitive tasks! The exact thing that programming was created to help eliminate! And you took this class in programming, so you should be all set! Follow the outline below in Excel and create your own macro that will automatically create charts for stocks. (This is actually what happened to me in my first job, and was the start to my being able to land my first big project.)

10.2.2. Tutorial

- We are starting our work life as a peon. Here is our job:
    - We have to import data from the web.
    - We have to chart the data.
    - We'll have to create 10 of these charts every day for different data sets.
    - Now just about any job could need to do this. That data could be anything. In this case, we'll use stock data.

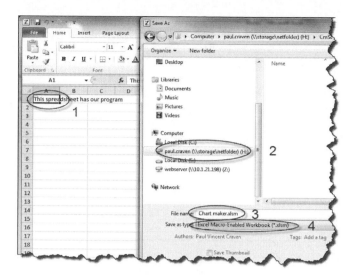

Figure 10.4.: Save As

- Great, our job is boring. Error prone. And takes way too long. Particularly if you want to make the charts look fancy.
  - But wait, we took Professor Craven's programming class. Let's try that.
  - Too bad we program Excel using Visual Basic, and Dr. Craven taught us Python. Ah well, let's not worry about details like that.
  - We'll create an Excel program that creates new stock charts from internet data.
- Outline of what we want our program to do:
  - Open a new file
  - Import data from web
  - Create chart
- Here are the steps to follow so we can program an Excel macro:
  - Open the Excel program. I'm using the 2010 version here.
  - Type in first cell "This spreadsheet has our program." This will make it obvious which spreadsheet has our program, and which spreadsheets have the charts.
  - Save this file and title it "chart maker" Important: Make sure to save as a Macro workbook! Otherwise your macro won't run. See Figure 10.4.
  - Click "view" tab
  - Click the down arrow on macros, then select "record macro." See Figure 10.5
  - Name the macro CreateChart, sec Figure 10.6.
    * You can't use a space in the name, because this is a function and has teh same rules Python has.
  - File tab...New...Blank workbook. See Figure 10.7.
  - Data tab...From web (Don't resize the window, it shows a bug in Excel.)

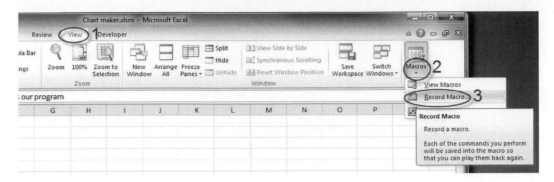

Figure 10.5.: Record Maco

Figure 10.6.: Set Macro Name

Figure 10.7.: Open a Blank Workbook

Figure 10.8.: Import Data

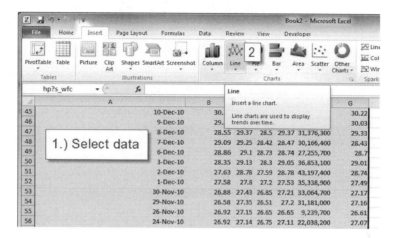

Figure 10.9.: Insert Line Chart

- Use Yahoo to get the stock information:
  http://finance.yahoo.com/q/hp?s=wfc
- Select the table we are interested in, and import. See Figure 10.8.
- Select the cells we want to chart. Do this by using the keyboard: ctrl-shift-left, then ctrl-shift-down, then up one.
- Insert tab...Line Chart. See Figure 10.9.
- Select the option to move to a new worksheet. See Figure 10.10.
- Right click on chart, "select data." See Figure 10.11.
- Modify the data so you only graph adjusted close. See Figure 10.12.
- Select "Layout" tab.
  * Set the axis labels.
  * Remove the legend.
  * Change the chart title to something better.
- Stop the recorder (view tab, macros button, stop recording.)
- Close the new spreadsheet we created. (Not the "chart maker" spreadsheet with our

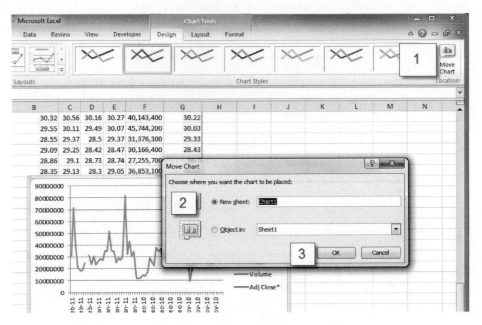

Figure 10.10.: Move Chart

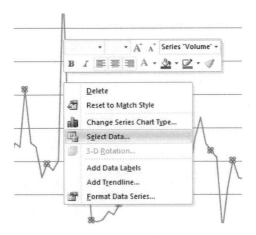

Figure 10.11.: Select Data

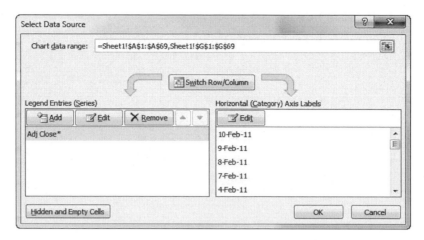

Figure 10.12.: Remove All But "Close"

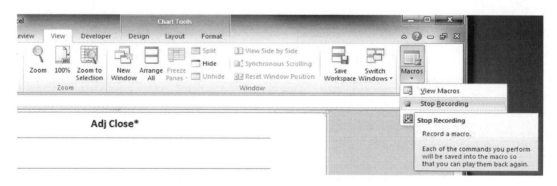

Figure 10.13.: Stop Recording

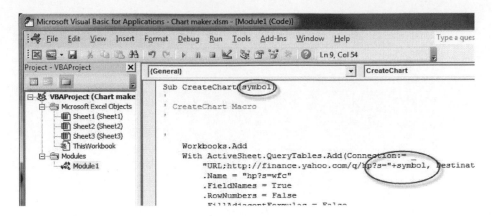

Figure 10.14.: Add a New Parameter

program.)

- Try it out:
  - Run the chart maker macro from the macro menu item.
  - Cool! It creates a chart, but what does this have to do with what we studied? Where's the code?
  - Glad you asked. Rather than play the macro, click edit.
  - Note first line. **Sub** is short for subroutine. Which is another name for function/method.
  - Look, **Workbooks.Add**, a function to add a workbook! Look at the parameters! Booleans! Objects!
  - What happens if we change the Ticker?
  - Cool! What if we could have a variable represent the ticker?
  - Ok, so what if we could make this into a function where we pass in the URL? See Figure 10.14.
  - And then we can create a new function that calls this with a whole batch of ticker symbols:

```
1 Sub CreateCharts ()
2     CreateChart ("WMT")
3     CreateChart ("INTC")
4     CreateChart ("WFC")
5     CreateChart ("BBY")
6     CreateChart ("FDX")
7 End Sub
```

This is what your Visual Basic script should look like after recording:

10.2.3. Code Listings

Listing 10.2: VBScript macro after recording

```
1  Sub CreateChart()
2  '
3  ' CreateChart Macro
4  '
5
6  '
7      Workbooks.Add
8      With ActiveSheet.QueryTables.Add(Connection:= _
9          "URL;http://finance.yahoo.com/q/hp?s=wfc", Destination:=Range("
              $A$1"))
10         .Name = "hp?s=wfc"
11         .FieldNames = True
12         .RowNumbers = False
13         .FillAdjacentFormulas = False
14         .PreserveFormatting = True
15         .RefreshOnFileOpen = False
16         .BackgroundQuery = True
17         .RefreshStyle = xlInsertDeleteCells
18         .SavePassword = False
19         .SaveData = True
20         .AdjustColumnWidth = True
21         .RefreshPeriod = 0
22         .WebSelectionType = xlSpecifiedTables
23         .WebFormatting = xlWebFormattingNone
24         .WebTables = "16"
25         .WebPreFormattedTextToColumns = True
26         .WebConsecutiveDelimitersAsOne = True
27         .WebSingleBlockTextImport = False
28         .WebDisableDateRecognition = False
29         .WebDisableRedirections = False
30         .Refresh BackgroundQuery:=False
31     End With
32     Range(Selection, Selection.End(xlToRight)).Select
33     Range(Selection, Selection.End(xlDown)).Select
34     ActiveSheet.Shapes.AddChart.Select
35     ActiveChart.ChartType = xlLine
36     ActiveChart.SetSourceData Source:=Range("Sheet1!$A$1:$G$69")
37     ActiveChart.Location Where:=xlLocationAsNewSheet
38     ActiveChart.ChartArea.Select
39     ActiveChart.Legend.Select
40     Selection.Delete
41     ActiveChart.ChartArea.Select
42     ActiveChart.SeriesCollection(5).Select
43     ActiveChart.SeriesCollection(1).Delete
44     ActiveChart.SeriesCollection(1).Delete
45     ActiveChart.SeriesCollection(1).Delete
```

```
46      ActiveChart.SeriesCollection(1).Delete
47      ActiveChart.SeriesCollection(1).Delete
48      ActiveChart.ChartArea.Select
49      ActiveChart.ChartTitle.Select
50      ActiveChart.ChartTitle.Text = "WFC"
51      Selection.Format.TextFrame2.TextRange.Characters.Text = "WFC"
52      With Selection.Format.TextFrame2.TextRange.Characters(1, 3).
            ParagraphFormat
53          .TextDirection = msoTextDirectionLeftToRight
54          .Alignment = msoAlignCenter
55      End With
56      With Selection.Format.TextFrame2.TextRange.Characters(1, 3).Font
57          .BaselineOffset = 0
58          .Bold = msoTrue
59          .NameComplexScript = "+mn-cs"
60          .NameFarEast = "+mn-ea"
61          .Fill.Visible = msoTrue
62          .Fill.ForeColor.RGB = RGB(0, 0, 0)
63          .Fill.Transparency = 0
64          .Fill.Solid
65          .Size = 18
66          .Italic = msoFalse
67          .Kerning = 12
68          .Name = "+mn-lt"
69          .UnderlineStyle = msoNoUnderline
70          .Strike = msoNoStrike
71      End With
72  End Sub
```

Once you modify the script to take a parameter so you can graph any stock, it should look like this:

Listing 10.3: Modified VBScript that uses a parameter

```
1  Sub CreateChart(ticker)
2  '
3  ' CreateChart Macro
4  '
5
6  '
7      Workbooks.Add
8      With ActiveSheet.QueryTables.Add(Connection:= _
9          "URL;http://finance.yahoo.com/q/hp?s=" + ticker, Destination:= _
            Range("$A$1"))
10         .Name = "hp?s=wfc"
11         .FieldNames = True
12         .RowNumbers = False
13         .FillAdjacentFormulas = False
14         .PreserveFormatting = True
```

```
15      .RefreshOnFileOpen = False
16      .BackgroundQuery = True
17      .RefreshStyle = xlInsertDeleteCells
18      .SavePassword = False
19      .SaveData = True
20      .AdjustColumnWidth = True
21      .RefreshPeriod = 0
22      .WebSelectionType = xlSpecifiedTables
23      .WebFormatting = xlWebFormattingNone
24      .WebTables = "16"
25      .WebPreFormattedTextToColumns = True
26      .WebConsecutiveDelimitersAsOne = True
27      .WebSingleBlockTextImport = False
28      .WebDisableDateRecognition = False
29      .WebDisableRedirections = False
30      .Refresh BackgroundQuery:=False
31   End With
32   Range(Selection, Selection.End(xlToRight)).Select
33   Range(Selection, Selection.End(xlDown)).Select
34   ActiveSheet.Shapes.AddChart.Select
35   ActiveChart.ChartType = xlLine
36   ActiveChart.SetSourceData Source:=Range("Sheet1!$A$1:$G$69")
37   ActiveChart.Location Where:=xlLocationAsNewSheet
38   ActiveChart.ChartArea.Select
39   ActiveChart.Legend.Select
40   Selection.Delete
41   ActiveChart.ChartArea.Select
42   ActiveChart.SeriesCollection(1).Select
43   ActiveChart.SeriesCollection(1).Delete
44   ActiveChart.SeriesCollection(1).Delete
45   ActiveChart.SeriesCollection(1).Delete
46   ActiveChart.SeriesCollection(1).Delete
47   ActiveChart.SeriesCollection(1).Delete
48   ActiveChart.ChartArea.Select
49   ActiveChart.ChartTitle.Select
50   ActiveChart.ChartTitle.Text = ticker
51   Selection.Format.TextFrame2.TextRange.Characters.Text = ticker
52   With Selection.Format.TextFrame2.TextRange.Characters(1, 3).
         ParagraphFormat
53      .TextDirection = msoTextDirectionLeftToRight
54      .Alignment = msoAlignCenter
55   End With
56   With Selection.Format.TextFrame2.TextRange.Characters(1, 3).Font
57      .BaselineOffset = 0
58      .Bold = msoTrue
59      .NameComplexScript = "+mn-cs"
60      .NameFarEast = "+mn-ea"
61      .Fill.Visible = msoTrue
```

143

```
62        .Fill.ForeColor.RGB = RGB(0, 0, 0)
63        .Fill.Transparency = 0
64        .Fill.Solid
65        .Size = 18
66        .Italic = msoFalse
67        .Kerning = 12
68        .Name = "+mn-lt"
69        .UnderlineStyle = msoNoUnderline
70        .Strike = msoNoStrike
71     End With
72 End Sub
```

Listing 10.4: VBScript function to create multiple charts

```
1 Sub CreateCharts()
2     CreateChart ("WMT")
3     CreateChart ("INTC")
4     CreateChart ("WFC")
5     CreateChart ("BBY")
6     CreateChart ("FDX")
7 End Sub
```

10.2.4. Review Questions

1. Write a function that prints out "Hello World."

2. Write code that will call the function in problem 1.

3. Write a function that prints out "Hello Bob", and will take a parameter to let the caller specify the name. Do not put an **input** statement inside the function! Use a parameter.

4. Write code that will call the function in problem 3.

5. Write a function that will take two numbers as parameters (not as input from the user) and print their product (i.e. multiply them).

6. Write code that will call the prior function.

7. Write a function that takes in two parameters. The first parameter will be a string named **phrase**. The second parameter will be a number named **count**. Print **phrase** to the screen **count** times. (e.g., the function takes in "Hello" and 5, then prints "Hello" five times.)

8. Write code to call the previous function.

9. Write code for a function that takes in a number, and returns the square of that number. Note, this function should return the answer, not print it out.

10. Write code to call the function above.

11. Write a function that takes three numbers as parameters, and returns the centrifugal force. The formula for centrifugal force is:
$F = mr\omega^2$
F is force, r is radius, ω is angular velocity, m is mass.

12. Write code to call the function above.

13. Write a function that takes a list of numbers as a parameter, and prints out each number individually using a `for` loop.

11. Controllers and Graphics

How do we get objects to move using the keyboard, mouse, or a game controller?

11.1. Introduction

So far, we've shown how to animate items on the screen, but not how to *interact* with them. How do we use a mouse, keyboard, or game controller to control the action on-screen? Thankfully this is pretty easy.

To begin with, it is necessary to have an object that can be moved around the screen. The best way to do this is to have a function that takes in an x and y coordinate, then draws an object at that location.

To give the function an x and y, we pass it to the function as a parameter. For example the following code defines a function that will draw a snowman when called:

Listing 11.1: Function to draw a snowman

```
1 def draw_snowman(screen,x,y):
2     # Draw a circle for the head
3     pygame.draw.ellipse(screen,white,[35+x,0+y,25,25])
4     # Draw the middle snowman circle
5     pygame.draw.ellipse(screen,white,[23+x,20+y,50,50])
6     # Draw the bottom snowman circle
7     pygame.draw.ellipse(screen,white,[0+x,65+y,100,100])
```

Then, in the main program loop, multiple snowmen can be drawn, as seen in Figure 11.1.

Listing 11.2: Calling draw_snowman

```
1 # Snowman in upper left
2 draw_snowman(screen,10,10)
3
4 # Snowman in upper right
5 draw_snowman(screen,300,10)
6
7 # Snowman in lower left
8 draw_snowman(screen,10,300)
```

Figure 11.1.: Snowmen drawn by a function

A full working example is available on-line at:

ProgramArcadeGames.com/python_examples/f.php?file=functions_and_graphics.py

Chances are, from a prior lab you already have a code that draws something cool. But how do you get that into a function? Let's take an example of code that draws a stick figure:

Listing 11.3: Code to draw a stickfigure

```
1  # Head
2  pygame.draw.ellipse(screen,black,[96,83,10,10],0)
3
4  # Legs
5  pygame.draw.line(screen,black,[100,100],[105,110],2)
6  pygame.draw.line(screen,black,[100,100],[95,110],2)
7
8  # Body
9  pygame.draw.line(screen,red,[100,100],[100,90],2)
10
11 # Arms
12 pygame.draw.line(screen,red,[100,90],[104,100],2)
13 pygame.draw.line(screen,red,[100,90],[96,100],2)
```

This code can easily be put in a function by adding a function def and indenting the code under it. We'll need to bring in all the data that the function needs to draw the stick figure. We need the screen variable to tell the function what window to draw on, and an x and y coordinate for where to draw the stick figure.

Figure 11.2.: Stick Figure

But we can't define the function in the middle of our program loop! The code should be removed from the main part of the program. Function declarations should go at the start of the program. We need to move that code to the top. See Figure 11.3 to help visualize.

Listing 11.4: Function that always draws a stickfigure in the same place

```
1 def draw_stick_figure(screen,x,y):
2     # Head
3     pygame.draw.ellipse(screen,black,[96,83,10,10],0)
4
5     # Legs
6     pygame.draw.line(screen,black,[100,100],[105,110],2)
7     pygame.draw.line(screen,black,[100,100],[95,110],2)
8
9     # Body
10    pygame.draw.line(screen,red,[100,100],[100,90],2)
11
12    # Arms
13    pygame.draw.line(screen,red,[100,90],[104,100],2)
14    pygame.draw.line(screen,red,[100,90],[96,100],2)
```

Right now, this code takes in an x and y coordinate. Unfortunately it doesn't actually do anything with them. You can specify any coordinate you want, the stick figure always draws in *in the same exact spot*. Not very useful. The next code example literally adds in the x and y coordinate to the code we had before.

Listing 11.5: Second attempt at stickfigure function

```
1 def draw_stick_figure(screen,x,y):
2     # Head
3     pygame.draw.ellipse(screen,black,[96+x,83+y,10,10],0)
4
5     # Legs
```

```
10    green     = (   0, 255,   0)
11    red       = ( 255,   0,   0)          New Function
12
13    def draw_stick_figure(screen,x,y):
14        # Head
15        pygame.draw.ellipse(screen,black,[96+x,83+y,10,10])
16
17        # Legs
18        pygame.draw.line(screen,black,[100+x,100+y],[105+x,110+y],2)
19        pygame.draw.line(screen,black,[100+x,100+y],[95+x,110+y],2)
20
21        # Body
22        pygame.draw.line(screen,red,[100+x,100+y],[100+x,90+y],2)
23
24        # Arms
25        pygame.draw.line(screen,red,[100+x,90+y],[104+x,100+y],2)
26        pygame.draw.line(screen,red,[100+x,90+y],[96+x,100+y],2)
27
28    pygame.init()
29
30    # Set the width and height of the screen [width,height]
31    size=[700,500]
32    screen=pygame.display.set_mode(size)
33
34    pygame.display.set_caption("My Game")
35
36    #Loop until the user clicks the close button.
37    done=False
38
39    # Used to manage how fast the screen updates
40    clock=pygame.time.Clock()
41
42    # --------- Main Program Loop -----------
43    while done==False:
44        # ALL EVENT PROCESSING SHOULD GO BELOW THIS COMMENT
45        for event in pygame.event.get(): # User did something
46            if event.type == pygame.QUIT: # If user clicked close
47                done=True # Flag that we are done so we exit this loop
48        # ALL EVENT PROCESSING SHOULD GO ABOVE THIS COMMENT
49
50        # ALL CODE TO DRAW SHOULD GO BELOW THIS COMMENT
51
52        # First, clear the screen to white. Don't put other drawing command
53        # above this, or they will be erased with this command.
54        screen.fill(white)
55
56        # Head
57        pygame.draw.ellipse(screen,black,[96+x,83+y,10,10],0
58
59        # Legs
60        pygame.draw.line(screen,black,[100+x,100+y],[105+x,110+y],2)
61        pygame.draw.line(screen,black,[100+x,100+y],[95+x,110+y],2)
62
63        # Body
64        pygame.draw.line(screen,red,[100+x,100+y],[100+x,90+y],2)
65
66        # Arms
67        pygame.draw.line(screen,red,[100+x,90+y],[104+x,100+y],2)
68        pygame.draw.line(screen,red,[100+x,90+y],[96+x,100+y],2)
69
70        # Call draw_stick_figure function         New function call
71        draw_stick_figure(screen, 50, 50)
72
```

Figure 11.3.: Making a Function and Putting it in the Right Place

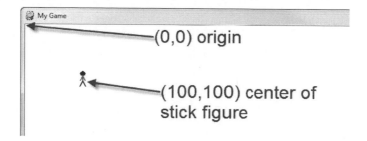

Figure 11.4.: Stick Figure

```
6    pygame.draw.line(screen,black,[100+x,100+y],[105+x,110+y],2)
7    pygame.draw.line(screen,black,[100+x,100+y],[95+x,110+y],2)
8
9    # Body
10   pygame.draw.line(screen,red,[100+x,100+y],[100+x,90+y],2)
11
12   # Arms
13   pygame.draw.line(screen,red,[100+x,90+y],[104+x,100+y],2)
14   pygame.draw.line(screen,red,[100+x,90+y],[96+x,100+y],2)
```

But the problem is that the figure is already drawn a certain distance from the origin. It assumes an origin of (0, 0) and draws the stick figure down and over about 100 pixels. See Figure 11.4 and how the stick figure is not drawn at the (0, 0) coordinate passed in.

By adding x and y in the function, we shift the origin of the stick figure by that amount. For example, if we call:

```
draw_stick_figure(screen,50,50)
```

The code does not put a stick figure at (50, 50). It shifts the origin down and over 50 pixels. Since our stick figure was already being drawn at about (100, 100), with the origin shift the figure is about (150, 150). How do we fix this so that the figure is actually drawn where the function call requests?

Find the smallest x value, and the smallest y value as shown in Figure 11.5. Then subtract that value from each x and y in the function. Don't mess with the height and width values. Here's an example where we subtracted the smallest x and y values:

Listing 11.6: Third attempt at stickfigure function

```
1 def draw_stick_figure(screen,x,y):
2     # Head
3     pygame.draw.ellipse(screen,black,[96-95+x,83-83+y,10,10],0)
4
5     # Legs
6     pygame.draw.line(screen,black,[100-95+x,100-83+y],[105-95+x,110-83+y
        ],2)
```

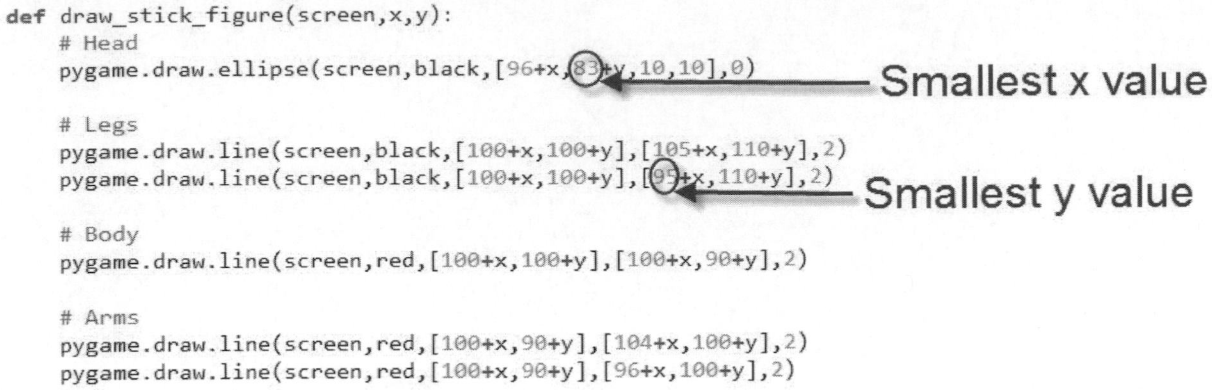

```
def draw_stick_figure(screen,x,y):
    # Head
    pygame.draw.ellipse(screen,black,[96+x,83+y,10,10],0)

    # Legs
    pygame.draw.line(screen,black,[100+x,100+y],[105+x,110+y],2)
    pygame.draw.line(screen,black,[100+x,100+y],[95+x,110+y],2)

    # Body
    pygame.draw.line(screen,red,[100+x,100+y],[100+x,90+y],2)

    # Arms
    pygame.draw.line(screen,red,[100+x,90+y],[104+x,100+y],2)
    pygame.draw.line(screen,red,[100+x,90+y],[96+x,100+y],2)
```

———Smallest x value

———Smallest y value

Figure 11.5.: Finding the Smallest X and Y Values

```
7   pygame.draw.line(screen,black,[100-95+x,100-83+y],[95-95+x,110-83+y
       ],2)
8
9   # Body
10  pygame.draw.line(screen,red,[100-95+x,100-83+y],[100-95+x,90-83+y],2)
11
12  # Arms
13  pygame.draw.line(screen,red,[100-95+x,90-83+y],[104-95+x,100-83+y],2)
14  pygame.draw.line(screen,red,[100-95+x,90-83+y],[96-95+x,100-83+y],2)
```

Or, to make a program simpler, do the subtraction yourself:

Listing 11.7: Final stickfigure function

```
1  def draw_stick_figure(screen,x,y):
2      # Head
3      pygame.draw.ellipse(screen,black,[1+x,y,10,10],0)
4
5      # Legs
6      pygame.draw.line(screen,black,[5+x,17+y],[10+x,27+y],2)
7      pygame.draw.line(screen,black,[5+x,17+y],[x,27+y],2)
8
9      # Body
10     pygame.draw.line(screen,red,[5+x,17+y],[5+x,7+y],2)
11
12     # Arms
13     pygame.draw.line(screen,red,[5+x,7+y],[9+x,17+y],2)
14     pygame.draw.line(screen,red,[5+x,7+y],[1+x,17+y],2)
```

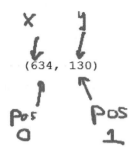

Figure 11.6.: Coordinates

11.2. Mouse

Great, now we know how to write a function to draw an object at specific coordinates. How do we get those coordinates? The easiest to work with is the mouse. It takes one line of code to get the coordinates:

```
pos = pygame.mouse.get_pos()
```

The trick is that coordinates are returned as a list, or more specifically a non-modifiable tuple. Both the x and y values are stored in the same variable. So if we do a **print(pos)** we get what is shown in Figure 11.6.

The variable **pos** is a tuple of two numbers. The x coordinate is in position 0 of array and the y coordinate is in the position 1. These can easily be fetched out and passed to the function that draws the item:

Listing 11.8: Controlling an object via the mouse

```
# Game logic
pos = pygame.mouse.get_pos()
x=pos[0]
y=pos[1]

# Drawing section
draw_stick_figure(screen,x,y)
```

Getting the mouse should go in the "game logic" part of the main program loop. The function call should go in the "drawing" part of the main program loop.

The only problem with this is that the mouse pointer draws right on top of the stick figure, making it hard to see, as shown in Figure ??.

The mouse can be hidden by using the following code right before the main program loop:

Listing 11.9: Hide the mouse cursor

```
# Hide the mouse cursor
pygame.mouse.set_visible(0)
```

Figure 11.7.: Stick Figure With Mouse Cursor On Top

A full working example can be found here:
`ProgramArcadeGames.com/python_examples/f.php?file=move_mouse.py`

11.3. Keyboard

Controlling with the keyboard is a bit more complex. We can't just grab the x and y from the mouse. The keyboard doesn't give us an x and y. We need to:

- Create an initial x and y for our start position.
- Set a "velocity" in pixels per frame when an arrow key is pressed down. (keydown)
- Reset the velocity to zero when an arrow key is released. (keyup)
- Adjust the x and y each frame depending on the velocity.

It seems complex, but this is just like the bouncing rectangle we did before, with the exception that the speed is controlled by the keyboard.

To start with, set the location and speed *before* the main loop starts:

```
# Speed in pixels per frame
x_speed=0
y_speed=0

# Current position
x_coord=10
y_coord=10
```

Inside the main `while` loop of the program, we need to add some items to our event processing loop. In addition to looking for a `pygame.QUIT` event, the program needs to look for keyboard events. An event is generated each time the user presses a key.

A `pygame.KEYDOWN` event is generated when a key is pressed down. A `pygame.KEYUP` event is generated when the user lets up on a key. When the user presses a key, the speed vector is set to 3 or -3 pixels per frame. When the user lets up on a key the speed vector is reset back to zero. Finally, the coordinates of the object are adjusted by the vector, and then the object is drawn. See the code example below:

Listing 11.10: Controlling an object via the keyboard

```
    for event in pygame.event.get():
```

```
        if event.type == pygame.QUIT:
            done = True

        # User pressed down on a key
        if event.type == pygame.KEYDOWN:
            # Figure out if it was an arrow key. If so
            # adjust speed.
            if event.key == pygame.K_LEFT:
                x_speed = -3
            if event.key == pygame.K_RIGHT:
                x_speed = 3
            if event.key == pygame.K_UP:
                y_speed = -3
            if event.key == pygame.K_DOWN:
                y_speed = 3

        # User let up on a key
        if event.type == pygame.KEYUP:
            # If it is an arrow key, reset vector back to zero
            if event.key == pygame.K_LEFT:
                x_speed = 0
            if event.key == pygame.K_RIGHT:
                x_speed = 0
            if event.key == pygame.K_UP:
                y_speed = 0
            if event.key == pygame.K_DOWN:
                y_speed = 0

    # Move the object according to the speed vector.
    x_coord += x_speed
    y_coord += y_speed

    # Draw the item where the mouse is.
    draw_stick_figure(screen, x_coord, y_coord)
```

For a full example see:
ProgramArcadeGames.com/python_examples/f.php?file=move_keyboard.py

Note that this example does not prevent the character from moving off the edge of the screen. To do this, in the game logic section, a set of if statements would be needed to check the x_coord and y_coord values. If they are outside the boundaries of the screen, then reset the coordinates to the edge. The exact code for this is left as an exercise for the reader.

11.4. Game Controller

Game controllers require a different set of code code, but the idea is still simple.

Figure 11.8.: Center (0,0)

Figure 11.9.: Up Left (-1,-1)

To begin, check to see if the computer has a joystick, and initialize it before use. This should only be done once. Do it ahead of the main program loop:

Listing 11.11: Initializing the game controller for use

```
# Current position
x_coord = 10
y_coord = 10

# Count the joysticks the computer has
joystick_count=pygame.joystick.get_count()
if joystick_count == 0:
    # No joysticks!
    print ("Error, I didn't find any joysticks.")
else:
    # Use joystick #0 and initialize it
    my_joystick = pygame.joystick.Joystick(0)
    my_joystick.init()
```

A joystick will return two floating point values. If the joystick is perfectly centered it will return (0,0). If the joystick is fully up and to the left it will return (-1,-1). If the joystick is down and to the right it will return (1,1). If the joystick is somewhere in between, values are scaled accordingly. See the controller images starting at Figure 11.8 to get an idea how it works.

Inside the main program loop, the values of the joystick returns may be multiplied according to how far an object should move. In the case of the code below, moving the joystick fully in a direction will move it 10 pixels per frame because the joystick values are multiplied by 10.

Figure 11.10.: Up (0,-1)

Figure 11.11.: Up Right (1,-1)

Figure 11.12.: Right (1,0)

Figure 11.13.: Down Right (1,1)

Figure 11.14.: Down (0,-1)

Figure 11.15.: Down Left (-1,1)

Figure 11.16.: Left (-1,0)

Listing 11.12: Controlling an object via a game controller

```
# As long as there is a joystick
if joystick_count != 0:

    # This gets the position of the axis on the game controller
    # It returns a number between -1.0 and +1.0
    horiz_axis_pos = my_joystick.get_axis(0)
    vert_axis_pos = my_joystick.get_axis(1)

    # Move x according to the axis. We multiply by 10 to speed up the
        movement.
    x_coord = int(x_coord+horiz_axis_pos * 10)
    y_coord = int(y_coord+vert_axis_pos * 10)

# Draw the item at the proper coordinates
draw_stick_figure(screen, x_coord, y_coord)
```

For a full example, see
ProgramArcadeGames.com/python_examples/f.php?file=move_game_controller.py.

Controllers have a lot of joysticks, buttons, and even "hat" switches. Below is an example program and screenshot that prints everything to the screen showing what each game controller is doing. Take heed that game controllers must be plugged in before this program starts, or the program can't detect them.

Listing 11.13: joystick_calls.py

```
1 # Sample Python/Pygame Programs
```

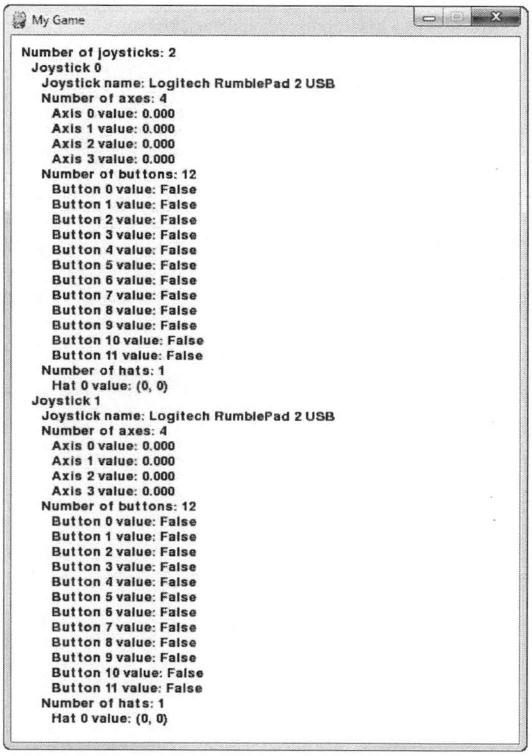

Figure 11.17.: Joystick Calls Program

```
2 # Simpson College Computer Science
3 # http://programarcadegames.com/
4 # http://simpson.edu/computer-science/
5
6 # Define some colors
7 BLACK    = (   0,   0,   0)
8 WHITE    = ( 255, 255, 255)
9
10 # This is a simple class that will help us print to the screen
11 # It has nothing to do with the joysticks, just outputing the
12 # information.
13 class TextPrint:
14     def __init__(self):
15         self.reset()
16         self.font = pygame.font.Font(None, 20)
17
18     def print(self, screen, textString):
19         textBitmap = self.font.render(textString, True, BLACK)
20         screen.blit(textBitmap, [self.x, self.y])
21         self.y += self.line_height
22
23     def reset(self):
24         self.x = 10
25         self.y = 10
26         self.line_height = 15
27
28     def indent(self):
29         self.x += 10
30
31     def unindent(self):
32         self.x -= 10
33
34
35 pygame.init()
36
37 # Set the width and height of the screen [width,height]
38 size = [500, 700]
39 screen = pygame.display.set_mode(size)
40
41 pygame.display.set_caption("My Game")
42
43 #Loop until the user clicks the close button.
44 done = False
45
46 # Used to manage how fast the screen updates
47 clock = pygame.time.Clock()
48
49 # Initialize the joysticks
```

```
50  pygame.joystick.init()
51
52  # Get ready to print
53  textPrint = TextPrint()
54
55  # -------- Main Program Loop -----------
56  while done==False:
57      # EVENT PROCESSING STEP
58      for event in pygame.event.get(): # User did something
59          if event.type == pygame.QUIT: # If user clicked close
60              done=True # Flag that we are done so we exit this loop
61
62          # Possible joystick actions: JOYAXISMOTION JOYBALLMOTION
                    JOYBUTTONDOWN JOYBUTTONUP JOYHATMOTION
63          if event.type == pygame.JOYBUTTONDOWN:
64              print("Joystick button pressed.")
65          if event.type == pygame.JOYBUTTONUP:
66              print("Joystick button released.")
67
68
69      # DRAWING STEP
70      # First, clear the screen to white. Don't put other drawing commands
71      # above this, or they will be erased with this command.
72      screen.fill(WHITE)
73      textPrint.reset()
74
75      # Get count of joysticks
76      joystick_count = pygame.joystick.get_count()
77
78      textPrint.print(screen, "Number of joysticks: {}".format(
            joystick_count) )
79      textPrint.indent()
80
81      # For each joystick:
82      for i in range(joystick_count):
83          joystick = pygame.joystick.Joystick(i)
84          joystick.init()
85
86          textPrint.print(screen, "Joystick {}".format(i) )
87          textPrint.indent()
88
89          # Get the name from the OS for the controller/joystick
90          name = joystick.get_name()
91          textPrint.print(screen, "Joystick name: {}".format(name) )
92
93          # Usually axis run in pairs, up/down for one, and left/right for
94          # the other.
95          axes = joystick.get_numaxes()
```

```
96          textPrint.print(screen, "Number of axes: {}".format(axes) )
97          textPrint.indent()
98
99          for i in range( axes ):
100             axis = joystick.get_axis( i )
101             textPrint.print(screen, "Axis {} value: {:>6.3f}".format(i,
                    axis) )
102         textPrint.unindent()
103
104         buttons = joystick.get_numbuttons()
105         textPrint.print(screen, "Number of buttons: {}".format(buttons) )
106         textPrint.indent()
107
108         for i in range( buttons ):
109             button = joystick.get_button( i )
110             textPrint.print(screen, "Button {:>2} value: {}".format(i,
                    button) )
111         textPrint.unindent()
112
113         # Hat switch. All or nothing for direction, not like joysticks.
114         # Value comes back in an array.
115         hats = joystick.get_numhats()
116         textPrint.print(screen, "Number of hats: {}".format(hats) )
117         textPrint.indent()
118
119         for i in range( hats ):
120             hat = joystick.get_hat( i )
121             textPrint.print(screen, "Hat {} value: {}".format(i, str(hat))
                    )
122         textPrint.unindent()
123
124         textPrint.unindent()
125
126
127     # ALL CODE TO DRAW SHOULD GO ABOVE THIS COMMENT
128
129     # Go ahead and update the screen with what we've drawn.
130     pygame.display.flip()
131
132     # Limit to 20 frames per second
133     clock.tick(20)
134
135 # Close the window and quit.
136 # If you forget this line, the program will 'hang'
137 # on exit if running from IDLE.
138 pygame.quit ()
```

11.5. Review Questions

1. What's wrong with this code that uses a function to draw a stick figure?

```
def draw_stick_figure(screen, x, y):
    # Head
    pygame.draw.ellipse(screen, black,[96,83,10,10], 0)

    # Legs
    pygame.draw.line(screen, black, [100,100], [105,110], 2)
    pygame.draw.line(screen, black, [100,100],[95,110], 2)

    # Body
    pygame.draw.line(screen, red, [100,100], [100,90], 2)

    # Arms
    pygame.draw.line(screen, red, [100,90], [104,100], 2)
    pygame.draw.line(screen, red, [100,90], [96,100], 2)
```

2. Show how to grab the x,y coordinate of where the mouse is.

3. To answer the following, go back to Chapter 5 where the event processing loop is discussed.

   a) Why is it important to keep the event processing loop "together"?

   b) Why is it important to only have one event processing loop?

4. When we created a bouncing rectangle, we multiplied the speed times -1 when the rectangle hit the edge of the screen. Explain why that technique won't work for moving an object with the keyboard.

5. Why does movement with the keyboard or game controller need to have a starting x,y location, but the mouse doesn't?

6. What values will a game controller return if it is held down and to the right?

12. Bitmapped Graphics and Sound

To move beyond the simplistic shapes offered by drawing circles and rectangles, our programs need the ability to work with *bitmapped graphics*. Bitmapped graphics can be photos or images created and saved from a drawing program.

But graphics aren't enough. Games need sound too! This chapter shows how to put graphics and sound in your game.

12.1. Storing The Program in a Folder

The programs we've made so far only involve one file. Now that we are including images and sounds, there are more files that are part of our program. It is easy to get these files mixed up with other programs we are making. The way to keep everything neat and separated out is to put each of these programs into its own folder. Before beginning any project like this, click the "new folder" button and use that new folder as a spot to put all the new files as shown in Figure 12.1.

12.2. Setting a Background Image

Need to set a background image for your game? Find an image like Figure 12.2. If you are looking on-line in a web browser, you can usually right-click on an image, and save it onto the computer. Save the image to the folder that we just created for our game.

Make sure you don't use copyrighted images! Using a reverse-image search it will be easy for your instructor to check to see if you did copy it. You are half-way through the class, don't risk failing now.

Any bitmap images used in a game should already be sized for how it should appear on the screen. Don't take a 5000x5000 pixel image from a high-resolution camera and then try to load it into a window only 800x600. Use a graphics program (even MS Paint will work) and resize/crop the image before using it in your Python program.

Loading an image is a simple process and involves only one line of code. There is a lot going on in that one line of code, so the explanation of the line will be broken into three parts. The first version of the our `load` command will load a file called `saturn_family1.jpg`. This file must be located in the same directory that the python program is in, or the computer will not find it:

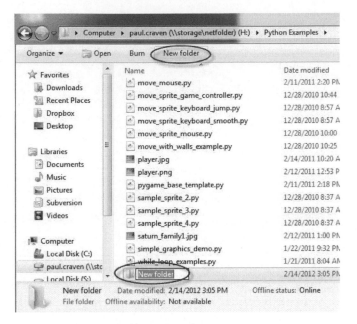

Figure 12.1.: Creating a new folder

Figure 12.2.: Background Image

Figure 12.3.: Player image

```
pygame.image.load("saturn_family1.jpg")
```

That code may load the image, but we have no way to reference that image and display it! We need a variable set equal to what the **load()** command returns. In the next version of our load command, we create a new variable named **background_image**. See below for version two:

```
background_image = pygame.image.load("saturn_family1.jpg")
```

Finally, the image needs to be converted to a format Pygame can more easily work with. To do that, we append **.convert()** to the command to call the convert function. The function **.convert()** is a method in the **Image** class. We'll talk more about classes, objects, and methods in Chapter 13.

All images should be loaded using code similar to the line below. Just change the variable name and file name as needed.

```
background_image = pygame.image.load("saturn_family1.jpg").convert()
```

Loading the image should be done *before* the main program loop. While it would be possible to load it in the main program loop, this would cause the program to fetch the image from the disk twenty or so times per second. This is completely unnecessary. It is only necessary to do it once at program start-up.

To display the image use the **blit** command. This "blits" the image bits to the screen. We've already used this command once before when displaying text onto a game window back in Chapter 5.

The **blit** command is a method in the **screen** variable, so we need to start our command by **screen.blit**. Next, we need to pass the image to blit, and where to blit it. This command should be done *inside* the loop so the image gets drawn each frame. See below:

```
screen.blit(background_image, [0,0])
```

This code blit's the image held in **background_image** to the screen starting at (0,0).

12.3. Moving an Image

Now we want to load an image and move it around the screen. We will start off with a simple red X. See Figure 12.3. The image for this red X may be downloaded from the book's website, or find a .gif or .png that you like with a white background. Don't use a .jpg.

To load the image we need the same type of command that we used with the background image. In this case, I'm assuming the file is saved as `player.png`.

```
player_image = pygame.image.load("player.png").convert()
```

Inside the main program loop, the mouse coordinates are retrieved, and passed to another `blit` function as the coordinates to draw the image:

```
# Get the current mouse position. This returns the position
# as a list of two numbers.
player_position = pygame.mouse.get_pos()
x = player_position[0]
y = player_position[1]

# Copy image to screen:
screen.blit(player_image, [x,y])
```

This demonstrates a problem. The image is a red X with a white background. So when the image is drawn the program shows Figure **??**.

We only want the red X, not the white background. But all images we can load are rectangles, so how do we show only the part of the image we want? The way to get around this is to tell the program to make one color "transparent" and not display. This can be done immediately after loading. The following makes the color white (assuming white is already defined as a variable) transparent:

```
player_image.set_colorkey(white)
```

This will work for most files ending in .gif and .png. This does not work well for most .jpg files. The jpeg image format is great for holding photographs, but it does subtly change the image as part of the algorithm that makes the image smaller. This means that not all of the

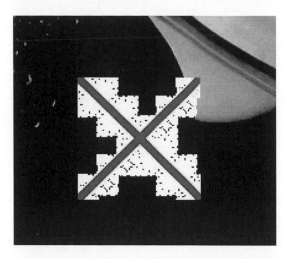

Figure 12.4.: JPEG Compression Artifacts

background color will be the same. In Figure 12.4 the X has been saved as a jpeg. The white around the X is not exactly (255, 255, 255), but just really close.

If you are picking out an image that will be transparent, choose a .gif or .png. These are the best formats for graphic art type of images. Photos should be .jpg. Keep in mind it is not possible to change a .jpg to another format just by renaming the file extension to .png. It is still a .jpg even if you call it something different. It requires conversion in a graphics program to change it to a different format. But once in a .jpg format, it has been altered and converting it to a .png won't fix those alterations.

Here are two great places to find free images to use in your program:

OpenGameArt.Org

HasGraphics.com

12.4. Sounds

In this section we'll play a clicking sound when the mouse button is clicked. You can download and save the sound here:

ProgramArcadeGames.com/python_examples/click.wav

Like images, sounds must be loaded before they are used. This should be done once sometime before the main program loop. The following command loads a sound file and creates a variable named click_sound to reference it:

```
click_sound = pygame.mixer.Sound("click.wav")
```

We can play the sound by using the following command:

```
click_sound.play()
```

But where do we put this command? If we put it in the main program loop it will play it twenty times or so per second. Really annoying. We need a "trigger." Some action occurs, then we play the sound. For example this sound can be played when the user hits the mouse button with the following code:

```
for event in pygame.event.get():
    if event.type == pygame.QUIT:
        done = True
    if event.type == pygame.MOUSEBUTTONDOWN:
        click_sound.play()
```

Uncompressed sound files usually end in .wav. These files are larger than other formats because no algorithm has been run on them to make them smaller. There is also the ever popular .mp3 format, although that format has patents that can make it undesirable for certain applications. Another format that is free to use is the OGG Vorbis format that ends in .ogg.

Pygame does not play all .wav files that can be found on the Internet. If you have a file that isn't working, you can try using the program **Audacity** to convert it to an ogg-vorbis type of sound file that ends in .ogg. This file format is small and reliable for use with pygame.

If you want background music to play in your program, then check out the on-line example section for:

ProgramArcadeGames.com/python_examples/f.php?file=background_music.py

Please note that you can't redistribute copyrighted music with your program. Even if you make a video of your program with copyrighted music in the background YouTube and similar video sights will flag you for copyright violation.

Great places to find free sounds to use in your program:

OpenGameArt.Org

www.freesound.org

12.5. Full Listing

Listing 12.1: bitmapped_graphics.py

```
1  # Sample Python/Pygame Programs
2  # Simpson College Computer Science
3  # http://programarcadegames.com/
4  # http://simpson.edu/computer-science/
5
6  # Explanation video: http://youtu.be/4YqIKncMJNs
7  # Explanation video: http://youtu.be/ONAK8VZIcI4
8  # Explanation video: http://youtu.be/_6c4o41BIms
9
10 import pygame
```

```
11
12 # Define some colors
13 white = (255, 255, 255)
14 black = (0, 0, 0)
15
16 # Call this function so the Pygame library can initialize itself
17 pygame.init()
18
19 # Create an 800x600 sized screen
20 screen = pygame.display.set_mode([800, 600])
21
22 # This sets the name of the window
23 pygame.display.set_caption('CMSC 150 is cool')
24
25 clock = pygame.time.Clock()
26
27 # Before the loop, load the sounds:
28 click_sound = pygame.mixer.Sound("click.wav")
29
30 # Set positions of graphics
31 background_position = [0,0]
32
33 # Load and set up graphics.
34 background_image = pygame.image.load("saturn_family1.jpg").convert()
35 player_image = pygame.image.load("player.png").convert()
36 player_image.set_colorkey(white)
37
38 done = False
39
40 while done == False:
41     clock.tick(10)
42
43     for event in pygame.event.get():
44         if event.type == pygame.QUIT:
45             done=True
46         if event.type == pygame.MOUSEBUTTONDOWN:
47             click_sound.play()
48
49     # Copy image to screen:
50     screen.blit(background_image, background_position)
51
52     # Get the current mouse position. This returns the position
53     # as a list of two numbers.
54     player_position = pygame.mouse.get_pos()
55     x = player_position[0]
56     y = player_position[1]
57
58     # Copy image to screen:
```

```
59      screen.blit(player_image, [x,y])
60
61      pygame.display.flip()
62
63 pygame.quit ()
```

12.6. Review Questions

For the following file extensions, write the extension next to the item that applies:

.jpg	.wav	.gif
.png	.ogg	.bmp
.mp3		

1. Photos

2. Graphic art

3. Uncompressed images

4. Songs and sound effects

5. Uncompressed sounds

What do the following Python programs print?

1.
```
def f():
    return 10

x = f()
print(x)
```

2.
```
def f(x):
    x = x + 10
    return x

x = 10
f(x)
print(x)
```

3.
```
def f(x):
    x = x + 10
    return x

def g(x):
```

```
        return x * 2

    print ( f( g(10) ) )
```

4.
```
def f(x):
    x = x + 10
    return x

def g(x):
    return x * 2

print ( g( f(10) ) )
```

5.
```
def f(x, y):
    return x / y

x=20
y=5
print ( f(y, x) )
```

6.
```
def f(x):
    return x * 2

def g(x):
    return x - 2

def h(x):
    return x + 10

print ( f(5) + g(f(5)) + h(g(10)) )
print ( h(g(f(10))) )
```

7.
```
x = len( [2,3,[5,6],[7,9]] )
print(x)
```

8. Write a function that prints "Hello."

9. Call the function in the prior problem.

10. Write a function that takes in a string as a parameter and counts the number of spaces in it.

11. Write a function that takes in an array as a parameter and prints each element individually.

12. Write a function that takes in an array as a parameter and returns the sum.

12.7. Lab

Complete **Lab 7** "Bitmapped Graphics and User Control" to control graphics and sound. You're getting close to creating a game!

13. Introduction to Classes

Package up related variables, and give them life!

13.1. Why Learn About Classes?

Each character in an adventure game needs data: a name, location, strength, are they raising their arm, what direction they are headed, etc. Plus those characters *do* things. They run, jump, hit, and talk.

Our Python code to store this data might look like:

```
1 name = "Link"
2 sex = "Male"
3 max_hit_points = 50
4 current_hit_points = 50
```

In order to do anything with this character, we'll need to pass that data to a function:

```
1 def display_character(name, sex, max_hit_points, current_hit_points):
2     print (name, sex, max_hit_points, current_hit_points)
```

Now imagine creating a program that has a set of variables like that for each character, monster, and item in our game. Then we need to create functions that work with those items. We've now waded into a quagmire of data. All of a sudden this doesn't sound like fun at all.

But wait, it gets worse! As our game expands, we may need to add new fields to describe our character. In this case we've added **max_speed**:

```
1 name = "Link"
2 sex = "Male"
3 max_hit_points = 50
4 current_hit_points = 50
5 max_speed = 10
6
7 def display_character(name, sex, max_hit_points, current_hit_points,
    max_speed):
8     print (name, sex, max_hit_points, current_hit_points)
```

In example above, there is only one function. But in a large video game, we might have hundreds of functions that deal with the main character. Adding a new field to help describe what character has and can do would require us to go through each one of those functions and add it to the parameter list. That would be a *lot* of work. And perhaps we need to add `max_speed` to different types of characters like monsters. There needs to be a better way. Somehow our program needs to package up those data fields so they can be managed easily.

13.2. Defining and Creating Simple Classes

A better way to manage multiple data attributes is to define a structure that has all of the information. Then we can give that "grouping" of information a name, like *Character* or *Address*. This can be easily done in Python and any other modern language by using a *class*.

For example, a class representing a character in a game:

```
1 class Character():
2     name = "Link"
3     sex = "Male"
4     max_hit_points = 50
5     current_hit_points = 50
6     max_speed = 10
7     armor_amount = 8
```

Here's another common example, holding all the fields for an address:

Listing 13.1: Define an address class

```
1 class Address():
2     name = ""
3     line1 = ""
4     line2 = ""
5     city = ""
6     state = ""
7     zip = ""
```

In the code above, `Address` is the *class name*. The variables in the class, such as `name` and `city`, are called *attributes* or *fields*. (Note the similarities and differences between declaring a class and declaring a function.)

Unlike functions and variables, class names should begin with an upper case letter. While it is possible to begin a class with a lower case letter, it is not considered good practice.

To better visualize classes and how they relate, programmers often make diagrams. A diagram for the `Address` class would look like Figure 13.1. See how the class name is on top with the name of each attribute listed below. To the right of each attribute is the data type, such as string or integer.

The class code *defines* a class but it does not actually create an *instance* of one. The code told the computer what fields an address has and what the initial default values will be. We don't actually have an address yet though. We can define a class without creating one just like we can define a function without calling it. To create a class and set the fields, look at the example below:

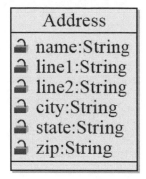

Figure 13.1.: Class Diagram

```
1 # Create an address
2 homeAddress = Address()
3
4 # Set the fields in the address
5 homeAddress.name = "John Smith"
6 homeAddress.line1 = "701 N. C Street"
7 homeAddress.line2 = "Carver Science Building"
8 homeAddress.city = "Indianola"
9 homeAddress.state = "IA"
10 homeAddress.zip = "50125"
```

An instance of the address class is created in line 2. Note how the class **Address** name is used, followed by parentheses. The variable name can be anything that follows normal naming rules.

To set the fields in the class, a program must use the *dot operator*. This operator is the period that is between the **homeAddress** and the field name. See how lines 5-10 use the dot operator to set each field value.

A very common mistake when working with classes is to forget to specify the which instance of the class you want to work with. If only one address is created, it is natural to assume the computer will know to use that address you are talking about. This is not the case however. See the example below:

```
1 class Address():
2     name = ""
3     line1 = ""
4     line2 = ""
5     city = ""
6     state = ""
7     zip = ""
8
9 # Create an address
```

```
10 my_address = Address()
11
12 # Alert! This does not set the address's name!
13 name = "Dr. Craven"
14
15 # This doesn't set the name for the address either
16 Address.name = "Dr. Craven"
17
18 # This does work:
19 my_address.name = "Dr. Craven"
```

A second address can be created and fields from both instances may be used. See the example below:

Listing 13.3: Working with two instances of address

```
1 class Address():
2     name = ""
3     line1 = ""
4     line2 = ""
5     city = ""
6     state = ""
7     zip = ""
8
9 # Create an address
10 homeAddress = Address()
11
12 # Set the fields in the address
13 homeAddress.name = "John Smith"
14 homeAddress.line1 = "701 N. C Street"
15 homeAddress.line2 = "Carver Science Building"
16 homeAddress.city = "Indianola"
17 homeAddress.state = "IA"
18 homeAddress.zip = "50125"
19
20 # Create another address
21 vacationHomeAddress = Address()
22
23 # Set the fields in the address
24 vacationHomeAddress.name = "John Smith"
25 vacationHomeAddress.line1 = "1122 Main Street"
26 vacationHomeAddress.line2 = ""
27 vacationHomeAddress.city = "Panama City Beach"
28 vacationHomeAddress.state = "FL"
29 vacationHomeAddress.zip = "32407"
30
31 print("The client's main home is in " + homeAddress.city)
32 print("His vacation home is in " + vacationHomeAddress.city)
```

Line 10 creates the first instance of **Address**; line 21 creates the second instance. The variable **homeAddress** points to the first instance and **vacationHomeAddress** points to the second.

Lines 24-29 set the fields in this new class instance. Line 31 prints the city for the home address, because **homeAddress** appears before the dot operator. Line 32 prints the vacation address because **vacationHomeAddress** appears before the dot operator.

In the example **Address** is called the *class* because it defines a new classification for a data object. The variables **homeAddress** and **vacationHomeAddress** refer to *objects* because they refer to actual instances of the class **Address**. A simple definition of an object is that it is an instance of a class. Like "Bob" and "Nancy" are instances of a Human class.

Putting lots of data fields into a class makes it easy to pass data in and out of a function. In the code below, the function takes in an address as a parameter and prints it out on the screen. It is not necessary to pass parameters for each field of the address.

```
31 # Print an address to the screen
32 def printAddress(address):
33     print(address.name)
34     # If there is a line1 in the address, print it
35     if( len(address.line1) > 0 ):
36         print (address.line1)
37     # If there is a line2 in the address, print it
38     if( len(address.line2) > 0 ):
39         print( address.line2 )
40     print( address.city+", "+address.state+" "+address.zip )
41
42 printAddress( homeAddress )
43 print()
44 printAddress( vacationHomeAddress )
```

13.2.1. Review Questions

1. Write code to create an instance of this class and set its attributes:

```
class Dog():
    age = 0
    name = ""
    weight = 0
```

2. Write code to create *two different* instances of this class and set attributes for both objects:

```
class Person():
    name = ""
    cellPhone = ""
    email = ""
```

3. For the code below, write a class that has the appropriate class name and attributes that will allow the code to work.

```
myBird = Bird()
myBird.color = "green"
myBird.name = "Sunny"
myBird.breed = "Sun Conure"
```

4. Create a class that would represent a character in a simple 2D game. Include attributes for the position, name, and strength.

5. The following code runs, but it is not correct. What did the programmer do wrong?

```
class Person:
    name = ""
    money = 0

nancy = Person()
name = "Nancy"
money = 100
```

6. Take a look at the code. It does not run. Can you spot the error?

```
class Person:
    name = ""
    money = 0

bob = Person()
print (bob.name, "has", money, "dollars.")
```

7. Even with the error fixed, the program will not print out the desired output:
   Bob has 0 dollars.
   Why is this the case?

13.3. Adding Methods to Classes

In addition to attributes, classes may have *methods*. A method is a function that exists inside of a class. Expanding the earlier example of a Dog class from the review problem 1 above, the code below adds a method for a dog barking.

```
1 class Dog():
2     age = 0
3     name = ""
4     weight = 0
5
6     def bark(self):
7         print("Woof")
```

The method definition is contained in lines 6-7 above. Method definitions in a class look almost exactly like function definitions. The big difference is the addition of a parameter `self` on line 6. The first parameter of any method in a class must be `self`. This parameter is required even if the function does not use it.

Here are the important items to keep in mind when creating methods for classes:
- Attributes should be listed first, methods after.
- The first parameter of any method must be `self`.
- Method definitions are indented exactly one tab stop.

Methods may be called in a manner similar to referencing attributes from an object. See the example code below.

```
1 myDog = Dog()
2
3 myDog.name = "Spot"
4 myDog.weight = 20
5 myDog.age = 3
6
7 myDog.bark()
```

Line 1 creates the dog. Lines 3-5 set the attributes of the object. Line 7 calls the `bark` function. Note that even through the `bark` function has one parameter, `self`, the call does not pass in anything. This is because the first parameter is assumed to be a reference to the dog object itself. Behind the scenes, Python makes a call that looks like:

```
# Example, not actually legal
Dog.bark(myDog)
```

If the `bark` function needs to make reference to any of the attributes, then it does so using the `self` reference variable. For example, we can change the `Dog` class so that when the dog barks, it also prints out the dog's name. In the code below, the name attribute is accessed using a dot operator and the `self` reference.

```
6     def bark(self):
7         print( "Woof says", self.name )
```

Attributes are adjectives, and methods are verbs. The drawing for the class would look like Figure 13.2.

13.3.1. Example: Ball Class

This example code could be used in Python/Pygame to draw a ball. Having all the parameters contained in a class makes data management easier. The diagram for the `Ball` class is shown in Figure 13.3.

```
1 class Ball():
2     # --- Class Attributes ---
```

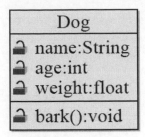

Figure 13.2.: Dog Class

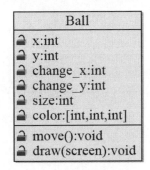

Figure 13.3.: Ball Class

```
3       # Ball position
4       x = 0
5       y = 0
6
7       # Ball's vector
8       change_x = 0
9       change_y = 0
10
11      # Ball size
12      size = 10
13
14      # Ball color
15      color = [255,255,255]
16
17   # --- Class Methods ---
18      def move(self):
19          self.x += self.change_x
20          self.y += self.change_y
21
22      def draw(self, screen):
23          pygame.draw.circle(screen, self.color, [self.x, self.y], self.size
                )
```

Below is the code that would go ahead of the main program loop to create a ball and set its attributes:

```
theBall = Ball()
theBall.x = 100
theBall.y = 100
theBall.change_x = 2
theBall.change_y = 1
theBall.color = [255,0,0]
```

This code would go inside the main loop to move and draw the ball:

```
theBall.move()
theBall.draw(screen)
```

13.4. References

Here's where we separate the true programmers from the want-to-be's. Understanding class references. Take a look at the following code:

```
1  class Person:
2      name = ""
3      money = 0
4
5  bob = Person()
6  bob.name = "Bob"
7  bob.money = 100
8
9  nancy = bob
10 nancy.name = "Nancy"
11
12 print(bob.name, "has", bob.money, "dollars.")
13 print(nancy.name, "has", nancy.money, "dollars.")
```

A common misconception when working with objects is to assume that the variable bob *is* the Person object. This is not the case. The variable bob is a *reference* to the Person object.

If bob actually was the object, then line 9 could create a *copy* of the object and there would be two objects in existence. The output of the program would show both Bob and Nancy having 100 dollars. But when run, the program outputs the following instead:

```
Nancy has 100 dollars.
Nancy has 100 dollars.
```

What bob stores is a *reference* to the object. Besides reference, one may call this *address*, *pointer*, or *handle*. A reference is an address in computer memory for where the object is stored. This address is a hexidecimal number which, if printed out, might look something like 0x1e504. When line 9 is run, the address is copied rather than the entire object the address points to. See Figure 13.4.

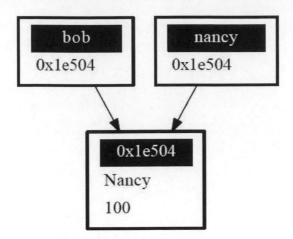

Figure 13.4.: Class References

13.4.1. Functions and References

Look at the code example below. Line 1 creates a function that takes in a number as a parameter. The variable **money** is a variable that contains a copy of the data that was passed in. Adding 100 to that number does not change the number that was stored in **bob.money** on line 10. Thus, the print statement on line 13 prints out 100, and not 200.

```
1  def giveMoney1(money):
2      money += 100
3
4  class Person:
5      name = ""
6      money = 0
7
8  bob = Person()
9  bob.name = "Bob"
10 bob.money = 100
11
12 giveMoney1(bob.money)
13 print(bob.money)
```

Look at the additional code below. This code does cause **bob.money** to increase and the print statement to print 200.

```
14 def giveMoney2(person):
15     person.money += 100
16
17 giveMoney2(bob)
18 print(bob.money)
```

Why is this? Because **person** contains a copy of the memory address of the object, not the actual object itself. One can think of it as a bank account number. The function has a copy of the bank account number, not a copy of the whole bank account. So using the copy of the bank account number to deposit 100 dollars causes Bob's bank account balance to go up.

Arrays work the same way. A function that takes in an array (list) as a parameter and modifies values in that array will be modifying the same array that the calling code created. The address of the array is copied, not the entire array.

13.4.2. Review Questions

1. Create a class called `Cat`. Give it attributes for name, color, and weight. Give it a method called `meow`.

2. Create an instance of the cat class, set the attributes, and call the meow method.

3. Create a class called `Monster`. Give it an attribute for name and an integer attribute for health. Create a method called `decreaseHealth` that takes in a parameter `amount` and decreases the health by that much. Inside that method, print that the animal died if health goes below zero.

13.5. Constructors

There's a terrible problem with our class for `Dog` listed below. When we create a dog, by default the dog has no name. Dogs should have names! We should not allow dogs to be born and then never be given a name. Yet the code below allows this to happen, and that dog will never have a name.

```
class Dog()
    name = ""

myDog = Dog()
```

Python doesn't want this to happen. That's why Python classes have a special function that is called any time an instance of that class is created. By adding a function called a *constructor*, a programmer can add code that is automatically run each time an instance of the class is created. See the example constructor code below:

Listing 13.4: Example of a class with a constructor

```
1  class Dog():
2      name=""
3
4      # Constructor
5      # Called when creating an object of this type
6      def __init__(self):
7          print("A new dog is born!")
```

```
 8
 9 # This creates the dog
10 myDog = Dog()
```

The constructor starts on line 6. It must be named __init__. There are two underscores before the init, and two underscores after. A common mistake is to only use one.

The constructor must take in `self` as the first parameter just like other methods in a class. When the program is run, it will print:

A new dog is born!

When a `Dog` object is created on line 10, the __init__ function is automatically called and the message is printed to the screen.

A constructor can be used for initializing and setting data for the object. The example `Dog` class above still allows the **name** attribute to be left blank after the creation of the dog object. How do we keep this from happening? Many objects need to have values right when they are created. The constructor function can be used to make this happen. See the code below:

Listing 13.5: Constructor that takes in data to initialize the class

```
 1 class Dog():
 2     name = ""
 3
 4     # Constructor
 5     # Called when creating an object of this type
 6     def __init__(self, newName):
 7         self.name = newName
 8
 9 # This creates the dog
10 myDog = Dog("Spot")
11
12 # Print the name to verify it was set
13 print(myDog.name)
14
15 # This line will give an error because
16 # a name is not passed in.
17 herDog = Dog()
```

On line 6 the constructor function now has an additional parameter named **newName**. The value of this parameter is used to set the **name** attribute in the `Dog` class on line 7. It is no longer possible to create a Dog class without a name. The code on line 17 tries this. It will cause a Python error and it will not run.

A common mistake is to name the parameter of the __init__ function the same as the attribute and assume that the values will automatically synchronize. This does not happen.

In the next example, there are two different variables that are both called **name**. They are printed on lines 8 and 10. The first variable **name** was created as a method parameter on line 6. That method variable goes away as soon as the method is done running. The second variable is the **name** attribute created (also known as *instance variable*) on line 2. It is a completely different variable from the one created on line 6. The variable **self.name** refers to attribute of this particular instance of the **Dog** class. That attribute will exist as long as this instance of the **Dog** class does.

```
1 class Dog():
2     name = "Rover"
3
4     # Constructor
5     # Called when creating an object of this type
6     def __init__(self, name):
7         # This will print "Rover"
8         print(self.name)
9         # This will print "Spot"
10        print(name)
11
12 # This creates the dog
13 myDog = Dog("Spot")
```

13.5.1. Review Questions

1. Should class names begin with an upper or lower case letter?

2. Should method names begin with an upper or lower case letter?

3. Should attribute names begin with an upper or lower case letter?

4. Which should be listed first in a class, attributes or methods?

5. What are other names for a reference?

6. What is another name for instance variable?

7. What is the name for an instance of a class?

8. Create a class called **Star** that will print out "A star is born!" every time it is created.

9. Create a class called **Monster** with attributes for health and a name. Add a constructor to the class that sets the health and name of the object with data passed in as parameters.

13.6. Inheritance

Another powerful feature of using classes and objects is the ability to make use of *inheritance*. It is possible to create a class and inherit all of the attributes and methods of a *parent class*.

For example, a program may create a class called `Boat` which has all the attributes needed to represent a boat in a game:

Listing 13.6: Class definition for a boat

```
1  class Boat():
2      tonnage = 0
3      name = ""
4      isDocked = True
5
6      def dock(self):
7          if isDocked:
8              print("You are already docked.")
9          else:
10             isDocked = True
11             print("Docking")
12
13     def undock(self):
14         if not isDocked:
15             print("You aren't docked.")
16         else:
17             isDocked = True
18             print("Undocking")
```

Our program also needs a submarine. Our submarine can do everything a boat can, plus we need a command for **submerge**. Without inheritance we have two options.

- One, add the **submerge()** command to our boat. This isn't a great idea because we don't want to give the impression that our boats normally submerge.
- Two, we could create a copy of the **Boat** class and call it **Submarine**. In this class we'd add the **submerge()** command. This is easy at first, but things become harder if we change the **Boat** class. A programmer would need to remember that we'd need to change not only the **Boat** class, but also make the same changes to the **Submarine** class. Keeping this code syncronized is time consuming and error-prone.

Luckily, there is a better way. Our program can create *child classes* that will inherit all the attributes and methods of the *parent class*. The child classes may then add fields and methods that correspond to their needs. For example:

```
1  class Submarine(Boat):
2      def submerge(self):
3          print("Submerge!")
```

Line 1 is the important part. Just by putting **Boat** in between the parentheses during the class declaration, we have automatically picked up every attribute and method that is in the **Boat** class. If we update **Boat**, then the child class **Submarine** will automatically get these updates. Inheritance is that easy!

The next code example is diagrammed out in Figure 13.5.

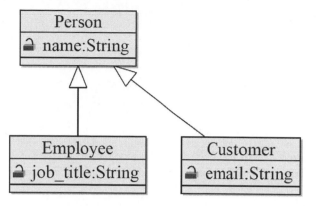

Figure 13.5.: Class Diagram

```
1 class Person():
2     name = ""
3
4 class Employee(Person):
5     job_title = ""
6
7 class Customer(Person):
8     email = ""
9
10 johnSmith = Person()
11 johnSmith.name = "John Smith"
12
13 janeEmployee = Employee()
14 janeEmployee.name = "Jane Employee"
15 janeEmployee.job_title = "Web Developer"
16
17 bobCustomer = Customer()
18 bobCustomer.name = "Bob Customer"
19 bobCustomer.email = "send_me@spam.com"
```

By placing **Person** between the parentheses on lines 4 and 7, the programmer has told the computer that **Person** is a parent class to both **Employee** and **Customer**. This allows the program to set the **name** attribute on lines 14 and 18.

Methods are also inherited. The code below will print out "Person created" three times because the employee and customer classes inherit the constructor from the parent class:

```
1 class Person():
2     name = ""
3
```

```
4      def __init__(self):
5          print("Person created")
6
7  class Employee(Person):
8      job_title = ""
9
10 class Customer(Person):
11     email = ""
12
13 johnSmith = Person()
14 janeEmployee = Employee()
15 bobCustomer = Customer()
```

Methods may be *overridden* by a child class to provide different functionality. In the code below, the child classes have their own constructors, so the parent's class will not be run:

Listing 13.9: Overriding constructors

```
1  class Person():
2      name = ""
3
4      def __init__(self):
5          print("Person created")
6
7  class Employee(Person):
8      job_title = ""
9
10     def __init__(self):
11         print("Employee created")
12
13 class Customer(Person):
14     email = ""
15
16     def __init__(self):
17         print("Customer created")
18
19 johnSmith = Person()
20 janeEmployee = Employee()
21 bobCustomer = Customer()
```

If the programmer desires to run both the parent and the child class's method, the child may explicitly call the parent's method:

Listing 13.10: Child class calling parent constructor

```
1  class Person():
2      name = ""
3
4      def __init__(self):
```

```
5          print("Person created")
6
7  class Employee(Person):
8      job_title = ""
9
10     def __init__(self):
11         Person.__init__(self)
12         print("Employee created")
13
14 class Customer(Person):
15     email = ""
16
17     def __init__(self):
18         Person.__init__(self)
19         print("Customer created")
20
21 johnSmith = Person()
22 janeEmployee = Employee()
23 bobCustomer = Customer()
```

13.6.1. Is-A and Has-A Relationships

Classes have two main types of relationships. They are "is a" and "has a" relationships.

A parent class should always be a more general, abstract version of the child class. This type of child to parent relationship is called an *is a* relationship. For example, a parent class Animal could have a child class Dog. The Dog class could have a child class Poodle. Another example, a dolphin *is a* mammal. It does not work the other way, a mammal is not necessarily a dolphin. So the class Dolphin should never be a parent to a class Mammal. Likewise a class Table should not be a parent to a class Chair because a chair is not a table.

The other type of relationship is the *has a* relationship. These relationships are implemented in code by class attributes. A dog has a name, and so the Dog class has an attribute for name. Likewise a person could have a dog, and that would be implemented by having the Person class have an attribute for Dog. The Person class would not derive from Dog because that would be some kind of insult.

Looking at the prior code example we can see:

- Employee is a person.
- Customer is a person.
- Person has a name.
- Employee has a job title.
- Customer has an e-mail.

13.6.2. Review Questions

Create the following program. Try writing it out before coding it. Download a worksheet for the questions in this chapter here.

1. Write code that defines a class named `Animal`:
   - Add an attribute for the animal name.
   - Add an `eat()` method for Animal that prints "Munch munch."
   - A `makeNoise()` method for Animal that prints "Grrr says [animal name]."
   - Add a constructor for the Animal class that prints "An animal has been born."

2. A class named `Cat`:
   - Make Animal the parent.
   - A `makeNoise()` method for Cat that prints "Meow says [animal name]."
   - A constructor for Cat that prints "A cat has been born." and it calls the parent constructor.

3. A class named `Dog`:
   - Make Animal the parent.
   - A `makeNoise()` method for Dog that prints "Bark says [animal name]."
   - A constructor for `Dog` that prints "A dog has been born." and it calls the parent constructor.

4. A main program with:
   - Code that creates a cat, two dogs, and an animal.
   - Sets the name for each animal.
   - Code that calls `eat()` and `makeNoise()` for each animal.

13.7. Lab

Complete `Lab` 8 "Classes and Graphics" to learn how to control hundreds of items, each going their own separate way.

14. Introduction to Sprites

Our games need support for handling objects that collide. Balls bouncing off paddles, laser beams hitting aliens, or our favorite character collecting a coin. All these examples require collision detection.

The Pygame library has support for *sprites*. A sprite is a two dimensional image that is part of the larger graphical scene. Typically a sprite will be some kind of object in the scene that will be interacted with like a car, frog, or little plumber guy.

Originally, video game consoles had built-in hardware support for sprites. Now this specialized hardware support is no longer needed, but we still use the term "sprite."

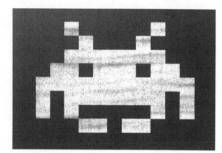

14.1. Basic Sprites and Collisions

Let's step through an example program that uses sprites. This example shows how to create a screen of black blocks, and collect them using a red block controlled by the mouse as shown in Figure 14.1. The program keeps "score" on how many blocks have been collected. The code for this example may be found at:

ProgramArcadeGames.com/python_examples/show_file.php?f=sprite_collect_blocks.py

The first few lines of our program start off like other games we've done:

```
1  # Sample Python/Pygame Programs
2  # Simpson College Computer Science
3  # http://simpson.edu/computer-science
4
5  import pygame
6  import random
7
8  # Define some colors
9  black    = (   0,   0,   0)
10 white    = ( 255, 255, 255)
11 red      = ( 255,   0,   0)
```

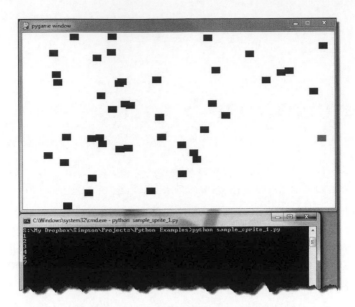

Figure 14.1.: Example Sprite Game

The pygame libary is imported for sprite support on line 5. The random library is imported for the random placement of blocks on line 6. The definition of colors is standard in lines 9-11; there is nothing new in this example yet.

```
13 # This class represents the ball
14 # It derives from the "Sprite" class in Pygame
15 class Block(pygame.sprite.Sprite):
```

Lines 13-15 start the definition of the Block class. Note that on line 15 this class is a child class of the Sprite class. The pygame.sprite. specifies the library and package, which will be discussed later in Chapter 15. All the default functionality of the Sprite class will now be a part of the Block class.

```
16     # Constructor. Pass in the color of the block,
17     # and its size
18     def __init__(self, color, width, height):
19         # Call the parent class (Sprite) constructor
20         pygame.sprite.Sprite.__init__(self)
```

The constructor for the Block class on line 18 takes in a parameter for self just like any other constructor. It also takes in parameters that define the object's color, height, and width.

It is important to call the parent class constructor in Sprite to allow sprites to initialize. This is done on line 20.

```
23         # Create an image of the block, and fill it with a color.
24         # This could also be an image loaded from the disk.
25         self.image = pygame.Surface([width, height])
```

```
26        self.image.fill(color)
```

Lines 25 and 26 create the image that will eventually appear on the screen. Line 25 creates a blank image. Line 26 fills it with black. If the program needs something other than a black square, these are the lines of code to modify.

For example, look at the code below:

```
16    # Ellipse Constructor. Pass in the color of the ellipse,
17    # and its size
18    def __init__(self, color, width, height):
19        # Call the parent class (Sprite) constructor
20        pygame.sprite.Sprite.__init__(self)
21
22        # Set the background color and set it to be transparent
23        self.image = pygame.Surface([width, height])
24        self.image.fill(white)
25        self.image.set_colorkey(white)
26
27        # Draw the ellipse
28        pygame.draw.ellipse(self.image,color,[0,0,width,height])
```

If the code above was substituted, then everything would be in the form of ellipses. Line 28 draws the ellipse and line 25 makes white a transparent color so the background shows up. This is the same concept used in Chapter 12 for making the white background of a red X transparent.

```
16    # Graphic Sprite Constructor.
17    def __init__(self):
18        # Call the parent class (Sprite) constructor
19        pygame.sprite.Sprite.__init__(self)
20
21        # Load the image
22        self.image = pygame.image.load("player.png").convert()
23
24        # Set our transparent color
25        self.image.set_colorkey(white)
```

If instead a bitmapped graphic is desired, substituting the lines of code in above will load a graphic and set white to the transparent background color. In this case, the dimensions of the sprite will automatically be set to the graphic dimensions, and it would no longer be necessary to pass them in. See how line 17 no longer has those parameters.

There is one more important line that we need in our constructor, no matter what kind of sprite we have:

```
27        # Fetch the rectangle object that has the dimensions of the
28        # image. The position of this object is updated
29        # by setting the values of rect.x and rect.y
30        self.rect = self.image.get_rect()
```

The attribute `rect` is a variable that is an instance of the `Rect` class that Pygame provides. The rectangle represents the dimensions of the sprite. This rectangle class has attributes for x and y that may be set. Pygame will draw the sprite where the x and y attributes are. So to move this sprite, a programmer needs to set `mySpriteRef.rect.x` and `mySpriteRef.rect.y` where `mySpriteRef` is the variable that points to the sprite.

We are done with the `Block` class. Time to move on to the initialization code.

```
32 # Initialize Pygame
33 pygame.init()
34
35 # Set the height and width of the screen
36 screen_width = 700
37 screen_height = 400
38 screen = pygame.display.set_mode([screen_width, screen_height])
```

The code above initializes Pygame and creates a window for the game. There is nothing new here from other Pygame programs.

```
40 # This is a list of 'sprites.' Each block in the program is
41 # added to this list.
42 # The list is managed by a class called 'Group.'
43 block_list = pygame.sprite.Group()
44
45 # This is a list of every sprite.
46 # All blocks and the player block as well.
47 all_sprites_list = pygame.sprite.Group()
```

A major advantage of working with sprites is the ability to work with them in groups. We can draw and move all the sprites with one command if they are in a group. We can also check for sprite collisions against an entire group.

The above code creates two lists. The variable `all_sprites_list` will contain every sprite in the game. This list will be used to draw all the sprites. The variable `ball_list` holds each object that the player can collide with. In this example it will include every object in the game but the player. We don't want the player in this list because when we check for the player colliding with objects in the `ball_list`, Pygame will go ahead and always return the player as colliding if it is part of that list.

```
49 for i in range(50):
50     # This represents a block
51     block = Block(black, 20, 15)
52
53     # Set a random location for the block
54     block.rect.x = random.randrange(screen_width)
55     block.rect.y = random.randrange(screen_height)
56
57     # Add the block to the list of objects
58     block_list.add(block)
59     all_sprites_list.add(block)
```

The loop starting on line 49 adds 50 black sprite blocks to the screen. Line 51 creates a new block, sets the color, the width, and the height. Lines 54 and 55 set the coordinates for where this object will appear. Line 58 adds the block to the list of blocks the player can collide with. Line 59 adds it to the list of all blocks. This should be very similar to the code you wrote back in Lab 8.

```
61 # Create a red player block
62 player = Block(red, 20, 15)
63 all_sprites_list.add(player)
```

Lines 61-63 set up the player for our game. Line 62 creates a red block that will eventually function as the player. This block is added to the all_sprites_list in line 63 so it can be drawn, but not the ball_list.

```
65 #Loop until the user clicks the close button.
66 done = False
67
68 # Used to manage how fast the screen updates
69 clock = pygame.time.Clock()
70
71 score = 0
72
73 # -------- Main Program Loop -----------
74 while done == False:
75     for event in pygame.event.get():
76         if event.type == pygame.QUIT:
77             done = True
78
79     # Clear the screen
80     screen.fill(white)
```

The code above is a standard program loop first introduced back in Chapter 5. Line 71 initializes our score variable to 0.

```
82     # Get the current mouse position. This returns the position
83     # as a list of two numbers.
84     pos = pygame.mouse.get_pos()
85
86     # Fetch the x and y out of the list,
87     # just like we'd fetch letters out of a string.
88     # Set the player object to the mouse location
89     player.rect.x = pos[0]
90     player.rect.y = pos[1]
```

Line 84 fetches the mouse position similar to other Pygame programs discussed before. The important new part is contained in lines 89-90 where the rectangle containing the sprite is moved to a new location. Remember this rect was created back on line 30 and this code won't work without that line.

```
92      # See if the player block has collided with anything.
93      blocks_hit_list = pygame.sprite.spritecollide(player,block_list,True)
```

This line of code takes the sprite referenced by **player** and checks it against all sprites in **block_list**. The code returns a list of sprites that overlap. If there are no overlapping sprites, it returns an empty list. The boolean **True** will remove the colliding sprites from the list. If it is set to **False** the sprites will not be removed.

```
95      # Check the list of collisions.
96      for block in blocks_hit_list:
97          score +=1
98          print(score)
```

This loops for each sprite in the collision list created back in line 93. If there are sprites in that list, increase the score for each collision. Then print the score to the screen. Note that the **print** on line 98 will not print the score to the main window with the sprites, but the console window instead. Figuring out how to make the score display on the main window is part of Lab 9.

```
100     # Draw all the spites
101     all_sprites_list.draw(screen)
```

The **Group** class that **all_sprites_list** is a member of has a method called **draw**. This method loops through each sprite in the list and calls that sprite's **draw** method. This means that with only one line of code, a program can cause every sprite in the **all_sprites_list** to draw.

```
103     # Limit to 20 frames per second
104     clock.tick(20)
105
106     # Go ahead and update the screen with what we've drawn.
107     pygame.display.flip()
108
109 pygame.quit()
```

Lines 103-109 flips the screen, and calls the **quit** method when the main loop is done.

14.2. Moving Sprites

In the example so far, only the player sprite moves. How could a program cause all the sprites to move? This can be done easily; just two steps are required.

The first step is to add a new method to the **Block** class. This new method is called **update**. The update function will be called automatically when **update** is called for the entire list.

Put this in the sprite:

```
def update(self):
    # Move the block down one pixel
    self.rect.y += 1
```

Put this in the main program loop:

```
# Call the update() method all all blocks in the block_list
block_list.update()
```

The code isn't perfect because the blocks fall off the screen and do not reappear. This code will improve the update function so that the blocks will reappear up top.

```
def update(self):
    # Move the block down one pixel
    self.rect.y += 1
    if self.rect.y > screen_height:
    self.rect.y = random.randrange(-100, -10)
    self.rect.x = random.randrange(0, screen_width)
```

If the program should reset blocks that are collected to the top of the screen, the sprite can be changed with the following code:

```
def reset_pos(self):
    self.rect.y = random.randrange(-100,-10)
    self.rect.x = random.randrange(0,screen_width)

def update(self):
    # Move the block down one pixel
    self.rect.y += self.change_y
    if self.rect.y > screen_height:
        self.reset_pos()
        self.game.score -= 1
```

Rather than destroying the blocks when the collision occurs, the program may instead call the reset_pos function and the block will move to the top of the screen ready to be collected.

```
# See if the player block has collided with anything.
blocks_hit_list = pygame.sprite.spritecollide(player,block_list,True)

# Check the list of collisions.
if len(blocks_hit_list) > 0:
    score +=len(blocks_hit_list)
    print(score)
```

Find the code above. Change the True to a False so the blocks are not destroyed. Change the if statement to a for loop that loops through each block the player has collided with. Call block.reset_pos() on that block.

14.3. Lab

Complete Lab 9 "Sprite Collecting" to create your first mini-game with sprites.

15. Libraries and Modules

A *library* is a collection of code for functions and classes. Often, these libraries are written by someone else and brought into the project so that the programmer does not have to "reinvent the wheel." In Python the term used to describe a library of code is *module*.

By using `import pygame` and `import random`, the programs created so far have already used modules. A library can be made up of multiple modules that can be imported. Often a library only has one module, so these words can sometimes be used interchangably.

Modules are often organized into groups of similar functionality. In this class programs have already used functions from the `math` module, the `random` module, and the `pygame` library. Modules can be organized so that individual modules contain other modules. For example, the `pygame` module contains submodules for `pygame.draw`, `pygame.image`, and `pygame.mouse`.

Modules are not loaded unless the program asks them to. This saves time and computer memory. This chapter shows how to create a module, and how to import and use that module.

15.1. Why Create a Library?

There are three major reasons for a programmer to create his or her own libraries:

1. It breaks the code into smaller, easier to use parts.

2. It allows multiple people to work on a program at the same time.

3. The code written can be easily shared with other programmers.

Some of the programs already created in this book have started to get rather long. By separating a large program into several smaller programs, it is easier to manage the code. For example, in the prior chapter's sprite example, a programmer could move the sprite class into a separate file. In a complex program, each sprite might be contained in its own file.

If multiple programmers work on the same project, it is nearly impossible to do so if all the code is in one file. However, by breaking the program into multiple pieces, it becomes easier.

One programmer could work on developing an "Orc" sprite class. Another programmer could work on the "Goblin" sprite class. Since the sprites are in separate files, the programmers do not run into conflict.

Modern programmers rarely build programs from scratch. Often programs are built from parts of other programs that share the same functionality. If one programmer creates code that can handle a mortgage application form, that code will ideally go into a library. Then any other program that needs to manage a mortgage application form at that bank can call on that library.

15.2. Creating Your Own Module/Library File:

In this example we will break apart a short program into multiple files. Here we have a function in a file named `test.py`, and a call to that function:

Listing 15.1: test.py with everything in it

```
1 # Foo function
2 def foo():
3     print ("foo!")
4
5 # Foo call
6 foo()
```

Yes, this program is not too long to be in one file. But if both the function and the main program code were long, it would be different. If we had several functions, each 100 lines long, it would be time consuming to manage that large of a file. But for this example we will keep the code short for clarity.

We can move the `foo` function out of this file. Then this file would be left with only the main program code. (In this example there is no reason to separate them, aside from learning how to do so.)

To do this, create a new file and copy the `foo` function into it. Save the new file with the name `my_functions.py`. The file must be saved to the same directory as `test.py`.

Listing 15.2: my_functions.py

```
1 # Foo function
2 def foo():
3     print ("foo!")
```

Listing 15.3: test.py that doesn't work

```
1 # Foo call that doesn't work
2 foo()
```

Unfortunately it isn't as simple as this. The file **test.py** does not know to go and look at the **my_functions.py** file and import it. We have to add the command to import it:

Listing 15.4: test.py that imports but still doesn't work

```
1 # Import the my_functions.py file
2 import my_functions
3
4 # Foo call that still doesn't work
5 foo()
```

That still doesn't work. What are we missing? Just like when we import pygame, we have to put the package name in front of the function. Like this:

Listing 15.5: test.py that finally works

```
1 # Import the my_functions.py file
2 import my_functions
3
4 # Foo call that does work
5 my_functions.foo()
```

This works because **my_functions.** is prepended to the function call.

15.3. Namespace

A program might have two library files that need to be used. What if the libraries had functions that were named the same? What if there were two functions named **print_report**, one that printed grades, and one that printed an account statement? For instance:

Listing 15.6: student_functions.py

```
1 def print_report():
2     print ("Student Grade Report:" )
```

Listing 15.7: financial_functions.py

```
1 def print_report():
2     print ("Financial Report:" )
```

How do you get a program to specify which function to call? Well, that is pretty easy. You specify the *namespace*. The namespace is the work that appears before the function name in the code below:

Listing 15.8: test.py that calls different print_report functions

```
1 import student_functions
```

```
2 import financial_functions
3
4 student_functions.print_report()
5 financial_functions.print_report()
```

So now we can see why this might be needed. But what if you don't have name collisions? Typing in a namespace each and every time can be tiresome. You can get around this by importing the library into the *local namespace*. The local namespace is a list of functions, variables, and classes that you don't have to prepend with a namespace. Going back to the `foo` example, let's remove the original import and replace it with a new type of import:

Listing 15.9: test.py

```
1 # import foo
2 from my_functions import *
3
4 foo()
```

This works even without `my_functions.` prepended to the function call. The asterisk is a wildcard that will import all functions from `my_functions`. A programmer could import individual ones if desired by specifying the function name.

15.4. Third Party Libraries

When working with Python, it is possible to use many libraries that are built into Python. Take a look at all the libraries that are available here:
`http://docs.python.org/3/py-modindex.html`

It is possible to download and install other libraries. There are libraries that work with the web, complex numbers, databases, and more.

- Pygame: The library used to create games.
  `http://www.pygame.org/docs/`
- wxPython: Create GUI programs, with windows, menus, and more.
  `http://www.wxpython.org/`
- pydot: Generate complex directed and non-directed graphs
  `http://code.google.com/p/pydot/`
- NumPy: Sophisticated library for working with matrices.
  `http://numpy.scipy.org/`

15.5. Review Questions

1. What is a Python library? What is a Python module?

2. What are some of the reasons why a programmer would want to create his/her own library file?

3. There are two ways to import library files in Python.

   - Give an example of each.
   - How do calls to functions and classes differ depending on how the library is imported?

4. Can library files import other library files?

5. First, try to write the code on paper. Then type it in.

   - Create a Monster() class with attributes for type and hit points. Create a print() method that prints what type of monster it is, and how many hit points it has.
   - Create child classes Orc() and Goblin(). Create an __init__ that sets the value for type to "Orc" or "Goblin". Also, set the hit points to random number between 5-10 for a Goblin, and 15-30 for an Orc.
   - Create a list of monsters and add a few orcs and goblins to the list. Then call the print() method for each item in the list.

6. Take the program from a prior lab. Make a copy of it. Separate the classes and functions into a separate file.

15.6. Lab

Complete **Lab** 10 "Sprite Moving" to expand your sprite game and use libraries for the sprites.

16. Searching

Searching is an important and very common operation that computers do all the time. Searches are used everytime someone does a ctrl-f for "find", when a user uses "type-to" to quickly select an item, or when a web server pulls information about a customer to present a customized web page with the customer's order.

There are a lot of ways to search for data. Google has based an entire multi-billion dollar company on this fact. This chapter introduces the two simplest methods for searching, the *linear search* and the *binary search*.

16.1. Reading From a File

Before discussing how to search we need to learn how to read data from a file. Reading in a data set from a file is *way* more fun than typing it in by hand each time.

Let's say we need to create a program that will allow us to quickly find the name of a super-villain. To start with, our program needs a database of super-villains. To download this data set, download and save this file:

http://ProgramArcadeGames.com/chapters/16_searching/super_villains.txt
These are random names generated by the nine.frenchboys.net website, although last I checked they no longer have a super-villain generator.

Save this file and remember which directory you saved it to.

In the same directory as super_villains.txt, create, save, and run the following python program:

```
1 file = open("super_villains.txt")
2
3 for line in file:
4     print(line)
```

There is only one new command in this code **open**. Because it is a built-in function like **print**, there is no need for an **import**. Full details on this function can be found in the **Python documentation** but at this point the documentation for that command is so technical it might not even be worth looking at.

The above program has two problems with it, but it provides a simple example of reading in a file. Line 1 opens a file and gets it ready to be read. The name of the file is in between the quotes. The new variable `file` is an object that represents the file being read. Line 3 shows how a normal `for` loop may be used to read through a file line by line. Think of `file` as a list of lines, and the new variable `line` will be set to each of those lines as the program runs through the loop.

Try running the program. One of the problems with the it is that the text is printed double-spaced. The reason for this is that each line pulled out of the file and stored in the variable `line` includes the carriage return as part of the string. Remember the carriage return and line feed introduced back in Chapter 1? The `print` statement adds yet another carriage return and the result is double-spaced output.

The second problem is that the file is opened, but not closed. This problem isn't as obvious as the double-spacing issue, but it is important. The Windows operating system can only open so many files at once. A file can normally only be opened by one program at a time. Leaving a file open will limit what other programs can do with the file and take up system resources. It is necessary to close the file to let Windows know the program is no longer working with that file. In this case it is not too important because once any program is done running, the Windows will automatically close any files left open. But since it is a bad habit to program like that, let's update the code:

```
1 file = open("super_villains.txt")
2
3 for line in file:
4     line = line.strip()
5     print(line)
6
7 file.close()
```

The listing above works better. It has two new additions. On line 4 is a call to the `strip` method built into every `String` class. This function returns a new string without the trailing spaces and carriage returns of the original string. The method does not alter the original string but instead creates a new one. This line of code would not work:

```
line.strip()
```

If the programmer wants the original variable to reference the new string, she must assign it to the new returned string as shown on line 4.

The second addition is on line 7. This closes the file so that the operating system doesn't have to go around later and clean up open files after the program ends.

16.2. Reading Into an Array

It is useful to read in the contents of a file to an array so that the program can do processing on it later. This can easily be done in python with the following code:

Listing 16.1: Read in a file from disk and put it in an array

```
1 # Read in a file from disk and put it in an array.
2 file = open("super_villains.txt")
3
4 name_list = []
5 for line in file:
6     line=line.strip()
7     name_list.append(line)
8
9 file.close()
```

This combines the new pattern of how to read a file, along with the previously learned pattern of how to create an empty array and append to it as new data comes in, which was shown back in Chapter 7. To verify the file was read into the array correctly a programmer could print the length of the array:

```
print( "There were",len(name_list),"names in the file.")
```

Or the programmer could bring the entire contents of the array:

```
for name in name_list:
    print(name)
```

Go ahead and make sure you can read in the file before continuing on to the different searches.

16.3. Linear Search

If a program has a set of data in an array, how can it go about finding where a specific element is? This can be done one of two ways. The first method is to use a *linear search*. This starts at the first element, and keeps comparing elements until it finds the desired element (or runs out of elements.)

16.3.1. Linear Search Algorithm

Listing 16.2: Linear search

```
1 # Linear search
2 i = 0
3 while i < len(name_list) and name_list[i] != "Morgiana the Shrew":
4     i += 1
```

```
5
6 if i < len(name_list):
7     print( "The name is at position",i)
8 else:
9     print( "The name was not in the list." )
```

The linear search is rather simple. Line 2 sets up an increment variable that will keep track of exactly where in the list the program needs to check next. The first element that needs to be checked is zero, so i is set to zero.

The next line is a bit more complex. The computer needs to keep looping until one of two things happens. It finds the element, or it runs out of elements. The first comparison sees if the current element we are checking is less than the length of the list. If so, we can keep looping. The second comparison sees if the current element in the name list is equal to the name we are searching for.

This check to see if the program has run out of elements *must occur first*. Otherwise the program will check against a non-existent element which will cause an error.

Line 4 simply moves to the next element if the conditions to keep searching are met in line 3.

At the end of the loop, the program checks to see if the end of the list was reached on line 6. Remember, a list of n elements is numbered 0 to n-1. Therefore if i is equal to the length of the list, the end has been reached. If it is less, we found the element.

16.3.2. Linear Search Review

Answer the following, assuming a program uses the linear search:

1. If a list has n elements, in the *best* case how many elements would the computer need to check before it found the desired element?

2. If a list has n elements, in the *worst* case how many elements would the computer need to check before it found the desired element?

3. If a list has n elements, how many elements need to be checked to determine that the desired element does not exist in the list?

4. If a list has n elements, what would the *average* number of elements be that the computer would need to check before it found the desired element?

5. Take the example linear search code and put it in a function. Take in the list along with the desired element. Return the position of the element, or -1 if it was not found.

16.4. Variations On The Linear Search

Variations on the linear search can be used to create several common algorithms. For example, say we had a list of aliens. We might want to check this group of aliens to see if one of the aliens green? Are all the aliens green? Which aliens are green?

To begin with, we'd need to define our alien:

Listing 16.3: Alien class

```
1  class Alien:
2    color = ""
3    name = ""
4    weight = 0
5    height = 0
```

Then we'd need to create a function to check and see if it has the property that we are looking for. In this case, is it green? We'll assume the color is a text string, and we'll convert it to upper case to eliminate case-sensitivity.

Listing 16.4: Alien class hasProperty method

```
1  def hasProperty(my_alien):
2    if my_alien.color.upper() == "GREEN":
3        return True
4    else:
5        return False
```

16.4.1. Does At Least One Item Have a Property?

Is at least one alien green? We can check. The basic algorithm behind this check:

Listing 16.5: Check if list has an item that has a property - while loop

```
1  def checkIfOneItemHasProperty1(list):
2    i = 0
3    while i < len(list) and not hasProperty(item):
4        i += 1
5
6    if i < len(list):
7        # Found an item with the property
8        return True
9    else:
10       # There is no item with the property
11       return False
```

This could also be done with a **for** loop. In this case, the loop will exit early by using a **return** once the item has been found. The code is shorter, but not every programmer would prefer it. Some programmers feel that loops should not be prematurely ended with a **return** or **break** statement. It all goes to personal preference, or the personal preference of the person that is footing the bill.

Listing 16.6: Check if list has an item that has a property - for loop

```
1 def checkIfOneItemHasProperty2(list):
2     for item in list:
3         if hasProperty(item):
4             return True
5     return False
```

16.4.2. Do All Items Have a Property?

Are all aliens green? This code is very similar to the prior example. Spot the difference and see if you can figure out the reson behind the change.

Listing 16.7: Check if all items have a property

```
1 def checkIfAllItemsHaveProperty(list):
2     for item in list:
3         if not hasProperty(item):
4             return False
5         return True
```

16.4.3. Create a List With All Items Matching a Property

What if you wanted a list of aliens that are green? This is a combination of our prior code, and the code to append items to a list that we learned about back in Chapter 7.

Listing 16.8: Create another list with all items matching a property

```
1 def getMatchingItems(list):
2     matchingList = []
3     for item in list:
4         if hasProperty(item):
5             matchingList.append(item)
6     return matchingList
```

These common algrithms can be used as part of a solution to a larger problem, such as find all the addresses in a list of customers that aren't valid.

16.5. Binary Search

A faster way to search a list is possible with the *binary search*. The process of a binary search can be described by using the classic number guessing game "guess a number between 1 and 100" as an example. To make it easier to understand the process, let's modify the game to be "guess a number between 1 and 128." The number range is inclusive, meaning both 1 and 128 are possibilities.

If a person were to use the linear search as a method to guess the secret number, the game would be rather long and boring.

```
Guess a number 1 to 128: 1
Too low.
Guess a number 1 to 128: 2
Too low.
Guess a number 1 to 128: 3
Too low.
....
Guess a number 1 to 128: 93
Too low.
Guess a number 1 to 128: 94
Correct!
```

Most people will use a binary search to find the number. Here is an example of playing the game using a binary search:

```
Guess a number 1 to 128: 64
Too low.
Guess a number 1 to 128: 96
Too high.
Guess a number 1 to 128: 80
Too low.
Guess a number 1 to 128: 88
Too low.
Guess a number 1 to 128: 92
Too low.
Guess a number 1 to 128: 94
Correct!
```

Each time through the rounds of the number guessing game, the guesser is able to eliminate one half of the problem space by getting a "high" or "low" as a result of the guess.

In a binary search, it is necessary to track an upper and a lower bound of the list that the answer can be in. The computer or number-guessing human picks the midpoint of those elements. Revisiting the example:

A lower bound of 1, upper bound of 128, mid point of $\dfrac{1+128}{2} = 64.5$.

```
Guess a number 1 to 128: 64
Too low.
```

A lower bound of 65, upper bound of 128, mid point of $\dfrac{65+128}{2} = 96.5$.

```
Guess a number 1 to 128: 96
Too high.
```

A lower bound of 65, upper bound of 95, mid point of $\frac{65 + 95}{2} = 80$.

```
Guess a number 1 to 128: 80
Too low.
```

A lower bound of 81, upper bound of 95, mid point of $\frac{81 + 95}{2} = 88$.

```
Guess a number 1 to 128: 88
Too low.
```

A lower bound of 89, upper bound of 95, mid point of $\frac{89 + 95}{2} = 92$.

```
Guess a number 1 to 128: 92
Too low.
```

A lower bound of 93, upper bound of 95, mid point of $\frac{93 + 95}{2} = 94$.

```
Guess a number 1 to 128: 94
Correct!
```

A binary search requires significantly fewer guesses. Worst case, it can guess a number between 1 and 128 in 7 guesses. One more guess raises the limit to 256. 9 guesses can get a number between 1 and 512. With just 32 guesses, a person can get a number between 1 and 4.2 billion.

To figure out how large the list can be given a certain number of guesses, the formula works out like $n = x^g$ where n is the size of the list and g is the number of guesses. For example:

$2^7 = 128$ (7 guesses can handle 128 different numbers)

$2^8 = 256$

$2^9 = 512$

$2^{32} = 4,294,967,296$

If you have the problem size, we can figure out the number of guesses using the *log* function. Specifically, *log base 2*. If you don't specify a base, most people will assume you mean the natural log with a base of $e \approx 2.71828$ which is not what we want. For example, using log base 2 to find how many guesses:

$log_2 128 = 7$

$log_2 65,536 = 16$

Enough math! Where is the code? The code to do a binary search is more complex than a linear search:

Listing 16.9: Binary search

```
1 # Binary search
2 key = "Morgiana the Shrew";
3 lower_bound = 0
4 upper_bound = len(name_list)-1
5 found = False
```

```
 6 while lower_bound < upper_bound and not found:
 7     middle_pos = (lower_bound+upper_bound) // 2
 8     if name_list[middle_pos] < key:
 9       lower_bound = middle_pos+1
10     elif name_list[middle_pos] > key:
11       upper_bound = middle_pos
12     else:
13         found = True
14
15 if found:
16     print("The name is at position", middle_pos)
17 else:
18     print("The name was not in the list.")
```

Since lists start at element zero, line 3 sets the lower bound to zero. Line 4 sets the upper bound to the length of the list minus one. So for a list of 100 elements the lower bound will be 0 and the upper bound 99.

The Boolean variable on line 5 will be used to let the while loop know that the element has been found.

Line 6 checks to see if the element has been found or if we've run out of elements. If we've run out of elements the lower bound will end up equalling the upper bound.

Line 7 finds the middle position. It is possible to get a middle position of something like 64.5. It isn't possible to look up position 64.5. (Although J.K. Rowling was rather clever in enough coming up with Platform $9\frac{3}{4}$, that doesn't work here.) The best way of handling this is to use the // operator first introduced way back in Chapter 5. This is similar to the / operator, but will only return integer results. For example, 11 // 2 would give 5 as an answer, rather than 5.5.

Starting at line 8, the program checks to see if the guess is high, low, or correct. If the guess is low, the lower bound is moved up to just past the guess. If the guess is to high, the upper bound is moved just below the guess. If the answer has been found, found is set to True ending the search.

16.5.1. Binary Search Review

Answer the following, assuming a program uses the binary search, and the search list is in order:

1. If a list has n elements, in the *best* case how many elements would the computer need to check before it found the desired element?

2. If a list has n elements, in the *worst* case how many elements would the computer need to check before it found the desired element?

3. If a list has n elements, how many elements need to be checked to determine that the desired element does not exist in the list?

4. If a list has n elements, what would the *average* number of elements be that the computer would need to check before it found the desired element?

5. Take the example linear search code and put it in a function. Take in the list along with the desired element. Return the position of the element, or -1 if it was not found.

16.6. Lab

Complete Lab 11 "Spell Check" and create your own spell-checker. This lab should really make it apparent how much faster the binary search is than the linear search.

17. Array-Backed Grids

17.1. Introduction

Games like minesweeper, tic-tac-toe, and many types of adventure games keep data for the game in a grid of numbers. For example, a tic-tac-toe board:

	O	O
	X	
X		

...can use a grid of numbers to represent the empty spots, the O's and the X's like this:

0	2	2
0	1	0
1	0	0

This grid of numbers can also be called a *two-dimensional array* or a *matrix*. (Finally, we get to learn about The Matrix.) The values of the numbers in the grid represent what should be displayed at each board location. In the prior example, 0 represents a spot where no one has played, a 1 represents an X, and a 2 represents an O.

Figure 17.1 is an example from the classic minesweeper game. This example has been modifed to show both the classic display on the left, and the grid of numbers used to display the board on the right.

The number 10 represents a mine, the number 0 represents a space that has not been clicked, and the number 9 represents a cleared space. The numbers 1 to 8 represent how many mines are within the surrounding eight squares, and is only filled in when the user clicks on the square.

Minesweeper can actually have two grids. One for the regular display, and a completely separate grid of numbers that will track if the user has placed "flags" on the board marking where she thinks the mines are.

Classic adventure game maps are created using a tiled map editor. These are huge grids where each location is simply a number representing the type of terrain that goes there. The terrain could be things like dirt, a road, a path, green grass, brown grass, and so forth. Programs like `Tiled Qt`shown in Figure 17.2 allow a developer to easily make these maps and write the grid to disk.

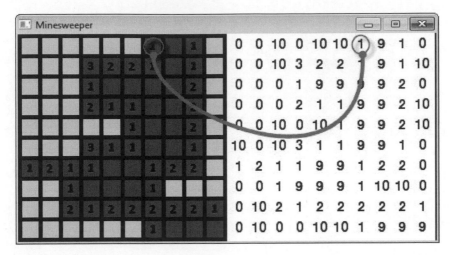

Figure 17.1.: Minesweeper game, showing the backing grid of numbers

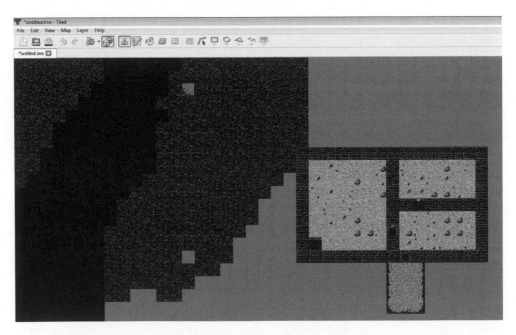

Figure 17.2.: Using Qt Tiles to create an adventure map

Adventure games also use multiple grids of numbers, just like minesweeper has a grid for the mines, and a separate grid for the flags. One grid, or "layer," in the adventure game represents terrain you can walk on; another for things you can't walk on like walls and trees; a layer for things that can instantly kill you, like lava or bottomless pits; one for objects that can be picked up and moved around; and yet another layer for initial placement of monsters.

Maps like these can be loaded in a Python program, but unfortunately a full description of how to manage is beyond the scope of this book. Projects like **PyTMX** that provide some of the code needed to load these maps.

17.2. Application

Enough talk, let's write some code. This example will create a grid that will trigger if we display a white or green block. We can change the grid value and make it green by clicking on it. This is a first step to a grid-based game like minesweeper, battleship, connect four, etc. (One year I had a student call me over and she had modified a program like this to show my name in flashing lights. That was . . . disturbing. So please use this knowledge only for good!)

Go to the **example code page** and download the base template file:
`ProgramArcadeGames.com/python_examples/f.php?file=pygame_base_template.py`

Starting with the blank template file, attempt to recreate this program following the instructions here. The final program is at the end of this chapter but don't skip ahead and copy it! If you do that you'll have learned nothing. Anyone can copy and paste the code, but if you can recreate this program you have skills people are willing to pay for. If you can only copy and paste, you've wasted your time here.

17.2.1. Drawing the Grid

1. Adjust the program's window size to 255x255 pixels.

2. Create variables named `width`, `height`, and `margin`. Set the width and height to 20. This will represent how large each grid location is. Set the margin to 5. This represents the margin between each grid location and the edges of the screen. Create these variables before the main program loop.

3. Draw a white box in the upper left corner. Draw the box drawn using the height and width variables created earlier. (Feel free to adjust the colors.) When you get done your program's window should look like Figure 17.3.

4. Use a `for` loop to draw 10 boxes in a row. Use `column` for the variable name in the `for` loop. The output will look like one long box until we add in the margin between boxes. See Figure 17.4.

Figure 17.3.: Step 3

Figure 17.4.: Step 4

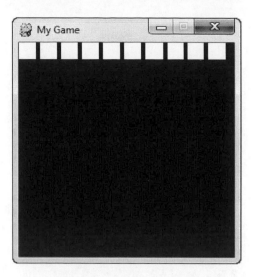

Figure 17.5.: Step 5

5. Adjust the drawing of the rectangle to add in the `margin` variable. Now there should be gaps between the rectangles. See Figure 17.5.

6. Add the margin before drawing the rectangles, in addition to between each rectangle. This should keep the box from appearing right next to the window edge. See Figure 17.6.

7. Add another `for` loop that also will loop for each row. Call the variable in this `for` loop `row`. Now we should have a full grid of boxes. See Figure 17.7.

17.2.2. Populating the Grid

8. Now we need to create a two-dimensional array. Creating a two-dimensional array in Python is, unfortunately, not as easy as it is in some other computer languages. There are some libraries that can be downloaded for Python that make it easy, but for this example they will not be used. To create a two-dimensional array and set an example, use the code below:

Listing 17.1: Create a 10x10 array of numbers

```
1 # --- Create grid of numbers
2 # Create an empty list
3 grid = []
4 # Loop for each row
5 for row in range(10):
6     # For each row, create a list that will
```

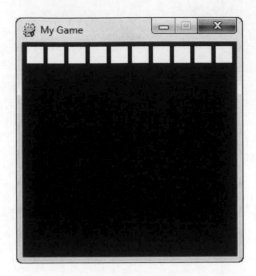

Figure 17.6.: Step 6

Figure 17.7.: Step 7

```
7        # represent an entire row
8        grid.append([])
9        # Loop for each column
10       for column in range(10):
11           # Add a the number zero to the current row
12           grid[row].append(0)
```

A much shorter example is below, but this example uses some odd parts of Python that I don't bother to explain in this book:

Listing 17.2: Create a 10x10 array of numbers

```
1 grid = [[0 for x in range(10)] for y in range(10)]
```

Use one of these two examples and place the code to create our array ahead of your main program loop.

9. Set an example location in the array to 1.

   Two dimensional arrays are usually represented addressed by first their row, and then the column. This is called a row-major storage. Most languages use row-major storage, with the exception of Fortran and MATLAB. Fortran and MATLAB use column-major storage.

   ```
   # Set row 1, column 5 to zero
   grid[1][5] = 1
   ```

   Place this code somewhere ahead of your main program loop.

10. Select the color of the rectangle based on the value of a variable named `color`. Do this by first finding the line of code where the rectangle is drawn. Ahead of it, create a variable named `color` and set it equal to white. Then replace the white color in the rectangle declaration with the `color` variable.

11. Select the color based on the value in the grid. After setting `color` to white, place an `if` statement that looks at the value in `grid[row][column]` and changes the color to green if the grid value is equal to 1. There should now be one green square. See Figure 17.8.

12. Print "click" to the screen if the user clicks the mouse button. See `bitmapped_graphics.py` for example code of how to detect a mouse click.

13. Print the mouse coordinates when the user clicks the mouse.
    See `move_mouse.py` for an example on getting the position of the mouse. See Figure 17.9.

Figure 17.8.: Step 11

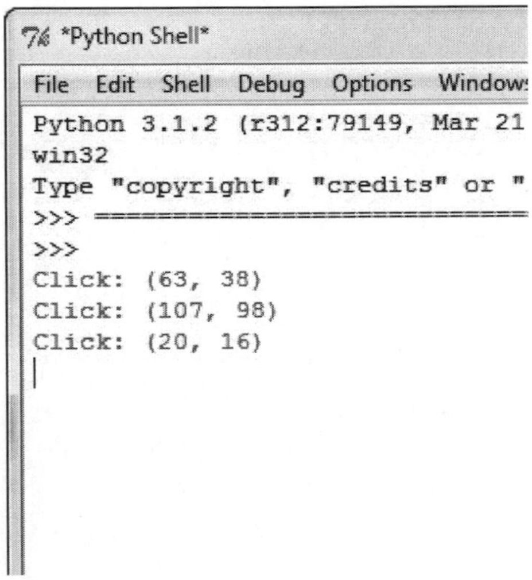

```
7% *Python Shell*
File  Edit  Shell  Debug  Options  Windows
Python 3.1.2 (r312:79149, Mar 21
win32
Type "copyright", "credits" or "
>>> ===========================
>>>
Click: (63, 38)
Click: (107, 98)
Click: (20, 16)
|
```

Figure 17.9.: Step 13

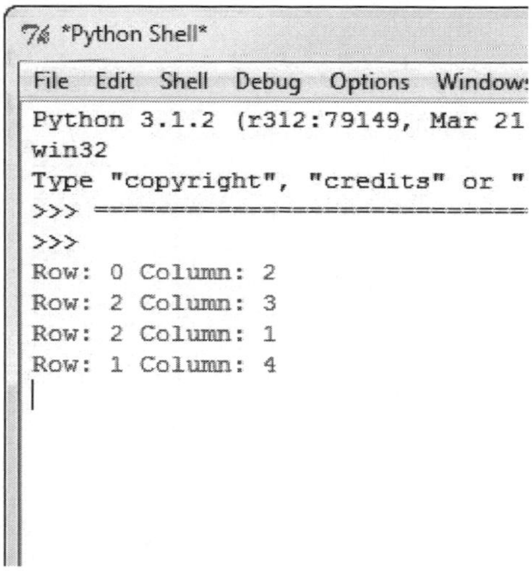

Figure 17.10.: Step 14

14. Convert the mouse coordinates into grid coordinates. Print those instead. Remember to use the width and height of each grid location combined with the margin. It will be necessary to convert the final value to an integer. This can be done by using `int` *or* by using the integer division operator `//` instead of the normal division operator `/`. See Figure 17.10.

15. Set the grid location at the row/column clicked to 1. See Figure 17.11.

17.2.3. Final Program

Listing 17.3: array_backed_grid.py

```
1  # Sample Python/Pygame Programs
2  # Simpson College Computer Science
3  # http://programarcadegames.com/
4  # http://simpson.edu/computer-science/
5
6  # Explanation video: http://youtu.be/mdTeqiWyFnc
7
8  import pygame
9
10 # Define some colors
11 black    = (   0,   0,   0)
12 white    = ( 255, 255, 255)
13 green    = (   0, 255,   0)
14 red      = ( 255,   0,   0)
15
```

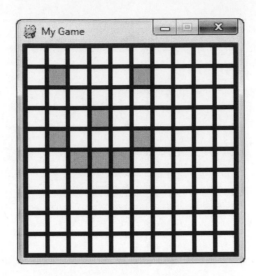

Figure 17.11.: Step 15

```
16 # This sets the width and height of each grid location
17 width  = 20
18 height = 20
19
20 # This sets the margin between each cell
21 margin = 5
22
23 # Create a 2 dimensional array. A two dimesional
24 # array is simply a list of lists.
25 grid = []
26 for row in range(10):
27     # Add an empty array that will hold each cell
28     # in this row
29     grid.append([])
30     for column in range(10):
31         grid[row].append(0) # Append a cell
32
33 # Set row 1, cell 5 to one. (Remember rows and
34 # column numbers start at zero.)
35 grid[1][5] = 1
36
37 # Initialize pygame
38 pygame.init()
39
40 # Set the height and width of the screen
41 size = [255, 255]
42 screen=pygame.display.set_mode(size)
43
44 # Set title of screen
```

```
45 pygame.display.set_caption("Array Backed Grid")
46
47 #Loop until the user clicks the close button.
48 done = False
49
50 # Used to manage how fast the screen updates
51 clock = pygame.time.Clock()
52
53 # -------- Main Program Loop -----------
54 while done == False:
55     for event in pygame.event.get(): # User did something
56         if event.type == pygame.QUIT: # If user clicked close
57             done = True # Flag that we are done so we exit this loop
58         if event.type == pygame.MOUSEBUTTONDOWN:
59             # User clicks the mouse. Get the position
60             pos = pygame.mouse.get_pos()
61             # Change the x/y screen coordinates to grid coordinates
62             column = pos[0] // (width + margin)
63             row = pos[1] // (height + margin)
64             # Sete t hat location to zero
65             grid[row][column] = 1
66             print("Click ", pos, "Grid coordinates: ", row, column)
67
68     # Set the screen background
69     screen.fill(black)
70
71     # Draw the grid
72     for row in range(10):
73         for column in range(10):
74             color = white
75             if grid[row][column] == 1:
76                 color = green
77             pygame.draw.rect(screen,
78                              color,
79                              [(margin+width)*column+margin,
80                               (margin+height)*row+margin,
81                               width,
82                               height])
83
84     # Limit to 20 frames per second
85     clock.tick(20)
86
87     # Go ahead and update the screen with what we've drawn.
88     pygame.display.flip()
89
90 # Be IDLE friendly. If you forget this line, the program will 'hang'
91 # on exit.
92 pygame.quit()
```

17.3. Lab

Go to Lab 12 "Final Lab Part 1" and start work on your own video game!

18. Sorting

Binary searches only work on lists that are in order. So how do programs get a list in order? How does a program sort a list of items when the user clicks a column heading, or otherwise needs something sorted?

There are several algorithms that do this. The two easiest algorithms for sorting are the *selection sort* and the *insertion sort*. Other sorting algorithms exist as well, such as the shell, merge, heap, and quick sorts.

The best way to get an idea on how these sorts work is to watch them. To see common sorting algorithms in action visit this excellent website:
`http://www.sorting-algorithms.com`

Each sort has advantages and disadvantages. Some sort a list quickly if the list is almost in order to begin with. Some sort a list quickly if the list is in a completely random order. Other lists sort fast, but take more memory. Understanding how sorts work is important in selecting the proper sort for your program.

18.1. Swapping Values

Before learning to sort, we need to learn how to swap values between two variables. This is a common operation in many sorting algorithms. Suppose a program has a list that looks like the following:

```
list = [15,57,14,33,72,79,26,56,42,40]
```

The developer wants to swap positions 0 and 2, which contain the numbers 15 and 14 respectively. See Figure 18.1.

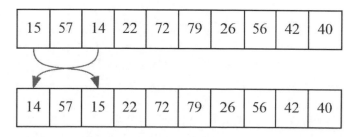

Figure 18.1.: Swapping values in an array

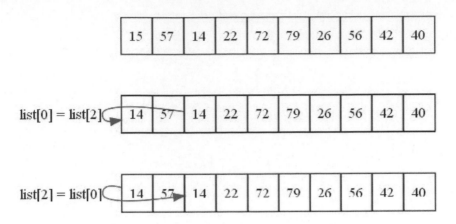

Figure 18.2.: Incorrect attempt to swap array values

A first attempt at writing this code might look something like this:

```
list[0] = list[2]
list[2] = list[0]
```

See Figure 18.2 to get an idea on what would happen. This clearly does not work. The first assignment `list[0] = list[2]` causes the value 15 that exists in position 0 to be overwritten with the 14 in position 2 and irretrievably lost. The next line with `list[2] = list[0]` just copies the 14 back to cell 2 which already has a 14.

To fix this problem, swapping values in an array should be done in three steps. It is necessary to create a temporary variable to hold a value during the swap operation. See Figure 18.3. The code to do the swap looks like the following:

Listing 18.1: Swapping two values in an array

```
1 temp = list[0]
2 list[0] = list[2]
3 list[2] = temp
```

The first line copies the value of position 0 into the `temp` variable. This allows the code to write over position 0 with the value in position 2 without data being lost. The final line takes the old value of position 0, currently held in the `temp` variable, and places it in position 2.

18.2. Selection Sort

The selection sort starts at the beginning of the list. Then code next scans the rest of the list to find the smallest number. The smallest number is swapped into location. The code then moves on to the next number. Graphically, the sort looks like Figure 18.4.

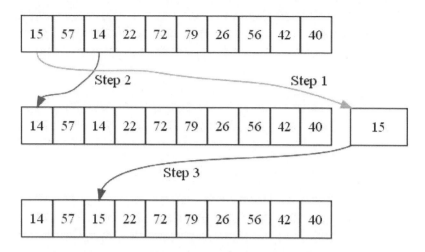

Figure 18.3.: Correct method to swap array values

The code for a selection sort involves two nested loops. The outside loop tracks the current position that the code wants to swap the smallest value into. The inside loop starts at the current location and scans to the right in search of the smallest value. When it finds the smallest value, the swap takes place.

Listing 18.2: Selection sort

```
1  # The selection sort
2  def selection_sort(list):
3
4      # Loop through the entire array
5      for curPos in range( len(list) ):
6          # Find the position that has the smallest number
7          # Start with the current position
8          minPos = curPos
9
10         # Scan left
11         for scanPos in range(curPos+1, len(list) ):
12
13             # Is this position smallest?
14             if list[scanPos] < list[minPos]:
15
16                 # It is, mark this position as the smallest
17                 minPos = scanPos
18
19         # Swap the two values
20         temp = list[minPos]
21         list[minPos] = list[curPos]
22         list[curPos] = temp
```

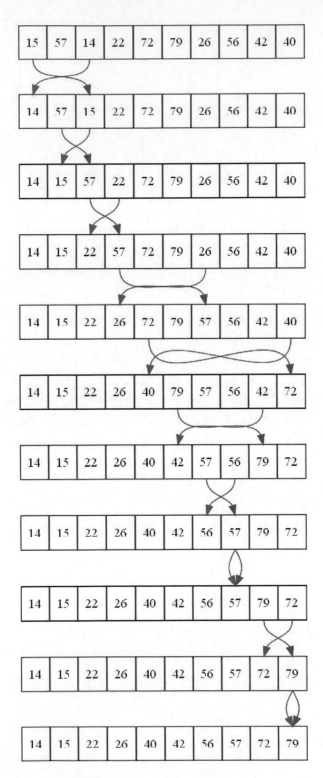

Figure 18.4.: Selection Sort

The outside loop will always run n times. The inside loop will run $n/2$ times. This will be the case regardless if the list is in order or not. The loops efficiency may be improved by checking if `minPos` and `curPos` are equal before line 16. If those variables are equal, there is no need to do the three lines of swap code.

In order to test the selection sort code above, the following code may be used. The first function will print out the list. The next code will create a list of random numbers, print it, sort it, and then print it again. On line 3 the `print` statement right-aligns the numbers to make the column of numbers easier to read. Formatting print statements will be covered in Chapter 21.

Listing 18.3: Swapping two values in an array

```
1  def print_list(list):
2      for item in list:
3          print("%3d" % item, end="")
4      print()
5
6  # Create a list of random numbers
7  list = []
8  for i in range(10):
9      list.append(random.randrange(100))
10
11 # Try out the sort
12 print_list(list)
13 selection_sort(list)
14 print_list(list)
```

18.3. Insertion Sort

The insertion sort is similar to the selection sort in how the outer loop works. The insertion sort starts at the left side of the array and works to the right side. The difference is that the insertion sort does not select the smallest element and put it into place; the insertion sort selects the next element to the right of what was already sorted. Then it slides up each larger element until it gets to the correct location to insert. Graphically, it looks like Figure 18.5.

The insertion sort breaks the list into two sections, the "sorted" half and the "unsorted" half. In each round of the outside loop, the algorithm will grab the next unsorted element and insert it into the list.

In the code below, the `keyPos` marks the boundary between the sorted and unsorted portions of the list. The algorithim scans to the left of `keyPos` using the variable `scanPos`. Note that in the insertion short, `scanPos` goes down to the left, rather than up to the right. Each cell location that is larger than `keyValue` gets moved up (to the right) one location.

When the loop finds a location smaller than `keyValue`, it stops and puts `keyValue` to the left of it.

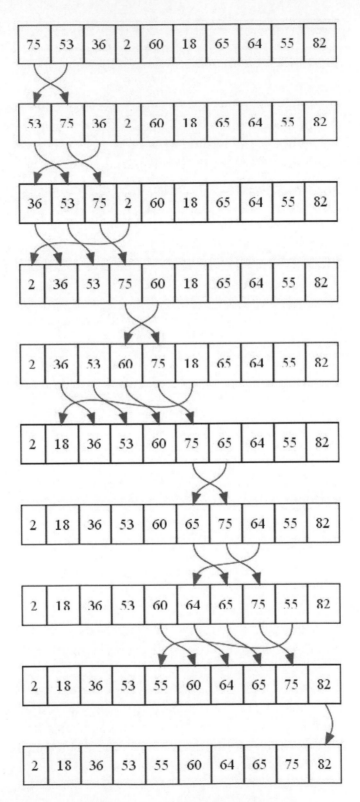

Figure 18.5.: Insertion Sort

The outside loop with an insertion sort will run n times. The inside loop will run an average of $n/2$ times if the loop is randomly shuffled. If the loop is close to a sorted loop already, then the inside loop does not run very much, and the sort time is closer to n.

Listing 18.4: Insertion sort

```python
def insertion_sort(list):

    # Start at the second element (pos 1).
    # Use this element to insert into the
    # list.
    for keyPos in range(1, len(list)):

        # Get the value of the element to insert
        keyValue = list[keyPos]

        # Scan to the left
        scanPos = keyPos - 1

        # Loop each element, moving them up until
        # we reach the position the
        while (scanPos >= 0) and (list[scanPos] > keyValue):
            list[scanPos + 1] = list[scanPos]
            scanPos = scanPos - 1

        # Everything's been moved out of the way, insert
        # the key into the correct location
        list[scanPos +  1] = keyValue
```

18.4. Review Questions

This review is divided into two parts. The second part covers this chapter. The first part covers Chapters 17 and before. Most students find it is a good idea to do some comprehensive review at this point.

18.4.1. Prior Chapters

1. Write a `for` loop that will print out a horizontal line of ten asterisks (*).

2. Write two nested `for` loops that will print a 10x10 box of asterisks.

3. Write Python code that will *create* an array of 100 zeros.

4. What is the difference between a class and an object?

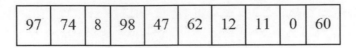

Figure 18.6.: Problem 13

5. What is the difference between a function and a method?

6. Write a function that prints your favorite number.

7. Call the function that prints your favorite number.

8. Write a function that takes three numbers and returns the average.

9. Programming classes:

    a) Write code for a class called `Ball`. Give it attributes for its position, and its velocity.

    b) Create a method called `update` that will move the ball's position according to its velocity.

    c) Create an instance of the `Ball` class, set its attributes.

    d) Create a `for` loop that will call the `update` method on ball 10 times, and print the ball's position.

18.4.2. Sorting Chapter

10. Write code to swap the values 25 and 40.

    ```
    list = [55, 41, 52, 68, 45, 27, 40, 25, 37, 26]
    ```

11. Write code to swap the values 2 and 27.

    ```
    list = [27, 32, 18,  2, 11, 57, 14, 38, 19, 91]
    ```

12. Why does the following code not work?

    ```
    list = [70, 32, 98, 88, 92, 36, 81, 83, 87, 66]
    temp = list[0]
    list[1] = list[0]
    list[0] = temp
    ```

13. Show how the numbers in Figure 18.6 are sorted, using the selection sort.

14. Show how the numbers in Figure 18.7 are sorted, using the selection sort.

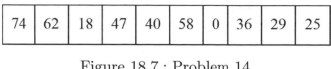

Figure 18.7.: Problem 14

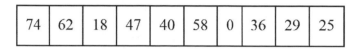

Figure 18.8.: Problem 15

15. Show how the numbers in Figure 18.8 are sorted, using the insertion sort.

16. Show how the numbers in Figure 18.9 are sorted, using the insertion sort.

17. Explain what `minPos` does in the selection sort.

18. Explain what `curPos` does in the selection sort.

19. Explain what `scanPos` does in the selection sort.

20. Explain what `keyPos` and `keyValue` are in the insertion sort.

21. Explain `scanPos` in the insertion sort.

22. Modify the sorts to print the number of times the inside loop is run, and the number of times the outside loop is run.

Figure 18.9.: Problem 16

19. Exceptions

When something goes wrong with your progam, do you want to keep the user from seeing a red Python error message? Do you want to keep your program from hanging? If so, then you need *exceptions*.

Exceptions are used to handle abnormal conditions that can occur during the execution of code. Exceptions are often used with file and network operations. This allows code to gracefully handle running out of disk space, network errors, or permission errors.

19.1. Vocabulary

There are several terms and phrases used while working with exceptions. Here are the most common:

* *Exception*: This term could mean one of two things. First, the condition that results in abnormal program flow. Or it could be used to refer to an object that represents the data condition. Each exception has an object that holds information about it.
* *Exception handling*: The process of handling an exception to normal program flow.
* *Catch block* or *exception block*: Code that handles an abnormal condition is said to "catch" the exception.
* *Throw* or *raise*: When an abnormal condition to the program flow has been detected, an instance of an exception object is created. It is then "thrown" or "raised" to code that will catch it.
* *Unhandled exception* or *Uncaught exception*: An exception that is thrown, but never caught. This usually results in an error and the program ending or crashing.
* *Try block*: A set of code that might have an exception thrown in it.

Most programming languages use the terms "throw" and "catch." Unfortunately Python doesn't. Python uses "raise" and "exception." We introduce the throw/catch vocabulary here because they are the most prevalent terms in the industry.

19.2. Exception Handling

The code for handling exceptions is simple. See the example below:

Listing 19.1: Handling division by zero

```
1 # Divide by zero
2 try:
3     x = 5/0
4 except:
5     print("Error dividing by zero")
```

On line two is the **try** statement. Every indented line below it is part of the "try block." There may be no *un*indented code below the **try** block that doesn't start with an **except** statement. The **try** statement defines a section of code that the code will attempt to execute.

If there is any exception that occurs during the processing of the code the execution will immediately jump to the "catch block." That block of code is indented under the **except** statement on line 4. This code is responsible for handling the error.

A program may use exceptions to catch errors that occur during a conversion from text to a number. For example:

Listing 19.2: Handling number conversion errors

```
1 # Invalid number conversion
2 try:
3     x = int("fred")
4 except:
5     print ("Error converting fred to a number")
```

An exception will be thrown on line 3 because "fred" can not be converted to an integer. The code on line 5 will print out an error message.

Below is an expanded version on this example. It error-checks a user's input to make sure an integer is entered. If the user doesn't enter an integer, the program will keep asking for one. The code uses exception handling to capture a possible conversion error that can occur on line 5. If the user enters something other than an integer, an exception is thrown when the conversion to a number occurs on line 5. The code on line 6 that sets **numberEntered** to **True** will not be run if there is an exception on line 5.

Listing 19.3: Better handling of number conversion errors

```
1 numberEntered = False
2 while numberEntered == False:
3     numberString = input("Enter an integer: ")
4     try:
5         n = int(numberString)
6         numberEntered = True
7     except:
8         print ("Error, invalid integer")
```

Files are particularly prone to errors during operations with them. A disk could fill up, a user could delete a file while it is being written, it could be moved, or a USB drive could be pulled out mid-operation. These types of errors may also be easily captured by using exception handling.

```
1 # Error opening file
2 try:
3     f = open("myfile.txt")
4 except:
5     print("Error opening file")
```

Multiple types of errors may be captured and processed differently. It can be useful to provide a more exact error message to the user than a simple "an error has occured."

In the code below, different types of errors can occur from lines 5-8. By placing IOError after except on line 9, only errors regarding Input and Output (IO) will be handled by that code. Likewise line 11 only handles errors around converting values, and line 13 covers division by zero errors. The last exception handling occurs on line 15. Since line 15 does not include a particular type of error, it will handle any error not covered by the except blocks above. The "catch-all" except must always be last.

Line 1 imports the sys library which is used on line 16 to print the type of error that has occured.

```
1 import sys
2
3 # Multiple errors
4 try:
5     f = open("myfile.txt")
6     s = f.readline()
7     i = int(s.strip())
8     x = 101/i
9 except IOError:
10     print ("I/O error")
11 except ValueError:
12     print ("Could not convert data to an integer.")
13 except ZeroDivisionError:
14     print ("Division by zero error")
15 except:
16     print ("Unexpected error:", sys.exc_info()[0])
```

A list of built-in exceptions is available from this web address: http://docs.python.org/library/exceptions.html

19.3. Example: Saving High Score

This shows how to save a high score between games. The score is stored in a file called high_score.txt.

Listing 19.5: high_score.py

```python
1  # Sample Python/Pygame Programs
2  # Simpson College Computer Science
3  # http://programarcadegames.com/
4  # http://simpson.edu/computer-science/
5
6  # Default high score
7  high_score = 0
8
9  # Try to read the high score from a file
10 try:
11     f = open("high_score.txt", "r")
12     high_score = int(f.read() )
13     f.close()
14     print ("The high score is",high_score)
15 except:
16     # Error reading file, no high score
17     print("There is no high score yet.")
18
19 # Get the score from the current game
20 current_score = 0
21 try:
22     # Ask the user for his/her score
23     current_score = int(input ("What is your score? "))
24 except:
25     # Error, can't turn what they typed into a number
26     print("I don't understand what you typed.")
27
28 # See if we have a new high score
29 if current_score > high_score:
30     print ("Yea! New high score!")
31
32     # We do! Save to disk
33     try:
34         # Write the file to disk
35         f = open("high_score.txt","w")
36         f.write(str(current_score))
37         f.close()
38     except:
39         # Hm, can't write it.
40         print("Too bad I couldn't save it.")
41 else:
42     print("Better luck next time.")
```

19.4. Exception Objects

More information about an error can be pulled from the *exception object*. This object can be retrieved while catching an error using the **as** keyword. For example:

Listing 19.6: Creating an exception

```
1 try:
2     x = 5 / 0
3 except ZeroDivisionError as e:
4     print(e)
```

The **e** variable points to more information about the exception that can be printed out. More can be done with exceptions objects, but unfortunately that is beyond the scope of this chapter.

19.5. Exception Generating

Exceptions may be generated with the **raise** command. For example:

Listing 19.7: Creating an exception

```
1 # Generating exceptions
2 def getInput():
3     userInput = input("Enter something: ")
4     if len(userInput) == 0:
5         raise IOError("User entered nothing")
6
7 getInput()
```

Try taking the code above, and add exception handling for the **IOError** raised.

It is also possible to create custom exceptions, but that is also beyond the scope of this book. Curious readers may learn more by going to:
http://docs.python.org/tutorial/errors.html#raising-exceptions

19.6. Proper Exception Use

Exceptions should not be used when **if** statements can just as easily handle the condition. Normal code should not raise exceptions when running the "happy path" scenario. Well-constructed try/catch code is easy to follow but code involving many exceptions and jumps in code to different handlers can be a nightmare to debug. (Once I was assigned the task of debugging code that read an XML document. It generated dozens of exceptions for each line of the file it read. It was incredibly slow and error-prone. That code should have never generated a single exception in the normal course of reading a file.)

19.7. Review Questions

1. Define the following terms:

   - Exception
   - Exception Handling
   - Try block
   - Catch block
   - Unhandled exception
   - Throw

2. Show how to modify the following code so that an error is printed if the number conversion is not successful:

```
1 user_input_string = input("Enter a number")
2 user_value = int(user_input_string)
```

3. What will the following code output?

```
1 x = 5
2 y = 0
3 print("A")
4 try:
5     print("B")
6     a = x / y
7     print("C")
8 except:
9     print("D")
10 print("E")
11 print(a)
```

4. What will the following code output?

```
1 x = 5
2 y = 10
3 print("A")
4 try:
5     print("B")
6     a = x / y
7     print("C")
8 except:
9     print("D")
10 print("E")
11 print(a)
```

20. Recursion

A child couldn't sleep, so her mother told her a story about a little frog,
who couldn't sleep, so the frog's mother told her a story about a little bear,
who couldn't sleep, so the bear's mother told her a story about a little weasel...
who fell asleep.
...and the little bear fell asleep;
...and the little frog fell asleep;
...and the child fell asleep.
(Source: `http://everything2.com/title/recursion`)

Recursion is an object or process that is defined in terms of itself. Mathematical patterns such as factorials and the fibonacci series are recursive. Documents that can contain other documents, which themselves can contain other documents, are recursive. Fractal images, and even certain biological processes are recursive in how they work.

20.1. Where is Recursion Used?

Documents, such as web pages, are naturally recusive. For example, Figure 20.1 shows a web document.

That web document can be contained in a "box," which can help layout the page as shown in Figure 20.2.

This works *recursively*. Each box can contain a web page, that can have a box, which could contain another web page as shown in Figure 20.3.

Web Page Title
Content for web page goes here Copyright © Info

Figure 20.1.: Web page

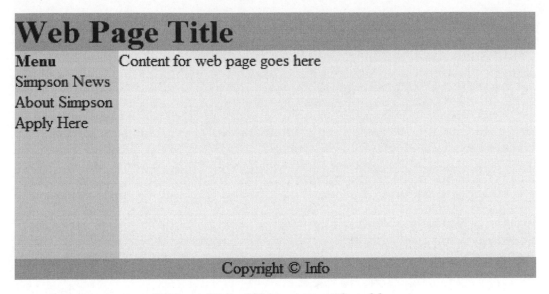

Figure 20.2.: Web page with tables

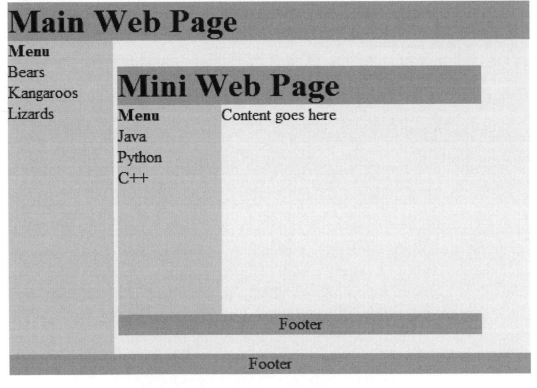

Figure 20.3.: Web page with recursion

Recursive functions are often used with advanced searching and sorting algorithms. We'll show some of that here and if you take a "data structures" class you will see a lot more of it.

Even if a person does not become a programmer, understanding the concept of recursive systems is important. If there is a business need for recursive table structures, documents, or something else, it is important to know how to specify this to the programmer up front.

For example, a person might specify that a web program for recipes needs the ability to support ingredients and directions. A person familiar with recursion might state that each ingredient could itself be a recipes with other ingredients (that could be recipes.) The second system is considerably more powerful.

20.2. How is Recursion Coded?

In prior chapters, we have used functions that call other functions. For example:

Listing 20.1: Functions calling other functions

```
1 def f():
2     g()
3     print("f")
4
5 def g():
6     print("g")
7
8 f()
```

It is also possible for a function to call itself. A function that calls itself is using a concept called *recursion*. For example:

Listing 20.2: Recursion

```
1 def f():
2     print("Hello")
3     f()
4
5 f()
```

The example above will print `Hello` and then call the `f()` function again. Which will cause another `Hello` to be printed out and another call to the `f()` function. This will continue until the computer runs out of something called *stack space*. When this happens, Python will output a long error that ends with:

`RuntimeError: maximum recursion depth exceeded`

The computer is telling you, the programmer, that you have gone too far down the rabbit hole.

20.3. Controlling Recursion Depth

To successfully use recursion, there needs to be a way to prevent the function from endlessly calling itself over and over again. The example below counts how many times it has been called, and uses an `if` statement to exit once the function has called itself ten times.

Listing 20.3: Controlling recursion levels

```
1 def f(level):
2     # Pring the level we are at
3     print("Recursion call, level",level)
4     # If we haven't reached level ten...
5     if level < 10:
6         # Call this function again
7         # and add one to the level
8         f(level+1)
9
10 # Start the recursive calls at level 1
11 f(1)
```

Output:

```
Recursion call, level 1
Recursion call, level 2
Recursion call, level 3
Recursion call, level 4
Recursion call, level 5
Recursion call, level 6
Recursion call, level 7
Recursion call, level 8
Recursion call, level 9
Recursion call, level 10
```

20.4. Recursion Factorial Calculation

Any code that can be done recursively can be done without using recursion. Some programmers feel that the recursive code is easier to understand.

Calculating the factorial of a number is a classic example of using recursion. Factorials are useful in probability and statistics. For example:

$10! = 10 \cdot 9 \cdot 8 \cdot 7 \cdot 6 \cdot 5 \cdot 4 \cdot 3 \cdot 2 \cdot 1$

Recursively, this can be described as:

$$n! = \begin{cases} 1 & \text{if } n = 0, \\ n \cdot (n-1)! & \text{if } n > 0. \end{cases}$$

Below are two example functions that calculate $n!$. The first one is non-recursive, the second is recursive.

Listing 20.4: Non-recursive factorial

```
1  # This program calculates a factorial
2  # WITHOUT using recursion
3  def factorial_nonrecursive(n):
4      answer = 1
5      for i in range(2,n+1):
6          answer = answer * i
7      return answer
```

Listing 20.5: Recursive factorial

```
1  # This program calculates a factorial
2  # WITH recursion
3  def factorial_recursive(n):
4      if( n == 1 ):
5          return n
6      else:
7          return n * factorial_recursive(n-1)
```

The functions do nothing by themselves. Below is an example where we put it all together. This example also adds some **print** statements inside the function so we can see what is happening.

Listing 20.6: Trying out recursive functions

```
1  # This program calculates a factorial
2  # WITHOUT using recursion
3
4  def factorial_nonrecursive(n):
5      answer = 1
6      for i in range(2,n+1):
7          print( i,"*",answer,"=", i*answer)
8          answer = answer * i
9      return answer
10
11 print("I can calculate a factorial!")
12 user_input = input ("Enter a number:")
13 n = int(user_input)
14 answer = factorial_nonrecursive(n)
15 print (answer)
16
17 # This program calculates a factorial
18 # WITH recursion
19
20 def factorial_recursive(n):
21     if( n == 1 ):
22         return n
```

```
23      else:
24          x = factorial_recursive(n-1)
25          print( n, "*", x, "=", n * x )
26          return n * x
27
28  print("I can calculate a factorial!")
29  user_input = input ("Enter a number:")
30  n = int(user_input)
31  answer = factorial_recursive(n)
32  print (answer)
```

Output:

```
I can calculate a factorial!
Enter a number:7
2 * 1 = 2
3 * 2 = 6
4 * 6 = 24
5 * 24 = 120
6 * 120 = 720
7 * 720 = 5040
5040
I can calculate a factorial!
Enter a number:7
2 * 1 = 2
3 * 2 = 6
4 * 6 = 24
5 * 24 = 120
6 * 120 = 720
7 * 720 = 5040
5040
```

20.5. Recursive Rectangles

Recursion is great to work with structured documents that are themselves recursive. For example, a web document can have a table divided into rows and columns to help with layout. One row might be the header, another row the main body, and finally the footer. Inside a table cell, might be another table. And inside of that can exist yet another table.

Another example is e-mail. It is possible to attach another person's e-mail to a your own e-mail. But that e-mail could have another e-mail attached to it, and so on.

Can we visually see recursion in action in one of our Pygame programs? Yes! Figure 20.4 shows an example program that draws a rectangle, and recursively keeps drawing rectangles inside of it. Each rectangle is 20% smaller than the parent rectangle. Look at the code. Pay close attention to the recursive call in the recursive_draw function.

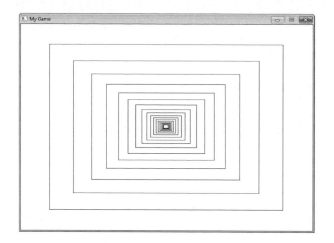

Figure 20.4.: Recursive Rectangles

Listing 20.7: recursive_rectangles.py

```python
1  # Sample Python/Pygame Programs
2  # Simpson College Computer Science
3  # http://programarcadegames.com/
4  # http://simpson.edu/computer-science/
5
6  import pygame
7
8  # Define some colors
9  black    = (   0,   0,   0)
10 white    = ( 255, 255, 255)
11 green    = (   0, 255,   0)
12 red      = ( 255,   0,   0)
13
14 def recursive_draw(x,y,width,height):
15     # Draw the rectangle
16     pygame.draw.rect(screen, black,
17                     [x,y,width,height],
18                     1)
19
20     # Is the rectangle wide enough to draw again?
21     if( width > 14 ):
22         # Scale down
23         x += width * .1
24         y += height * .1
25         width *= .8
26         height *= .8
27         # Recursively draw again
28         recursive_draw(x, y, width, height)
29
```

```
30 pygame.init()
31
32 # Set the height and width of the screen
33 size = [700, 500]
34 screen = pygame.display.set_mode(size)
35
36 pygame.display.set_caption("My Game")
37
38 #Loop until the user clicks the close button.
39 done=False
40
41 # Used to manage how fast the screen updates
42 clock = pygame.time.Clock()
43
44 # -------- Main Program Loop -----------
45 while done == False:
46     for event in pygame.event.get(): # User did something
47         if event.type == pygame.QUIT: # If user clicked close
48             done = True # Flag that we are done so we exit this loop
49
50     # Set the screen background
51     screen.fill(white)
52
53     # ALL CODE TO DRAW SHOULD GO BELOW THIS COMMENT
54     recursive_draw(0, 0, 700, 500)
55     # ALL CODE TO DRAW SHOULD GO ABOVE THIS COMMENT
56
57     # Limit to 20 frames per second
58     clock.tick(20)
59
60     # Go ahead and update the screen with what we've drawn.
61     pygame.display.flip()
62
63 # Be IDLE friendly. If you forget this line, the program will 'hang'
64 # on exit.
65 pygame.quit()
```

20.6. Fractals

Fractals are defined recursively. Here is a very simple fractal, showing how it changes depending on how "deep" the recursion goes.

Listing 20.8: fractal.py

```
1 # Sample Python/Pygame Programs
2 # Simpson College Computer Science
```

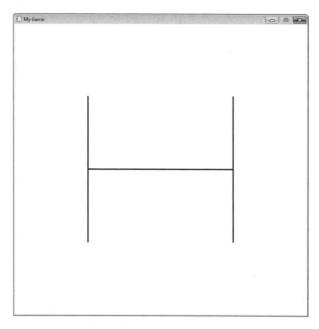

Figure 20.5.: Recursive Fractal Level 0

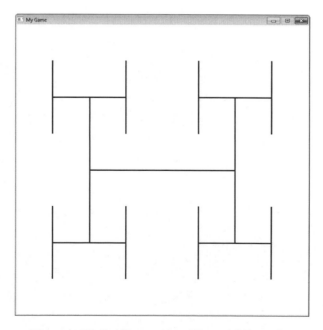

Figure 20.6.: Recursive Fractal Level 1

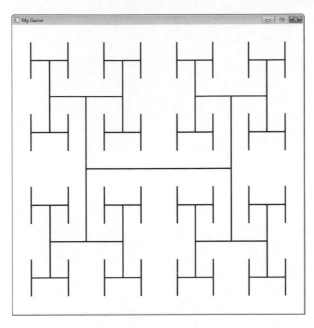

Figure 20.7.: Recursive Fractal Level 2

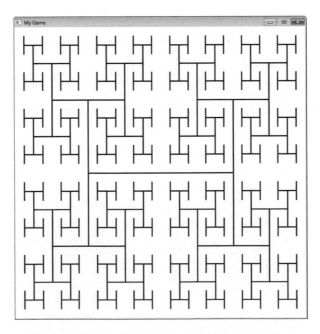

Figure 20.8.: Recursive Fractal Level 3

```
3  # http://programarcadegames.com/
4  # http://simpson.edu/computer-science/
5
6  import pygame
7
8  # Define some colors
9  black     = (   0,   0,   0)
10 white     = ( 255, 255, 255)
11 green     = (   0, 255,   0)
12 red       = ( 255,   0,   0)
13
14 def recursive_draw(x,y,width,height,count):
15     # Draw the rectangle
16     #pygame.draw.rect(screen,black,[x,y,width,height],1)
17     pygame.draw.line(screen,
18                      black,
19                      [x+width*.25,height//2+y],
20                      [x+width*.75,height//2+y],
21                      3)
22     pygame.draw.line(screen,
23                      black,
24                      [x+width*.25,(height*.5)//2+y],
25                      [x+width*.25,(height*1.5)//2+y],
26                      3)
27     pygame.draw.line(screen,
28                      black,
29                      [x+width*.75,(height*.5)//2+y],
30                      [x+width*.75,(height*1.5)//2+y],
31                      3)
32
33     if count > 0:
34         count -= 1
35         # Top left
36         recursive_draw(x,y,                        width//2,height//2,count)
37         # Top right
38         recursive_draw(x+width//2,y,               width//2,height//2,count)
39         # Bottom left
40         recursive_draw(x,y+width//2,               width//2,height//2,count)
41         # Bottom right
42         recursive_draw(x+width//2,y+width//2,   width//2,height//2,count)
43
44
45 pygame.init()
46
47 # Set the height and width of the screen
48 size = [700,700]
49 screen = pygame.display.set_mode(size)
50
```

```
51 pygame.display.set_caption("My Game")
52
53 #Loop until the user clicks the close button.
54 done = False
55
56 # Used to manage how fast the screen updates
57 clock = pygame.time.Clock()
58
59 # -------- Main Program Loop ----------
60 while done == False:
61     for event in pygame.event.get(): # User did something
62         if event.type == pygame.QUIT: # If user clicked close
63             done=True # Flag that we are done so we exit this loop
64
65     # Set the screen background
66     screen.fill(white)
67
68     # ALL CODE TO DRAW SHOULD GO BELOW THIS COMMENT
69     fractal_level = 3
70     recursive_draw(0, 0, 700, 700, fractal_level)
71     # ALL CODE TO DRAW SHOULD GO ABOVE THIS COMMENT
72
73     # Limit to 20 frames per second
74     clock.tick(20)
75
76     # Go ahead and update the screen with what we've drawn.
77     pygame.display.flip()
78
79 # Be IDLE friendly. If you forget this line, the program will 'hang'
80 # on exit.
81 pygame.quit()
```

20.7. Recursive Binary Search

Recursion can be also be used to perform a binary search. Here is a non-recursive binary search from Chapter 17:

Listing 20.9: Non-recursive binary search

```
1 def binary_search_nonrecursive(search_list,key):
2     lower_bound = 0
3     upper_bound = len(search_list)-1
4     found = False
5     while lower_bound < upper_bound and found == False:
6         middle_pos = (lower_bound+upper_bound) // 2
7         if search_list[middle_pos] < key:
```

```
8              lower_bound = middle_pos+1
9          elif list[middle_pos] > key:
10             upper_bound = middle_pos
11         else:
12             found = True
13
14     if found:
15         print( "The name is at position",middle_pos)
16     else:
17         print( "The name was not in the list." )
18
19 binary_search_nonrecursive(name_list,"Morgiana the Shrew")
```

This same binary search written in a recusive manner:

Listing 20.10: Recursive binary search

```
1 def binary_search_recursive(search_list,key, lower_bound, upper_bound):
2     middle_pos = (lower_bound+upper_bound) // 2
3     if search_list[middle_pos] < key:
4         binary_search_recursive(search_list,
5                                 key,
6                                 middle_pos+1,
7                                 upper_bound)
8     elif search_list[middle_pos] > key:
9         binary_search_recursive(search_list,
10                                key,
11                                lower_bound,
12                                middle_pos )
13    else:
14        print("Found at position", middle_pos)
15
16 lower_bound = 0
17 upper_bound = len(name_list)-1
18 binary_search_recursive(name_list,
19                         "Morgiana the Shrew",
20                         lower_bound,
21                         upper_bound)
```

20.8. Review Questions

1. "To understand recursion, one must first understand recursion." Explain the joke.

2. Two mirrors face each other. Explain how their reflections demonstrate the property of recursion.

3. Explain how Multi-Level Marketing uses recursion.

4. Explain how the "sweep" function in the classic minesweeper game could be done with recursion. If you don't know, ask!

5. Explain how finding your way out of a maze could be done with recursion.

6. Use the Chrome browser and create your own screenshot at:
   `http://juliamap.googlelabs.com`
   Use `alt-PrtScr` to capture the image.

7. Write a recursive function `f(n)` that takes in a value n and returns the value for `f`, given the following definition:
$$f_n = \begin{cases} 6 & \text{if } f = 1, \\ \frac{1}{2}f_{n-1} + 4 & \text{if } f > 1. \end{cases}$$
Then write a `for` loop that prints out the answers for values of n from 1 to 10. It should look like:

```
n= 1  ,  a= 6
n= 2  ,  a= 7.0
n= 3  ,  a= 7.5
n= 4  ,  a= 7.75
n= 5  ,  a= 7.875
n= 6  ,  a= 7.9375
n= 7  ,  a= 7.96875
n= 8  ,  a= 7.984375
n= 9  ,  a= 7.9921875
n= 10  ,  a= 7.99609375
```

8. Write recursive code that will print out the first 10 terms of the sequence:
$$f_n = \begin{cases} 1 & \text{if } f = 1, \\ 1 & \text{if } f = 2, \\ f(n-1) + f(n-2) & \text{if } f > 2. \end{cases}$$

21. Formatting

Here is a quick table for reference when doing text formatting. For a detailed explanation of how text formatting works, keep reading.

Number	Format	Output	Description
3.1415926	{:.2f}	3.14	2 decimal places
3.1415926	{:+.2f}	+3.14	2 decimal places with sign
-1	{:+.2f}	-1.00	2 decimal places with sign
3.1415926	{:.0f}	3	No decimal places (will round)
5	{:0>2d}	05	Pad with zeros on the left
1000000	{:,}	1,000,000	Number format with comma separator
0.25	{:.2%}	25.00%	Format percentage
1000000000	{:.2e}	1.00e+09	Exponent notation
11	{:>10d}	11	Right aligned
11	{:<10d}	11	Left aligned
11	{:^10d}	11	Center aligned

21.1. Decimal Numbers

Try running the following program, which prints out several random numbers.

```
1 import random
2
3 for i in range(10):
4     x = random.randrange(20)
5     print(x)
```

The output is left justified and numbers look terrible:

```
13
2
0
10
3
18
1
14
```

5

We can use string formatting to make the list of numbers look better by right-justifying them. The first step is to use the **format** command on the string. See below:

```
1 import random
2
3 for i in range(10):
4     x = random.randrange(20)
5     print("{}".format(x) )
```

This gets our program closer right-justify the number, but we aren't quite there yet. See how the string ends with `.format(x)`. All strings are actually an instances of a class named **String**. That class has methods that can be called. One of them is **format**.

The **format** function will not print out the curly braces {} but instead replaces them with the value in **x**. The output (below) looks just like what we had before.

```
15
4
12
3
8
7
15
12
8
```

To right justify, we add more information about how to format the number between the curly braces {}:

Listing 21.1: Right justified list of numbers

```
1 import random
2
3 for i in range(10):
4     x = random.randrange(20)
5     print("{:2}".format(x) )
```

```
15
 4
12
 3
 8
 7
15
12
 8
```

This is better; we have right justified numbers! But how does it work? The `:2` that we added isn't exactly intuitive.

Here's the breakdown: The { } tells the computer we are going to format a number. After the : inside the curly braces will be formatting information. In this case we give it a 2 to specify a *field width* of two characters. The field width value tells the computer to try to fit the number into a field two characters wide. By default, it will try to right-justify numbers and left-justify text.

Even better, the program no longer needs to call **str( )** to convert the number to a string. Leave the string conversions out.

What if you had large numbers? Let's make bigger random numbers:

```
1 import random
2
3 for i in range(10):
4     x = random.randrange(100000)
5     print( "{:6}".format(x) )
```

This gives output that is right justified, but still doesn't look good:

```
18394
72242
97508
21583
11508
76064
88756
77413
 7930
81095
```

Where are the commas? This list would look better with separators between each three digits. Take a look at the next example to see how they are added in:

```
1 import random
2
3 for i in range(10):
4     x = random.randrange(100000)
5     print( "{:6,}".format(x) )
```

```
65,732
30,248
13,802
17,177
 3,584
 7,598
21,672
82,900
72,838
48,557
```

We added a comma after the field width specifier, and now our numbers have commas. That comma must go *after* the field width specifier, not before. Commas are included in calculating the field width. For example, 1,024 has a field width of 5, not 4.

We can print multiple values, and combine the values with text. Run the code below.

```
1 x = 5
2 y = 66
3 z = 777
4 print ("A - '{}' B - '{}' C - '{}'".format(x,y,z) )
```

The program will substitute numbers in for the curly braces, and still print out all of the other text in the string:

```
A - '5' B - '66' C - '777'
```

If there are three sets of curly braces, the computer will expect three values to be listed in the `format` command. The first value given will replace the first curly brace.

Sometimes we may want to print the same value twice. Or show them in a different order than how they were fed into the `format` function.

```
1 x = 5
2 y = 66
3 z = 777
4 print ("C - '{2}' A - '{0}' B - '{1}' C again - '{2}'".format(x,y,z) )
```

See that by placing a number in the curly braces, we can specify which parameter passed into the `format` function we want printed out. Parameters are numbered starting at 0, so x is considered parameter 0.

We can still specify formatting information after a colon. For example:

```
1 x = 5
2 y = 66
3 z = 777
4 print ("C - '{2:4}' A - '{0:4}' B - '{1:4}' C again - '{2:4}'".format(x,y,
    z) )
```

We can see that the code above will show the values right justified with a field width of four:

```
C - ' 777' A - '   5' B - '  66' C again - ' 777'
```

21.2. Strings

Let's look at how to format strings.

The following list looks terrible.

```
1 my_fruit = ["Apples","Oranges","Grapes","Pears"]
2 my_calories = [4,300,70,30]
3
```

```
4 for i in range(4):
5     print(my_fruit[i],"are",my_calories[i],"calories.")
```

```
Apples are 4 calories.
Oranges are 300 calories.
Grapes are 70 calories.
Pears are 30 calories.
```

Now try it using the **format** command. Note how we can put additional text and more than one value into the same line.

Listing 21.2: Formatting a list of fruit

```
1 my_fruit = ["Apples","Oranges","Grapes","Pears"]
2 my_calories = [4,300,70,30]
3
4 for i in range(4):
5     print("{:7} are {:3} calories.".format(my_fruit[i],my_calories[i]) )
```

```
Apples    are    4 calories.
Oranges   are  300 calories.
Grapes    are   70 calories.
Pears     are   30 calories.
```

That's pretty cool, and it looks the way we want it. But what if we didn't want the numbers right justified, and the text left justified? We can use < and > characters like the following example:

```
1 my_fruit = ["Apples","Oranges","Grapes","Pears"]
2 my_calories = [4,300,70,30]
3
4 for i in range(4):
5     print("{:>7} are {:<3} calories.".format(my_fruit[i],my_calories[i]) )
```

```
 Apples are 4   calories.
Oranges are 300 calories.
 Grapes are 70  calories.
  Pears are 30  calories.
```

21.3. Leading Zeros

This produces output that isn't right:

```
1 for hours in range(1,13):
2     for minutes in range(0,60):
3         print( "Time {}:{}".format(hours, minutes) )
```

```
Time 8:56
Time 8:57
Time 8:58
Time 8:59
Time 9:0
Time 9:1
Time 9:2
```

We need to use leading zeros for displaying numbers in clocks. Rather than specify a 2 for the field width, instead use 02. This will pad the field with zeros rather than spaces.

Listing 21.3: Formatting time output

```
1 for hours in range(1,13):
2     for minutes in range(0,60):
3         print( "Time {:02}:{:02}".format(hours, minutes) )
```

```
Time 08:56
Time 08:57
Time 08:58
Time 08:59
Time 09:00
Time 09:01
Time 09:02
```

21.4. Floating Point Numbers

We can also control floating point output. Examine the following code and its output:

Listing 21.4: Formatting float point numbers

```
1 x = 0.1
2 y = 123.456789
3 print( "{:.1}   {:.1}".format(x,y) )
4 print( "{:.2}   {:.2}".format(x,y) )
5 print( "{:.3}   {:.3}".format(x,y) )
6 print( "{:.4}   {:.4}".format(x,y) )
7 print( "{:.5}   {:.5}".format(x,y) )
8 print( "{:.6}   {:.6}".format(x,y) )
9 print()
10 print( "{:.1f}   {:.1f}".format(x,y) )
11 print( "{:.2f}   {:.2f}".format(x,y) )
12 print( "{:.3f}   {:.3f}".format(x,y) )
13 print( "{:.4f}   {:.4f}".format(x,y) )
14 print( "{:.5f}   {:.5f}".format(x,y) )
15 print( "{:.6f}   {:.6f}".format(x,y) )
```

```
0.1   1e+02
0.1   1.2e+02
0.1   1.23e+02
0.1   123.5
0.1   123.46
0.1   123.457

0.1   123.5
0.10   123.46
0.100   123.457
0.1000   123.4568
0.10000   123.45679
0.100000   123.456789
```

A format of .2 means to display the number with two digits of precision. Unfortunately this means if we display the number 123 which has three significant numbers rather than rounding it we get the number in scientific notation: 1.2e+02.

A format of .2f (note the f) means to display the number with two digits after the decimal point. So the number 1 would display as 1.00 and the number 1.5555 would display as 1.56.

A program can also specify a field width character:

```
1 x = 0.1
2 y = 123.456789
3 print( "'{:10.1}'   '{:10.1}'".format(x,y) )
4 print( "'{:10.2}'   '{:10.2}'".format(x,y) )
5 print( "'{:10.3}'   '{:10.3}'".format(x,y) )
6 print( "'{:10.4}'   '{:10.4}'".format(x,y) )
7 print( "'{:10.5}'   '{:10.5}'".format(x,y) )
8 print( "'{:10.6}'   '{:10.6}'".format(x,y) )
9 print()
10 print( "'{:10.1f}'   '{:10.1f}'".format(x,y) )
11 print( "'{:10.2f}'   '{:10.2f}'".format(x,y) )
12 print( "'{:10.3f}'   '{:10.3f}'".format(x,y) )
13 print( "'{:10.4f}'   '{:10.4f}'".format(x,y) )
14 print( "'{:10.5f}'   '{:10.5f}'".format(x,y) )
15 print( "'{:10.6f}'   '{:10.6f}'".format(x,y) )
```

The format 10.2f does not mean 10 digits before the decimal and two after. It means a total field width of 10. So there will be 7 digits before the decimal, the decimal which counts as one more, and 2 digits after.

```
'       0.1'   '     1e+02'
'       0.1'   '   1.2e+02'
'       0.1'   '  1.23e+02'
'       0.1'   '     123.5'
'       0.1'   '    123.46'
'       0.1'   '   123.457'
```

```
'      0.1'    '     123.5'
'      0.10'   '    123.46'
'     0.100'   '   123.457'
'    0.1000'   '  123.4568'
'   0.10000'   ' 123.45679'
'  0.100000'   '123.456789'
```

21.5. Printing Dollars and Cents

If you want to print a floating point number for cost, you use an **f**. See below:

```
1 cost1  = 3.07
2 tax1   = cost1 * 0.06
3 total1 = cost1 + tax1
4
5 print("Cost:  ${0:5.2f}".format(cost1) )
6 print("Tax:    {0:5.2f}".format(tax1) )
7 print("------------")
8 print("Total: ${0:5.2f}".format(total1) )
```

Remember! It would be easy to think that **%5.2f** would mean five digits, a decimal, followed by two digits. But it does not. It means a total field width of five, including the decimal and the two digits after. Here's the output:

```
Cost:  $ 3.07
Tax:     0.18
------------
Total: $ 3.25
```

Danger! The above code has a mistake that is very common when working with financial transactions. Can you spot it? Try spotting it with the expanded code example below:

```
1  cost1  = 3.07
2  tax1   = cost1 * 0.06
3  total1 = cost1 + tax1
4
5  print("Cost:  ${0:5.2f}".format(cost1) )
6  print("Tax:    {0:5.2f}".format(tax1) )
7  print("------------")
8  print("Total: ${0:5.2f}".format(total1) )
9
10 cost2  = 5.07
11 tax2   = cost2 * 0.06
12 total2 = cost2 + tax2
13
14 print()
15 print("Cost:  ${0:5.2f}".format(cost2) )
16 print("Tax:    {0:5.2f}".format(tax2) )
```

```
17 print("------------")
18 print("Total: ${0:5.2f}".format(total2) )
19
20
21 print()
22 grand_total = total1 + total2
23 print("Grand total: ${0:5.2f}".format(grand_total) )
```

Here's the output:

```
Cost:   $ 3.07
Tax:       0.18
------------
Total: $ 3.25

Cost:   $ 5.07
Tax:       0.30
------------
Total: $ 5.37

Grand total: $ 8.63
```

Spot the mistake? You have to watch out for rounding errors! Look at that example, it seems like the total should be $ 8.62 but it isn't.

Print formatting doesn't change the number, only what is output! If we changed the print formatting to include three digits after the decimal the reason for the error becomes more apparent:

```
Cost:   $3.070
Tax:       0.184
------------
Total: $3.254

Cost:   $5.070
Tax:       0.304
------------
Total: $5.374

Grand total: $8.628
```

Again, formating for the display does not change the number. Use the **round** command to change the value and truely round. See below:

```
1 cost1 = 3.07
2 tax1 = round(cost1 * 0.06,2)
3 total1 = cost1 + tax1
4
5 print("Cost:   ${0:5.2f}".format(cost1) )
6 print("Tax:    {0:5.2f}".format(tax1) )
7 print("------------")
```

```
 8 print("Total: ${0:5.2f}".format(total1) )
 9
10 cost2 = 5.07
11 tax2 = round(cost2 * 0.06,2)
12 total2 = cost2 + tax2
13
14 print()
15 print("Cost:  ${0:5.2f}".format(cost2) )
16 print("Tax:    {0:5.2f}".format(tax2) )
17 print("------------")
18 print("Total: ${0:5.2f}".format(total2) )
19
20
21 print()
22 grand_total = total1 + total2
23 print("Grand total: ${0:5.2f}".format(grand_total) )
```

```
Cost:   $ 3.07
Tax:      0.18
------------
Total: $ 3.25

Cost:   $ 5.07
Tax:      0.30
------------
Total: $ 5.37

Grand total: $ 8.62
```

The round command controls how many digits after the decimal we round to. It returns the rounded value but does not change the original value. See below:

```
1 x = 1234.5678
2 print( round(x,2) )
3 print( round(x,1) )
4 print( round(x,0) )
5 print( round(x,-1) )
6 print( round(x,-2) )
```

See below to figure out how feeding the **round()** function values like −2 for the digits after the decimal affects the output:

```
1234.57
1234.6
1235.0
1230.0
1200.0
```

21.6. Use in Pygame

We don't just have to format strings for print statements. The example `timer.py` uses string formatting and blit's the resulting text to the screen to make an on-screen timer:

```
1 # Use python string formatting to format in leading zeros
2 output_string = "Time: {0:02}:{1:02}".format(minutes,seconds)
3
4 # Blit to the screen
5 text = font.render(output_string,True,black)
6 screen.blit(text, [250,250])
```

21.7. Review

1. Take the following program:

   ```
   1 score = 41237
   2 highscore = 1023407
   3
   4 print("Score:        "+str(score) )
   5 print("High score: "+str(highscore) )
   ```

   Which right now outputs:

   ```
   Score:        41237
   High score: 1023407
   ```

   Use print formatting so that the output instead looks like:

   ```
   Score:            41,237
   High score:  1,023,407
   ```

2. Create a program that loops from 1 to 20 and lists the decimal equivilant of their inverse. Use print formatting to exactly match the following output:

   ```
   1/1  = 1.0
   1/2  = 0.5
   1/3  = 0.333
   1/4  = 0.25
   1/5  = 0.2
   1/6  = 0.167
   1/7  = 0.143
   1/8  = 0.125
   1/9  = 0.111
   1/10 = 0.1
   1/11 = 0.0909
   1/12 = 0.0833
   ```

```
1/13 = 0.0769
1/14 = 0.0714
1/15 = 0.0667
1/16 = 0.0625
1/17 = 0.0588
1/18 = 0.0556
1/19 = 0.0526
1/20 = 0.05
```

3. Write a recursive function that will calculate the fibonacci series, and use output formatting. Your result should look like:

```
 1  -          0
 2  -          1
 3  -          1
 4  -          2
 5  -          3
 6  -          5
 7  -          8
 8  -         13
 9  -         21
10  -         34
11  -         55
12  -         89
13  -        144
14  -        233
15  -        377
16  -        610
17  -        987
18  -       1597
19  -       2584
20  -       4181
21  -       6765
22  -      10946
23  -      17711
24  -      28657
25  -      46368
26  -      75025
27  -     121393
28  -     196418
29  -     317811
30  -     514229
31  -     832040
32  -    1346269
33  -    2178309
34  -    3524578
35  -    5702887
```

4. Why does this run so slow? How could it be made to run faster?

A. Labs

B. Lab 1: Custom Calculators

In this lab we'll create three custom calculator programs. To help create these labs check the code in Chapter 1. In particular, the example program at the end of that chapter provides a good template for the code needed in this lab.

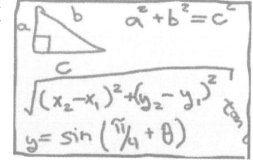

Make sure you can write out simple programs like what is assigned in this lab. Be able to do it from memory, and on paper. These programs follow a very common pattern in computing:

1. Take in data

2. Perform calculations

3. Output data

Programs take in data from sources like databases, 3D models, game controllers, keyboards, and the internet. They perform calculations and output the result. Sometimes we even do this in a loop thousands of times a second.

It is a good idea to do the calculations separate from the output of the data. While it is possible to do the calculation inside the print statement, it is better to do the calculation, store it in a variable, and then output it later. This way calculations and output aren't mixed together.

When writing programs it is a good idea to use blank lines to separate logical groupings of code. For example, place a blank line between the input statements, the calculation, and the output statement.

For this lab you will create three short programs. If you are using a version control system, remember to commit and push your changes to the server. Click the "Send the lab for grading" button when you are done.

B.1. Part A

Create a program that asks the user for a temperature in Fahrenheit, and then prints the temperature in Celsius. Search the internet for the correct calculation. Look at Chapter 1 for the miles-per-gallon example to get an idea of what should be done.

Sample run:

```
Enter temperature in Fahrenheit:32
The temperature in Celsius: 0.0
```

Sample run:

```
Enter temperature in Fahrenheit:72
The temperature in Celsius: 22.2222222222
```

The numbers from this program won't be formatted nicely. That is ok. But if it bothers you, look ahead to **Chapter 21** and see how to make your output look great!

B.2. Part B

Create a new program that will ask the user for the information needed to find the area of a trapezoid, and then print the area. The formula for the area of a trapezoid is:

$$A = \frac{1}{2}(x_1 + x_2)h$$

Sample run:

```
Area of a trapezoid
Enter the height of the trapezoid:5
Enter the length of the bottom base:10
Enter the length of the top base:7
The area is: 42.5
```

B.3. Part C

Create your own original problem and have the user plug in the variables. If you are not in the mood for anything original, choose an equation from this list:

Area of a circle	$A = \pi r^2$
Area of an ellipse	$A = \pi r_1 r_2$
Area of an equilateral triangle	$A = \dfrac{h^2 \sqrt{3}}{3}$
Volume of a cone	$V = \dfrac{\pi r^2 h}{3}$
Volume of a sphere	$V = \dfrac{4 \pi r^3}{3}$
Area of an arbitrary triangle	$A = \dfrac{1}{2} ab \sin C$

When done, turn in the assignment according to your teacher's instructions. If you are using a version control system, make sure to commit the files, and push them to the server.

C. Lab 2: Create-a-Quiz

Now is your chance to write your *own* quiz. Use these quizzes to filter job applicants, weed out potential mates, or just plain have a chance to sit on the other side of the desk and make, rather than take, the quiz.

This lab applies the material used in **Chapter 3** on using **if** statements. It also requires a bit of **Chapter 1** because the program must calculate a percentage.

C.1. Description

This is the list of features your quiz needs to have:

1. Create your own quiz with five or more questions. You can ask questions that require:

   - a number as an answer (e.g., What is 1+1?)
   - text (e.g. What is Harry Potter's last name?)
   - a selection (Which of these choices are correct? A, B, or C?)

2. If you have the user enter non-numeric answers, think and cover the different ways a user could enter a correct answer. For example, if the answer is "a", would "A" also be acceptable? See **Section 3.6** for a reminder on how to do this.

3. Let the user know if he or she gets the question correct. Print a message depending on the user's answer.

4. You need to keep track of how many questions they get correct.

5. At the end of the program print the percentage of questions the user gets right.

Keep the following in mind when creating the program:

1. Variable names should start with a lower case letter. Upper case letters work, but it is not considered proper. (Right, you didn't realize that programming was going to be like English Tea Time, did you?)

2. To create a running total of the number correct, create a variable to store this score. Set it to zero. With an `if` statement, add one to the variable each time the user gets a correct answer. (How do you know if they got it correct? Remember that if you are printing out "correct" then you have aleady done that part. Just add a line there to add one to the number correct.) If you don't remember how to add one to a variable, go back and review `Section 1.5`.

3. Treat true/false questions like multiple choice questions, just compare to "True" or "False." Don't try to do `if a:` we'll implent `if` statements like that later on in the class, but this isn't the place.

4. Calculate the percentage by using a formula at the end of the game. Don't just add 20% for each question the user gets correct. If you add 20% each time, then you have to change the program 5 places if you add a 6th question. With a formula, you only need 1 change.

5. To print a blank line so that all the questions don't run into each other, use the following code:

```
print()
```

6. Remember the program can print multiple items on one line. This can be useful when printing the user's score at the end.

```
print("The value in x is", x)
```

When you are done turn in the assignment according to your teacher/mentor's instructions.

C.2. Example Run

Here's an example from my program. Please create your own original questions. I like to be entertained while I check these programs.

Output:

```
Quiz time!

How many books are there in the Harry Potter series? 7
Correct!

What is 3*(2-1)? 3
Correct!

What is 3*2-1? 5
Correct!
```

```
Who sings Black Horse and the Cherry Tree?
1. Kelly Clarkson
2. K.T. Tunstall
3. Hillary Duff
4. Bon Jovi
? 2
Correct!

Who is on the front of a one dollar bill
1. George Washington
2. Abraham Lincoln
3. John Adams
4. Thomas Jefferson
? 2
No.

Congratulations, you got 4 answers right.
That is a score of 80.0 percent.
```

D. Lab 3: Create-a-Picture

D.1. Description

Your assignment: Draw a pretty picture. The goal of this lab is to get practice using functions, using `for` loops, and introduce computer graphics.

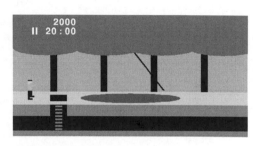

To get full credit:

* You must use multiple colors.
* You must have a coherent picture. I am not interested in abstract art with random shapes.
* You must use multiple types of graphic functions (e.g. circles, rectangles, lines, etc.)
* You must use a `while` or `for` loop to create a repeating pattern. Do not just redraw the same thing in the same location 10 times. Actually use that index variable as an offset to displace what you are drawing. Remember that you can contain multiple drawing commands in a loop, so you can draw multiple train cars for example.

For a template program to modify, look at the following example programs:

`ProgramArcadeGames.com/python_examples/f.php?file=pygame_base_template.py`
`ProgramArcadeGames.com/python_examples/f.php?file=simple_graphics_demo.py`

See **Chapter 5** for an explanation of the template. For official documentation on the draw module:

`http://www.pygame.org/docs/ref/draw.html`

To select new colors, either use

`http://www.colorpicker.com/`

or open up the Windows Paint program and click on "Edit Colors." Copy the values for Red, Green, and Blue. Do not worry about colors for hue, Saturation, or Brilliance.

Please use comments and blank lines to make it easy to follow your program. If you have 5 lines that draw a robot, group them together with blank lines above and below. Then add a comment at the top telling the reader what you are drawing.

E. Lab 4: Loopy Lab

E.1. Part 1

Write a Python program named `part_1.py` that will print the following:

```
10
11 12
13 14 15
16 17 18 19
20 21 22 23 24
25 26 27 28 29 30
31 32 33 34 35 36 37
38 39 40 41 42 43 44 45
46 47 48 49 50 51 52 53 54
```

E.1.1. Tips for Part 1

- Generate the output for part one using two nested `for` loops.
- Create a separate variable to store numbers that will be printed.

This problem requires a bit of an "a-ha" to get. Make sure to ask around if you have problems. My students often find it to be one of the harder problems in this course.

E.2. Part 2

Write a program named `part_2.py` that:

1. Takes a list of five numbers from the user

2. Prints the list

3. Prints the average

4. Modifies the list so each element is one greater than it was before

5. Prints the modified list

Example:

```
Part 2
Enter 5 numbers:
Enter a number: 4
Enter a number: 8
Enter a number: 2
Enter a number: 3
Enter a number: 5
You entered: [4, 8, 2, 3, 5]
The average of those numbers is: 4.4
That same list with 1 added to each number: [5, 9, 3, 4, 6]
```

E.2.1. Tips for Part 2

- Allow the user to enter a number.
- Add the number to a list.
- At the end of the loop, print the list.
- Use a loop to total all numbers entered. (Yes, there is a **sum** command, but practice using the **for** loop please.
- Divide the total by five to get the average.
- Use a loop to add one to each number in the list
- Print the resulting list (with the 1 added to each element).

This part demonstrates how to create a list, how to total a list, and how to change each item in a list.

E.3. Part 3

Start with the pygame template code:

`pygame_base_template.py`

Rename the file to `part_3.py`. Use nested **for** loops to draw small green rectangles. Make the image look like Figure E.1.

Do not create the grid by drawing lines, use a grid created by rectangles.

If this is too boring, create a similar grid of something else. It is ok to change the color, size, and type of shape drawn. Just get used to using nested **for** loops to generate a grid.

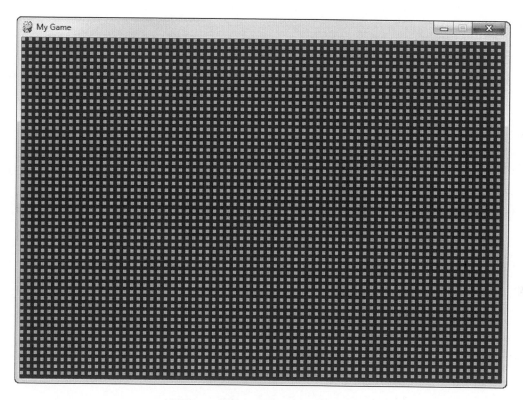

Figure E.1.: Pygame Grid

F. Lab 5: Animation

F.1. Requirements

Modify the prior Create-a-Picture lab, or start a new one.

Animate the image. Try one or more of the following:

- Move an item across the screen.
- Move an item back and forth.
- Move up/down/diagonally.
- Move in circles.
- Have a person wave his/her arms.
- Create a stoplight that changes colors.

Remember, the more flair the better! Have fun with this lab, and take time to see what you can do.

G. Lab 6: Functions

Create a set of four separate Python programs. Here is a description of each program:

1. Write a function called **min** that will take three numbers and *return* the smallest value. If more than one number tied for smallest, still return that smallest number. Copy/Paste the following code and make sure that it runs against the function you created:

```
1 print ( min (4,7,5) )
2 print ( min (4,5,5) )
3 print ( min (4,4,4) )
4 print ( min (-2,-6,-100) )
5 print ( min ("Z","B","A"))
```

You should get this result:

Output:

```
4
4
4
-100
A
```

The function should return the value, not print the value. Also, while there is a **min** function built into Python, don't use it. Please use **if** statements and practice creating it yourself.

2. Write a function called **box** that will output boxes given a height and width. Copy and paste the following code and make sure it works with the function you wrote:

```
1 box(7,5)   # Print a box 7 high, 5 across
2 print()    # Blank line
3 box(3,2)   # Print a box 3 high, 2 across
4 print()    # Blank line
5 box(3,10)  # Print a box 3 high, 10 across
```

You should get the following results:

Output:

```
*****
*****
*****
*****
*****
*****
*****

**
**
**

*********
*********
*********
```

3. Write a function called **find** that will take a list of numbers, **list**, along with one other number, **key**. Have it search the list for the value contained in **key**. Each time your function finds the key value, print the array position of the key. You will need to juggle three variables, one for the list, one for the key, and one for the position of where you are in the list.

   Copy/Paste this code to test it:

```
1 list=[36, 36, 79, 96, 36, 91, 77, 33, 19, 3, 34, 70, 12, 12, 54, 98,
      86, 11, 17, 17]
2
3 find(list,12)
4 find(list,91)
5 find(list,80)
```

   ...check for this output:

Output:

```
Found 12 at position 12
Found 12 at position 13
Found 91 at position 5
```

   Use a **for** loop with an index variable and a **range**. Inside the loop use an **if** statement. The function can be written in about four lines of code.

4. Write one program that has the following:

   - Functions:

— Write a function named `create_list` that takes in a list size and return as list of random numbers from 1-6. i.e., calling `create_list(5)` should return 5 random numbers from 1-6. (Remember, Chapter 7 has code showing how to do something similar, creating a list out of five numbers the user enters. Here, you need to create random numbers rather than ask the user.)

To test, use this code against the function you wrote:

```
1 my_list = create_list(5)
2 print(my_list)
```

And you should get output of five random elements that looks something like:
Output:

```
[2,5,1,6,3]
```

— Write a function called `count_list` that takes in a list and a number. Have the function return the number of times the specified number appears in the list.

To test, use this code against the function you wrote:

```
1 count = count_list([1,2,3,3,3,4,2,1],3)
2 print(count)
```

And you should get output something like:
Output:

```
3
```

— Write a function called `average_list` that returns the average of the list passed into it.

To test, use this code against the function you wrote:

```
1 avg = average_list([1,2,3])
2 print(avg)
```

And you should get output something like:
Output:

```
2
```

• Now that the functions have been created, use them all in a main program that will:
   — Create a list of 10,000 random numbers from 1 to 6.
   — Print the count of 1 through 6. (That is, print the number of times 1 appears in the 10,000. And then do the same for 2-6.)
   — Print the average of all 10,000 random numbers.

H. Lab 7: Bitmapped Graphics and User Control

Create a graphics based program. You can start a new program, or continue with a prior lab. This is the checklist for completing this lab:

- Make sure this program is created in its own directory.
- Incorporate at least one function that draws an item on the screen. The function should take position data that specifies where to draw the item. (Note: You will also need to pass a reference to the "screen." Another note, this is difficult to do with images loaded from a file. I recommend doing this only with regular drawing commands.)
- Add the ability to control an item via mouse, keyboard, or game controller.
- Include some kind of bit-mapped graphics. Do not include bit-mapped graphics as part of your "draw with a function." That won't work well until we've learned a bit more.
- Include sound. You could make a sound when the user clicks the mouse, hits a key, moves to a certain location, etc. If the sound is problematic, you may skip this part.
- Make sure all files are added to version control. If instead you need to send the program to someone, the entire directory must be zipped. See Figure H.1.

Example Code:

`ProgramArcadeGames.com/index.php?chapter=example_code`

Sounds and bitmaps you can use:

`opengameart.org`

It is ok to use code from prior labs, such as Lab 5.

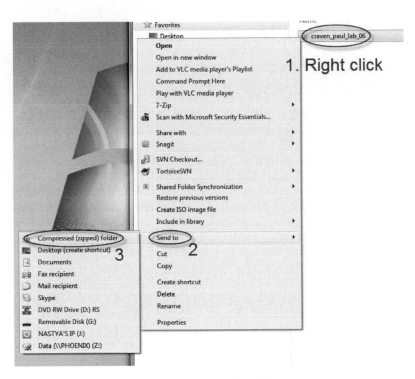

Figure H.1.: How to zip all the files in a directory

I. Lab 8: Classes and Graphics

Graphics provide an excellent opportunity to use classes. Each graphic object can be represented by an *object*. Each type of graphic object can be represented by a *class*. An object's location, speed, and color can be stored in *attributes*.

I.1. Instructions

1. Start a new program with:
   ProgramArcadeGames.com/python_examples/f.php?file=pygame_base_template.py

2. Name your program `lastname_firstname_labs_08.py` or something similar.

3. Right after the default colors are defined in the example program, create a class called `Rectangle`.

   - Add `x` and `y` attributes, which will be used for storing the object's position.
   - Create a `draw` method. Have the method create a green 10x10 rectangle at the location stored in `x` and `y`. Don't forget to use `self.` before the variables. The method will need to take in a reference to `screen` so that the `pygame.draw.rect` function can draw the rectangle to the correct screen.

4. Before the program loop, create a variable called `myObject` and set it equal to a new instance of `Rectangle`.

5. Inside the main program loop, call myObject's `draw()` method.

6. Checkpoint: Make sure your program works, and the output looks like Figure I.1.

7. Right after the program creates the instance of `Rectangle`, set the x and y values to something new, like 100, 200. Run the program again to make sure it works and the rectangle moves to the new coordinates.

8. Add attributes to the class for height and width. Draw the rectangle using these new attributes. Run the program and make sure it works.

9. Get the object to move:

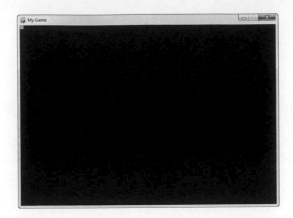

Figure I.1.: Rectangle in top left corner

- Add attributes for change_x and change_y
- Create a new method called **move()**, that adjusts x and y based on change_x and change_y. (Note that the move method will not need screen as a parameter because it doesn't draw anything to the screen.)
- Set myObject's change_x and change_y to values, like 2 and 2.
- Call the **move()** method in the main program loop.
- Test to make sure the object moves.

10. Randomize the object

- Import the random library
- Set the x location to a random number between 0 and 700. Do this in the loop where you create the object. Do not do it where the field is defined in the class. The class template is only created once and will use the same random numbers for each object we create.
- Set the y location to a random number between 0 and 500
- Set the height and width to a random number between 20 and 70
- Set the change_x and change_y to random numbers between -3 and 3
- Test and make sure it looks like Figure I.2.

11. Create and display a list of objects

- Before the code that creates the myObject, create an empty list, called **myList**
- Create a for loop that loops 10 times.
- Put the code that creates myObject into the for loop
- Append myObject to myList.
- Inside the main program loop, loop through each item of myList.
- Call the draw and move methods for each item of the list.

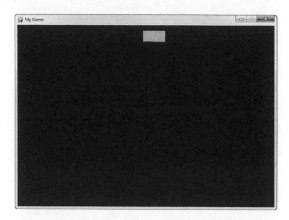

Figure I.2.: Rectangle in random spot

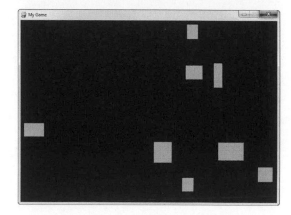

Figure I.3.: Ten rectangles

- Make sure that the code calls the draw method of the element pulled out by the for loop, don't just use myObject.draw()
- Test and see if your program looks like Figure I.3.

12. Use inheritance

- After the Rectangle class, create a new class called Ellipse.
- Set Rectangle to be the parent class of Ellipse.
- Create a new draw method that draws an ellipse instead of a rectangle.
- Create a new for loop that adds 10 instances of Ellipse to `myList` in addition to the 10 rectangles. (Just use two separate for loops.)
- Test and see if your program looks like Figure I.4.

13. Make it more colorful

- Adjust the program, so that color is an attribute of `Rectangle`.

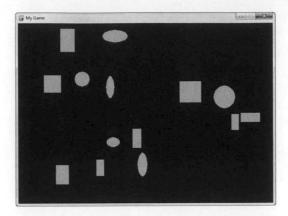

Figure I.4.: Rectangles and ellipses

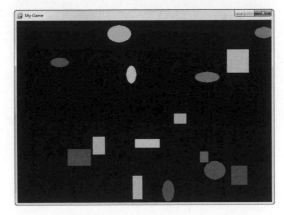

Figure I.5.: Colorful shapes

- Draw the rectangles and ellipsies using the new color.
- In the for loops, set the shapes to random colors. Remember, colors are specified by three numbers in a list, so you need a list of three random numbers (r, g, b)
- Test and see if your program looks like Figure I.5.

14. Try it with more than 10 items of each type. Figure I.6 shows 1,000 shapes.

15. You are done! Turn in your program.

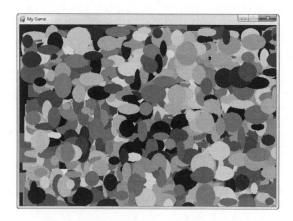

Figure I.6.: Shapes gone crazy

J. Lab 9: Sprite Collecting

This lab practices using Pygame sprites as described in `Chapter 14`.

- Start with an empty directory and put all of the lab-related files in this directory.
- Start with the following program:
  `ProgramArcadeGames.com/python_examples/f.php?file=sprite_collect_blocks.py`
- Modify it so the player moves with the keyboard rather than the mouse. Take a look at the `move_sprite_keyboard_smooth.py` program also available on the example page.
- Create another list of sprites, one that decreases the player score instead.
- Color the player blue, the good sprites green, and the bad sprites red. Or use graphics to signify good/bad sprites as shown in the `sprite_collect_graphic.py` example file.
- Rather than simply use `print` to display the score on the console, display the score on the graphics window. Go back to `simple_graphics_demo.py` for an example of displaying text.
- Add sound effects for when the user hits good blocks, or bad blocks. Here are a couple from `OpenGameArt.org`:
  `ProgramArcadeGames.com/labs/sprite_collecting/good_block.wav`
  `ProgramArcadeGames.com/labs/sprite_collecting/bad_block.wav`
- Add a check and make sure the player doesn't slide off the end of the screen.
- Download a wav file and have it play a sound if the user tries to slide off the screen. Here's one sound you can use:
  `ProgramArcadeGames.com/labs/sprite_collecting/bump.wav`

K. Lab 10: Sprite Moving

This lab practices uses Pygame sprites as described in **Chapter 14**, and separates the classes into different files as described in **Chapter 15**.

- Start in an empty directory and put all of the lab-related files in this directory.
- Start with a copy of the program you wrote for **Lab 9: Sprite Collecting**.
- Move the **Block** class into a new file.
- Make sure your program runs like before. Adjust **import** statements as needed.
- Define a **GoodBlock** class in a new file, and inherit from your **Block** class. (Define the class, don't create an instance of it. Your **for** loop that creates the instances does not move.)
- Add a new **update** method. Make the good block randomly move up, down, left or right each update. (Change **self.rect.x** and **self.rect.y** randomly each time the **update** function is called. Not to a completely new number, but add a random number from -3 to 3 or so. Remember that **random.randrange(-3,3)** does not generate a random number from -3 to 3.)
- Change your **for** loop so that it creates instances of the **GoodBlock** class and not your old regular **Block** class.
- Call **update** on the list of all the sprites you have. Do this in the main program loop so the blocks keep moving, not just once at the start of the program.
- Test and make sure it works.
- Make sure the blocks don't wiggle outside the screen.
- Test and make sure it works.
- Create a **BadBlock** class in a new file and inherit from the **Block** class.
- Make an **update** function and have the bad block sprites move down the screen, similar to what was done at the end of Chapter 14. Extra kudos if you make a bouncing rectangle.
- Test, make sure it works.
- Double check to make sure each class is in its own file.

L. Lab 11: Spell Check

This lab shows how to create a spell checker. To prepare for the lab, go to:
ProgramArcadeGames.com/index.php?chapter=examples list
...and download the files listed below. The files are in the "Searching and Sorting Examples" section.

- `AliceInWonderLand.txt` - Text of "Alice In Wonderland"
- `AliceInWonderLand200.txt` - First chapter of "Alice In Wonderland"
- `dictionary.txt` - A list of words

L.1. Requirements

Write a single program in Python that checks the spelling of the first chapter of "Alice In Wonderland." First use a linear search, then use a binary search. Print the line number along with the word that does not exist in the dictionary.

L.2. Steps to complete:

1. Create a file for your program, such as `lab_11_lastname_first.py`.

2. It is necessary to split apart the words in the story so that they may be checked individually. It is also necessary to remove extra punctuation and white-space. Unfortunately, there is not any good way of doing this with what the book has covered so far. The code to do this is short, but a full explanation is beyond the scope of this class. Include the following function in your program.

Listing L.1: Function to split apart words in a string and return them as a list

```
1 import re
2
3 # This function takes in a line of text and returns
4 # a list of words in the line.
5 def split_line(line):
6     return re.findall('[A-Za-z]+(?:\'[A-Za-z]+)?',line)
```

This code uses a *regular expression* to split the text apart. Regular expressions are very powerful and relatively easy to learn. To learn more about regular expressions, see: `http://en.wikipedia.org/wiki/Regular_expression`

3. Read the file `dictionary.txt` into an array. Go back to the chapter on Searching, or see the `searching_example.py` for example code on how to do this. This does *not* have anything to do with the `import` command, libraries, or modules.

4. Close the file.

5. Print `--- Linear Search ---`

6. Open the file `AliceInWonderLand200.txt`

7. Start a `for` loop to iterate through each line.

8. Call the `split_line` function to split apart the line of text in the story that was just read in. Store the list that the function returns in a new variable named `words`.

9. Start a nested `for` loop to iterate through each word in the line.

10. Using a linear search, check the current word against the words in the dictionary. Check the chapter on searching or the `searching_example.py` for example code on how to do this. When comparing to the words in the dictionary, convert the word to uppercase first. For example: `word.upper()`.

11. If the word was not found, print the word and the line that it was on.

12. Close the file.

13. Make sure the program runs successfully before moving on to the next step.

14. Print `--- Binary Search ---`

15. The linear search takes quite a while to run. To temporarily disable it, it may be commented out by using three quotes before and after that block of code. Ask if you are unsure how to do this.

16. Repeat the same pattern of code as before, but this time use a binary search. Much of the code from the linear search may be copied, and it is only necessary to replace the lines of code that represent the linear search with the binary search.

17. Note the speed difference between the two searches.

18. Make sure the linear search is re-enabled, if it was disabled while working on the binary search.

19. Upload the final program or check in the final program.

L.3. Example Run

```
--- Linear Search ---
Line 3   possible misspelled word: Lewis
Line 3   possible misspelled word: Carroll
Line 46  possible misspelled word: labelled
Line 46  possible misspelled word: MARMALADE
Line 58  possible misspelled word: centre
Line 59  possible misspelled word: learnt
Line 69  possible misspelled word: Antipathies
Line 73  possible misspelled word: curtsey
Line 73  possible misspelled word: CURTSEYING
Line 79  possible misspelled word: Dinah'll
Line 80  possible misspelled word: Dinah
Line 81  possible misspelled word: Dinah
Line 89  possible misspelled word: Dinah
Line 89  possible misspelled word: Dinah
Line 149  possible misspelled word: flavour
Line 150  possible misspelled word: toffee
Line 186  possible misspelled word: croquet
--- Binary Search ---
Line 3   possible misspelled word: Lewis
Line 3   possible misspelled word: Carroll
Line 46  possible misspelled word: labelled
Line 46  possible misspelled word: MARMALADE
Line 58  possible misspelled word: centre
Line 59  possible misspelled word: learnt
Line 69  possible misspelled word: Antipathies
Line 73  possible misspelled word: curtsey
Line 73  possible misspelled word: CURTSEYING
Line 79  possible misspelled word: Dinah'll
Line 80  possible misspelled word: Dinah
Line 81  possible misspelled word: Dinah
Line 89  possible misspelled word: Dinah
Line 89  possible misspelled word: Dinah
Line 149  possible misspelled word: flavour
Line 150  possible misspelled word: toffee
Line 186  possible misspelled word: croquet
```

M. Lab 12: Final Lab Part 1

This is it! This is your chance to use your creativity and really show off what you can create in your own game. More than just passing a test, in this class you actually get to do something, and create something real.

This final lab is divided into three parts. Each part raises the bar on what your game needs to be able to do.

M.0.1. Requirements for part 1:

- Open up a screen.
- Set up the items to be drawn on the screen.
- Provide some sort of rudimentary player movement via mouse, keyboard, or game controller.

M.0.2. Tips:

- If your program will involve things running into each other, start by using sprites. Do not start by using drawing commands, and expect to add in sprites later. It won't work and you'll need start over from scratch. This will be sad.
- If you are coding a program like mine sweeper or connect four, do not use sprites. Since collision detection is not needed, there is no need to mess with sprites.
- Under "longer game examples" I have two programs that show how to create pong or breakout style games. Don't just turn these in as Part 1 though; you'll need to add a lot before it really qualifies.
- `OpenGameArt.org` has a lot of images and sounds you can use royalty-free.

M.0.3. Looking ahead:

- Including this lab, there will be a total of three parts.
  - Part 1 - Get the screen set up and some basic interaction.
  - Part 2 - Get the game mostly functional.
  - Part 3 - Add items like the display of the score, sound, and make it look nice.

N. Lab 13: Final Lab Part 2

For Final Lab Part 2, your game should be mostly functional. A person should be able to sit down and play the game for a few minutes and have it feel like a real game. Here are some things you might want to add:

- Be able to collide with objects.
- Players can lose the game if something bad happens.
- On-screen score.
- Some initial sound effects.
- Movement of other characters in the screen.
- The ability to click on mines or empty spots.

O. Lab 14: Final Lab Part 3

For the final part, add in the last polish for your game. Here are some things you might want to add:

- Multiple levels
- Sounds
- Multiple "lives"
- Title and instruction screens
- Background music
- Heat seeking missiles
- Hidden doors
- A "sweep" action in a minesweeper game or the ability to place "flags"

Listings

About the author: Paul Vincent Craven graduated with a bachelors degree from Simpson College, a masters from the Missouri University of Science and Technology, and a doctorate from the University of Idaho. He worked in the industry for fifteen years before deciding to teach full time at Simpson College in Indianola, Iowa.

Printed in Great Britain
by Amazon.co.uk, Ltd.,
Marston Gate.